CONSE~~RVATION~~
PIECES

Humphrey Mackworth-Praed

PACKARD PUBLISHING LIMITED
CHICHESTER

CONSERVATION PIECES

First published in 1991 by Packard Publishing Limited,
16 Lynch Down, Funtington, Chichester, West Sussex PO18 9LR.

ISBN 1 85341 046 2

A CIP cataloguing record of this book is available from the British Library.

Cover design by Cecil Smith.

Typeset by Inforum Typesetting, Portsmouth, Hampshire.
Printed and bound in the United Kingdom.

Contents

Foreword

These stories about wildlife conservation were written some years after the events described, using various records available to me, chiefly the slides I had taken at the time as a quick form of diary. They are not in chronological order; many of the events overlapped, and some I have run together.

I would like to express gratitude to all who helped in the work we undertook, and not only those whom, for ease of narrative, I have mentioned by name. These include at least a dozen different Johns, while Davids and Kens are also numerous.

I have drawn, with its late Editor's permission, on the articles I wrote over many years for *Birds & Country*, as well as some that appeared in the *Surrey Naturalist*.

There is a glossary of acronyms and some other terms at the end. I am most grateful to Margaret for typing and to Vanessa for advice and support.

H.W.M-P.
Tunbarr, Headley 1991

Dedicated to all Conservation Volunteers

ONE

Stepping Up Box Hill

David drove his crowbar into the chalk and it went in deep. I knocked a stake into the hole with a sledge and it stood firm, projecting a foot or so. We worked our way across the gully putting the stakes in a rough line *(see Photo 1)*. Ken and the others were fetching the bundles of stakes and brushwood, that I had driven up in my old landrover and trailer on to the Gun Road above us, and the girls wove the brushwood between the stakes like a sort of trellis. We made another line a yard further down, and so on down to the foot of the gully. It took all day and the result was a bit irregular, but the stakes were firm, and the brushwood looked as if it would stay in place.

It was 8 March, 1975. All through the winter, I had put a few of each working party on to cutting these stakes, of whatever wood was available, and using the triangular bow saws 20 inches (500 mm – see Glossary) long as a guide to length. They had to be at least an inch in width. We had nearly 1000 in all, pointed and tied in bundles of 50. I had tried them out elsewhere, but it was a relief to find they worked. Not everything works on Box Hill.

Above us was the retaining wall that Brian had put in four months earlier with his JCB. He'd used oak uprights, and elm planks – there was plenty of dead elm about then with the disease having come to stay the year before. He'd filled in the gullies in the Gun Road behind, some of them nearly half its width, and pounded them down with the bucket. The retaining wall was fine, but it stood out as a slanting silver-grey line from the hill opposite, so I had got a lot of cans of spray paint, black, green, brown and ochre, and tried to camouflage it as we did to lorries in the war. It wasn't too successful, as you had to put the black patches near where the uprights came, to hide the shadow, and of course these were at regular intervals, so showed up rather. It did break the line up a bit though.

I ought to explain that this Gun Road, or Fort Road, as it's sometimes called, runs up the south side of the Zig-Zag valley, and was made to drag guns up to the Fort. This was all around 1900 when a chain of these forts was made along the North Downs to protect London. They were really more like mobilization centres, and the idea was that arms would be stored there and when the invasion came, troops would spread out between them to form a defensive line. They were never used because it didn't happen. In fact I don't think this road was ever used for guns. It's a riding track now.

Round this whole area, and along the top of the wall, we had a fence. We'd used plain wire, because barbed is 'aggro,' and invites retaliation. I'd got ³⁄₁₆" angles; ⅛" could have bent with people swinging on them. This fence was also put up by Brian, and the cost of this, and the retaining wall, came to about £650, including the materials I got for him cheap. There were a lot of notices too. The Countryside Commission was paying 75 per cent of the cost, and it was keen on notices. The idea is that if you explain it to people, they'll appreciate your endeavour, and not take it apart. It depends on the people though. I didn't think notices would last so I made them simple, just photostated sheets in Nyrex holders, with holes punched and string at the corners. Some people may have got the message, but mostly they just tore them down. I replaced them once a week.

Later on, we put up painted wooden ones, but they weren't much good either, even though I wired them and put grease where you'd grip them. One even had the lettering wiped off it, clean as a whistle. I never found out how that was done – who carries paint-stripper round on walks? Or may be it was sun-oil or hair-spray. Anything can happen on Box Hill.

This was a Countryside Commission project administered from London then, before the head office moved to Cheltenham. Box Hill was about the nearest country park, and the Commissioners didn't like the erosion scars on it. They were a bit new at the game then, so they said what they wanted, and left the details to us. They still had to learn about costing too, and were frightened of being taken for a ride. It was public money after all.

The scars had been there some time, generations probably *(Photo 5)*. Some people were quite fond of them; part of the character they said. But the CC wanted to prove the damage could be repaired, and it was doing parallel work elsewhere: the Lake District and so forth, on harder soil. Chalk is easier, as all you have to do is to put soil over it. The problem is to make the soil stick. Hence the trellis-work.

Brian had collected a big pile of topsoil up by the Fort. I'd made sure it was the right sort, from another Upper Chalk site where he'd been working. It doesn't do to mix types, because it confuses people, particularly the botanists. On the next day he brought it down the Gun Road in the bucket of his JCB, a ton at a time, and dropped it over the fence along the wall. We raked it down over the lines of trellis, and spread it around. It worked out about six to nine inches deep, though it tailed off a bit lower down. We'd thought if we did it like that, the shrubs, and there were quite a few in and between the gullies, would grow up through it, and spread into it. Then in a year or two we could raise it all some more.

It took some time for him to go up and down, so between his trips we staked the next gully. We'd been told to try different methods, so for this one we put the stakes dotted all over it, and we got some tangles of Travellers' Joy (*Clematis vitalba*) and slung it all over, with yew branches mixed up in it. We raked the soil down over this too.

I never knew why it was called Travellers' Joy until, a year or two later, Sandy was managing Box Hill, and started to tear it off the yews, as he thought it was doing them no good, and adding to the amount of snow that could lodge and break branches. He got a rash on his hands and asked me if it came from doing this. As I knew it was in the buttercup family, and as most of them are toxic somehow, I thought it probably was, and looked it up. English textbooks are fine for describing plants but French ones say what good the plant is to man, such as if you can eat it. They give more of the biochemistry too. The French name for Travellers' Joy is *Vigne blanche* according to Coste, and he says it is "âcre et très irritante", but other books call it *Herbe aux gueux*, the beggars' plant, so my guess is that it's what they used to give them sores to show people when they went begging, and our Travellers' Joy comes from that sense of the word.

It took us the whole weekend to fill in these two gullies. They are the ones called 3 and 2 in the write-up that David put in *Countryside Recreation Review*, Vol. 2 of 1977, from information we supplied. I took a lot of photos for the record, and so did Ken, and some of the others. The cost was only about £100, including the BTCV party and all incidentals. All the material was free of course. Actually gully 2 was in two sections, marked A and B, because it forked at the top, but we ran it all together, and hoped the bushes between would spread. Looking back from the hill the other side, it seemed quite an improvement.

I'd been glad to see David and Ken on that job, because I'd worked with them before, and I'd asked for the BTCV because they were the best for this sort of work, which hadn't been tried out before, and we had to make the rules as we went along. They had the intelligence and versatility for this. The National Trust wardens then were still in the billhook age, though they got a lot better a few years later with training colleges like Merrist Wood coming along.

Not much happened for a while, apart from replacing the notices, and mending the fence when it was cut. Then in November 1975 the Countryside Commission thought it wanted the original slope restored more. So further along, on Gulleys 1 A and B, they got Brian to put in a series of timber revetments down the slope at intervals. He used spruce thinnings for this from the plantations.

I got photos of this too *(Photo 2)*; there were three of these revetments, with spruce posts in front, and thinnings laid end-wise, heads and tails, behind them, about seven in the top one, then four in the next down, and one or two in the lowest one. The chalk was laid up to the level of the uppermost of the thinnings, so it was quite deep, and then he spread earth over it all to get the slope even and graded to the level of the line of the hill, as if it hadn't been eroded. So the soil was only inches deep, on top of two or three feet of chalk rubble.

This cost £400 and it looked good at first, but I think it was trying to do too much at once, because the chalk rubble stifled what plants there were, and we had to plant it up. This happened in January 1976. We'd been given a list of native plants to be put in, and a plan of order in which to plant them, the prickly ones outside. Actually some of them weren't obtainable commercially, so we made do with what we could get. Hawthorn was easy to buy, because people use it for hedges. For ash and yew we could dig up young plants elsewhere. Buckthorn, wayfaring tree and field maple weren't so easy, but we did manage to find a few small enough to try to move, mostly from the woods round Polesden Lacey. Nowadays you can buy all these, and more, from specialized nurseries, but you couldn't then.

I got the BTCV again to do the work, but the weather wasn't good, and I didn't take photos. The hawthorns looked the most likely to succeed, as they were quicks grown for hedging, but the others that we'd dug up had a lot of torn roots. Actually 1976 was a very dry summer, so unless we'd been able to keep them watered, there wasn't much hope for them, with the soil so thin over the chalk. A few came through, and there was a good wayfaring tree growing already, with yews all around too.

I don't know where Brian got that soil from, but when I looked at it in mid-July there was a larkspur flowering, with a hummingbird hawk-moth flying round it. This was about the last job he did with that JCB, because it got burnt. He kept it in an old shed by the tea-room on top of the hill, and it all went up one day. He hadn't got it insured for much either, so it put him out of business, and he moved away. A pity, as he was a great help on the hill.

This was the last time we used the BTCV on this job, as by then the National Trust had set up a base camp near Leith Hill, so we had Acorn parties from that. John brought the first one to Box Hill in that July of 1976, and they spent two or three days making steps of round timber where there was a gap to the side of the gullies to the right as you look up. Repairing erosion is all very well, but it is caused by traffic, and the traffic has to go somewhere. So you have to provide for this, and it has to be somewhere that people can see, otherwise they will break through again elsewhere. We'd had a lot of trouble with people coming down through the gullies we'd repaired, despite the notices. Once a teacher was seen to read them, and then take his whole class down through the fences. So these steps gave them a way to go, and they led to a fairly well-marked path that slanted up the hill anyway. In fact this became too much used, and one day I watched a lot of kids from a school going up and down it time and again. I couldn't see what they were at, until I realized there was a teacher at the bottom with a marking board, and they were being sponsored for the number of times they went up and down. Sponsored erosion!

People usually talk as though erosion was caused by going up hill, but I think more is done coming down. It depends on how you do it of course, walking, or sitting on your backside. Or if you have a horse with you. Some years there were crazes for sliding down the slopes of Box Hill, and kids came for miles with bits of tin, or plastic or cardboard, or just their jeans, and they'd climb up, and slide down. We didn't think it mattered all that much at first, in fact on one visit the Director General of the Trust was heard to say to the Chairman, "The only thing wrong with that is that we're too old for it". Then we had a student; one of the many writing a thesis on 'The effect of human pressure on chalk turf' or words to that effect. Most of them put in little pegs and tapes and come back later and find they've been kicked about. This one was different. She just sat on one slope and made a sketch of all the possible sliding routes on the hill opposite. There were about twenty-seven. Then she counted the number of times each was used, and she showed me her results. When we found that some of the slides were used over two hundred times in a day, we realized there was a problem.

These 1976 steps took some of the traffic, but they were a bit rough, and the Committee didn't like the way the turf had been cut putting them in, and the soil heaped to one side. Also there were a lot of man orchids just below them, and musk orchids on the slope above them, above the Gun Road. They asked Sandy and me to make a report about it all. So we looked at it from all angles and recommended that we should have two flights of steps from the Gun Road right down to the valley floor, and that these should be not straight but curving, with flat sections, to take advantage of various yews and clumps of bushes that would hide them from the view from the hill opposite. This alignment would also take account of where there were orchid colonies, man and musk in particular, but as far as possible all the common spotted, fragrant and pyramid orchids that grow in patches on these slopes.

The two flights of steps would be each side of the gully area. The right-hand one would be based on the 1976 Acorn's steps, of which there were 21, but the bottom part of this would be swung to the right, to keep clear of the man orchids, and brought down to the road just below the first hairpin, keeping close to a clump of yew and shrubs which would shade it most of the day.

The left-hand flight would use the uppermost gully, marked 4 on the Countryside Commission's plan, and which they had meant to keep as a control, but it seemed better to use it, as we couldn't see people from below traversing to the right-hand steps, even if they were the only ones, and people from above coming down the Gun Road would just take the first way down that they saw, which happened to be this gully. We could curl it inwards a bit, behind bushes, so that it would come out pretty well below the centre of the gullies. We thought these left-hand steps should be made first.

We also recommended that the wire fence around the restored gullies should be left up until 1979 and that repair of it should be part of the warden's duties, also that the two flights of steps when made should be considered for extension above the Gun Road, as a lot of the traffic came from up there, off the main ridge track above the Whites. Also we didn't agree with the Countryside Commission report that the gully the contractor filled right up would be the best in the long term, and we thought that raising the level gradually, plants and all, would turn out to be better.

Our suggestions were agreed, including starting with the left-hand steps. The gullies we'd repaired had greened over by then, and when you looked from the hill opposite the chief features that hit you were the short, white, eroded tracks on the slope above the Gun Road, and the many tracks leading up to the gullies, and particularly now to the 1976 steps. None was through to the chalk yet, but would be soon. The actual gullies themselves weren't so noticeable, but if you looked at them closely, you could see there had been movement through them, despite the thorn bushes and things we put in them to dissuade people, not to mention the notices.

We started these steps on 7 May 1977, and for various reasons we began at two places, one at the foot, and one in the middle. This was partly to show the Acorn party how to do the work on fairly easy sections, and to split them into two groups so all 14 of them didn't fall over each other; and partly because these sections were relatively screened from view, just in case we made a mess of it. Also two parties gave a bit of a spur to competition. Another change we made was to use squared 2″ thick timber planks, about 8″ wide, cut to a metre in length, and square pegs 18″ long to go in front of them. You can buy these in bundles ready pointed for surveyors, which is cheaper than making them yourself. For some reason square timber looks a lot better in chalk, though in sandstone I don't think round timber looks so bad. The Acorns were about even in sexes, and sizes too for that matter. They soon got the idea. John took the ones in the middle, and I took the ones below. We each got four or five steps finished that first day *(Photo 3)*.

There are various things about putting in steps. Firstly unless you're careful you tend to bring the pegs in closer and closer as you work down, so it looks constricted. Secondly the pegs try to twist as you drive them in, and don't keep square to the step – you often have to take them out and crowbar again. Then you have to use a spirit-level and rule all the time to keep them level and equal distances apart. You also have to avoid making one step higher than others – you should be able to put a straight edge down a flight so that it touches each step. Then you must decide where to put the turf you cut. We thought it looked best if we made a low mound of spoil alongside the downhill side, and turfed on top of that – it screened the steps a bit in the view from the hill opposite. Filling up the steps too needs a bit of care as they tend to hollow out in use; even though you use mells or punners to compact them initially, you probably have to fill them more later on when they've been used a bit.

I went on leave the next week, but John carried on and joined the two lots up, so the bottom half was finished. Later with other camps we took it further, up through the gully, and it was a bit tricky there because we had to angle some of them, and put in a handrail or two. We also found we had to alter some we'd made, especially where there was a flat section, because people tend to come off the steps there and go straight down the hill if it's clear. We tried to bring them onto the flat traverses at an angle so that they kept going to the next set of steps – we didn't want to put up barricades, as they would have shown up. Anyway the kids would only have swung under them. But by the end of 1978 we had a good flight going all the way up, some 115 steps in all.

We began the right-hand steps on Sunday, 25 March 1979, and we started by making a flat track parallel to the road up to the hairpin, where there was a small car park then by the Dawyck beech. This track would allow parkers there to reach the steps.

There had been a big dogwood patch in the way, but I'd sprayed it with Krenite the year before. Making this track was straightforward, but at first the weekend motorbikers were a bit of a pain. This was before the police clamped down on them, so one had strings of bikes going up and down all the time. A thousand motorbikers are quite an impressive sight, though most of them were just there to show off their bikes to each other at the car park at the foot of the hill – the girl friends on the pillions were secondary. But every so often about twenty or so would rev up, and start off up the hill. Then they'd come down again. After half an hour of this we got used to it, and didn't bother to look at them.

Making this track first helped us in getting material to the site, as we couldn't park on the road. We started the flight up the hill, and we also put steps to connect to the road below. Again to spread the party we began halfway up as well, though it meant some work in barrowing uphill with a rope tied to the front of the barrow. We also had to steer a tricky course between orchid patches, while still keeping in as much cover as we could from a yew tree which was there.

John had moved to warden another patch by then, and Nigel had taken over the base camp. In May '79 he had a camp of engineering apprentices from a Midlands firm. Two of its staff came down too – it was a good firm. The lads were a bit surprised at first, when they saw the job, but in fact it was good basic training for them, and they soon had ideas for improving technique. We were using tanalised timber by then, but they started undercutting the turves along the edges, so that they could be bent down afterwards along the sides, and not leave a raw edge. They put in some rather classy barriers at the foot, and turned it, so that no-one could run down straight into the road. Then at the top they re-did the 1976 Acorns' steps and turned them to lead into the new flight. They made a very good job of it all, and went back right pleased. There were 132 steps in this flight when it was finished (*Photo 4*).

We had a grass fire that spring, though it didn't reach the steps. For many years the usual practice at Box Hill had been to burn all the long grass the first week in March. There was nearly always a dry period then, and sometimes they had a thorough inferno, with it running up into the yews, and burning their lower branches. They maintained that if they didn't burn then, someone would do it for them later in the summer, and it would get into the woods. The Committee members said they liked the look of the fresh green grass coming up afterwards. I told them that's what Attila felt. Apart from burning the invertebrates, so that Box Hill always had fewer butterflies than Colley Hill for instance, not that that was very well managed at the time, it didn't really do what they thought. It made the grasses spread more, particularly the *Brachypodium*. Luckily the silver-spotted skippers, which were about the rarest butterflies there, used the *Festuca ovina* on the fairly bare patches for egg-laying and the fire didn't spread to these. So they still survived – just.

Anyway we'd changed the policy, and this fire was the first big one since. It was started by some rockers who had gone to the New Forest, and there'd been a fight in which someone had got knifed, so part of the group had quit and come to camp on Box Hill. They'd made a campfire in the valley, and left it to run up the hillsides. However it didn't do as much damage as feared, and hadn't spread into the woodland. The woods there are mostly deciduous, and don't burn as easily as that, even though there is a lot of box in them. So while it made a mess of several acres, it wasn't enough to prove it was right to burn deliberately each year. Now the grass doesn't get long enough, with the winter sheep-grazing. But that is another story.

We didn't put in any more steps, except for an incomplete flight above the Gun Road which we didn't finish. I think this was because we couldn't really work out how to indicate to the people on the ridge where the steps down were, unless one made a proper path to them. It wouldn't be any good putting notices up, as they'd spoil the view, and anyway they'd get torn down.

Nor did we do anything much to the ridge track itself, though it was frequently suggested. It is worn right through to the chalk, but in most weathers it isn't too bad. There are just a few days in the year when it is really sticky. On appearances, a made-up track might look worse, and because it is shown in a lot of old drawings and paintings of Box Hill people are inclined to say it is part of the place, and leave it. I think it could be drained, but they would need to be underground drains, because if you made drainage channels either way from the ridge, you'd get more erosion. Personally I would have liked to try camouflets, that is driving a hole down about 10 feet, with the sort of machine they use for prospecting for motorway routes, and then blowing a small explosive charge at the bottom, so it makes a chamber. If you then filled this hole with hardcore I think you'd get drainage into the fissures in the chalk itself. I did suggest this, but it wasn't tried.

Lower down George used to try to break up the eroded line of the track by putting hawthorn bushes in, and this worked a bit, though a new track soon formed round them. Probably one day something will be done, but it didn't seem a priority at that time. Malcolm is in charge of Box Hill now, and there have been a good many changes in recent years. You can still get the odd excitement with a car burnt, or rolled down the hill, or both. But it isn't the free-for-all it used to be. The slopes opposite the Council car park at the bottom further along have been fenced off and stepped now, so kids can't push each other down into the road. Though I saw a skier come through not long ago; at least I saw her put into the ambulance afterwards. Malcolm says he doesn't get more casualties than the average ski resort.

I had a look at our steps recently to see how 12 years had treated them. They've had some attention from time to time, but in general they are much as we made them. The timbers seem good for as long again, and the edges have healed; some are growing orchids. From the other side they are hardly noticeable, especially the left-hand one, which we were able to take behind more clumps of shrubs. The short flight above the Gun Road has been taken up to the top, 21 steps in all, and a marker post put in, but there is clearly still a difficulty in getting people to come down at the right place to find them *(Photo 6)*.

The gullies have grown up a lot too. The fence has been left along the top of Brian's retaining wall, which is just as well because the part he filled right up with chalk and soil is fairly open still and people could easily go down that way, except that old yew boughs have been laid across to dissuade them. These don't look good. The bits we did are much thicker in comparison, though soil hasn't been added to them. This is a pity, because the elm planks are rotting now, so there is already a drop-down forming. But I think Sandy and I were right that this would be the better job in the long run. There is a possible track through at one place still, but you would have to be determined to follow it, and the shrubs are closing over it. The sheep-grazing fence now runs below this too, and adds to the obstacles.

So I suppose the lesson is that erosion can be cured, but it is quite a long job, and it needs an initial impetus which the Countryside Commission gave, to get things started. Otherwise people just talk about it forever. But I'm not too happy about one thing, which is that people use steps going up, but coming down, unless it's wet, they prefer to walk down the side to avoid the jarring feeling each time. So you get an eroded track forming alongside the steps, at least where there is a long straight flight, and this is happening at Box Hill. I don't know the answer, except possibly to avoid long straight flights. I saw one once at a place called Monte Bré in the south of Switzerland, where they had gone the whole hog, and made a straight flight of several hundred steps in concrete up a ridge slope. This had had a side path formed alongside it all the way down, and everyone tended to go up by the steps and down to their side, because of that jarring feeling. So I expect there is still a lot to be learnt about this sort of thing.

The costs have gone up too, and nowadays you have to reckon on about £2 per step for the timber alone, which is quite a factor, though if you call it £500 for the 250 steps we put in on Box Hill perhaps it doesn't sound so bad. After all, we were probably putting right 50 years of erosion, and stopping as much again which would have happened in the future. Then there was the cost of filling up the gullies. Still if you compare it with what gets spent on restoring paintings and so forth, you are probably laughing all the way up the hill. It makes it a lot easier for visitors to get round too, as well as the amenity aspect.

Anyway it was an interesting exercise, because that sort of thing hadn't really been done seriously before, so it was quite fun working it out. We'd thought we'd have trouble from people taking up the planks, but that never happened, though they could easily have pulled them out when they were new. Later on, when the planks settled in and became part of the place, it probably didn't occur to people to do this. Since then we've done a lot of steps at other places, Leith Hill and Cissbury for instance, and they certainly reduce the erosion eyesores.

TWO

The Giant Rhubarb

When I first visited the common, it had belonged to the National Trust for over sixty years, and you could tell it belonged to them by the notice at its narrow entrance. On closer inspection the fact that the notice was of an obsolete pattern, and embellished, though not unfavourably, by the addition of a green edging indicated that it was not without some touch of more local attention. Reference to the Trust's Handbook showed indeed that it was in the custodianship of the Parish Council of the neighbourhood, and one presumes that this arrangement had been made as a satisfactory method of local management at the time of its acquisition, since when no change had seemed necessary in the case of such a small property.

It was indeed small in comparison with other properties of the Trust, being only seven acres in extent, but it was not without interest. It was shaped like a P, facing backwards, and with the bottom of the letter touching the main road. The upright was formed by a narrow strip with a gravel drive, which served a line of houses. This strip appeared chiefly notable for the variety of garden escapes that had become established along it. Actually these were not so much escapes as throw-outs, and as I watched, on my first visit, a lady wheel-barrowed a further contribution from her garden for deposition on this convenient dumping-ground, placing it not of course immediately in front of her own house, but towards the further side of the strip, where there was a ditch and hedge. Beyond this one could see a collection of small fields, some farmed, some forming paddocks for horses, and one where an underground reservoir had been built, for this common was on a ridge of high ground. The access road to this reservoir ran across the strip, and a Water Board lorry was occupying it. Other paths ran across it too, apparently much used, no doubt mainly for the purpose of the lady with the wheel-barrow, or for the convenient walking of dogs before shutting them up each evening.

I suppose this narrow strip or spine took up some 3 acres of the total, and the rest, forming the head of the backwards P, was of a size and shape that might have contained a small village cricket ground, with quite a chance of scoring a six beyond its confines. Later I found that this had once been the case, and that its situation on a ridge then commanding good views in all directions had given it a local reputation as a beauty spot, which had presumably led to the decision to bestow it on the National Trust. Times however had changed, and no doubt the players had moved to some larger arena. The cricket ground had reverted to a rough field, and heather had become established on its acid soil. Birch and oak had taken root, with whortleberry coming up in their shade. Molinia tussocks had begun to form, and at the time I first saw it, these and bracken were the prevailing ground cover, with the heather reduced to two patches where the shade of the birches was less intense. Within ten years, these patches were to dwindle away, and even the whortleberry needed to struggle to survive under the developing canopy of the trees. These had been supplemented by some spot-planting, perhaps in a policy of reinforcing success, of further birches of the weeping variety.

The species list which I made on that first visit, and added to on my occasional later ones, comprised some 35 kinds of bird, 10 of butterflies, and about 70 of plants, not including grasses, so that there was really quite a varied collection present within the seven acres. Fox and badger seemed to visit, common lizard survived, and no doubt there were other smaller animals. The birds were of garden or woodland kinds, the two larger woodpeckers, pigeons of course, and occasionally a pheasant, but mostly thrushes, finches and tits. Jays, magpies and crows, even rooks and jackdaws, were not unusual, and one could often see a nuthatch or treecreeper, while robins and wrens were frequent. The plants were more complicated, because one had difficulty in deciding what had come by natural means and what had been assisted by ladies with wheelbarrows.

One assumed that the hazel, rowan and alder buckthorn had made its own way to the common, even if it had not been there all the time, as appeared likely in the case of the holly, honeysuckle and gorse. The broom was probably less original, but possible, so was the raspberry. The daffodils and Solomon's seal were clearly throw-outs, though doing well, as was the variegated yellow dead-nettle, which formed the ground cover over a quarter of an acre. Laburnum and laurel must have spread from the gardens, and also the rhododendron, possibly also the cherry and cherry-plum. Pride of place had however to be yielded to the knotweeds. The Japanese variety (*Reynoutria japonica*) which is such a common and pestiferous introduction that it is included in the banned list in Section 14 of the *Wildlife and Countryside Act*, though present here, looked relatively harmless beside its enormous Chinese relative, the Giant Knotweed (*R. sachalinensis*) which towered to ten feet or more over a large part of the spine of the common. It was known to the locals as the Giant Rhubarb.

Legend had it that a green-fingered lady, some thirty or forty years ago, had brought in one or two roots, which she had planted on the common because her garden was full of plants already. Whether she then uttered a blessing or a curse is unrecorded. I did not meet anyone who said they liked the plant, though some said it brought recollections of war-time experiences in Burmese jungles. One could imagine it might be a useful feature of a landscape planting on a fairly massive scale, with its thick forest of stems and large leaves topped in autumn by sprays of creamy-white flowers. In the narrow confines of a small common this attraction was lost because there was no room to stand back sufficiently from it for admiration to be excited, even for its vigour. It covered the whole width from the drive on one side to the paddock on the other, into which it had spread. In fact it was still spreading into this, and reducing the grazing space of the two resident donkeys, since it was not palatable even to them. I suppose in all it must have covered more than half an acre, but although one could not walk through it, because the stems were too close together, it was divided into two sections by one of the cross-tracks which was used sufficiently often to remain clear, and in walking along this, one was translated into another land.

Each spring, or perhaps I should say summer because the Giant Knotweed comes up in May, a month later than the Japanese kind, it grew steadily and quickly up to its height of ten feet or more, and each autumn it died down to leave a forest of brown stems. At this stage the local practice was to cut these down and burn them, so that for six months of the year visibility across the common was restored. But each year the weed had spread, and the work was greater. Nothing grew in its shade, and as it spread, it forced itself into neighbouring vegetation, and swamped it. Even a patch of tough blackthorn was undermined by its massive roots, with the knotweed stems coming up through the middle of the blackthorn boughs, and spreading above them. Nothing could stand against it.

However the situation at the wider head of the common seemed to me to be most in need of attention, where the diminishing heather needed relief from shading, and the birch and oak needed thinning. A neighbouring farmer was using one of the cross tracks as access to his field, rutting it badly in the process. There were other problems too, with the spread of bracken and rhododendron. Agreement was reached with the Parish Council, and a plan of work by volunteer members of the Young National Trust group was arranged. It was at this stage that I became aware of Nobby.

He was a short, thick-set man, reputedly intolerant of any activities in his domain being conducted by anyone except himself. He had been in the employment of the Parish Council for longer than anyone could remember, and was referred to as The Ranger. No doubt at one time his responsibilities were more widely spread, but now in his retirement he lived in a cottage adjoining the common, halfway along the gravel drive, from which he exercised his authority. In this he was supported by a large family, extending to grandchildren or further, who ensured that he did not go too far onto the seven acres but stayed, unless accompanied, within eyeshot of the cottage. His dog, which in some ways resembled him, as people's dogs frequently do, was of the brown wire-haired terrier breed which looks rather like a small Airedale. It was immensely fat, and its four legs – one at each corner – gave it the appearance of the sort of dog that one sees in drawings by children. No doubt it also had been more active in its time, but now it was happy to walk slowly behind its master, or observe while Nobby trimmed the grass of the verges of the drive with a sickle and short crooked stick, which he did most beautifully.

Nobby was very willing to talk of his expertise, and his toolshed bore ample witness to his mastery of the use of edged tools in a surprising array of shapes and sizes, all appropriate to their purpose, and showing evidence of past use, probably through many lifetimes. I privately hoped that such a collection would find a worthy home in some rural museum when he finally abandoned their use. He told me something of the history of the cricket ground, though I thought he over-estimated in saying that it was the third highest place in the county, as I had been on others considerably higher, though not all visible from where we stood. His local patriotism was enormous, and it was interesting that the gravel of the drive had come from a seaside beach, some twenty miles away, being brought on the return journey of carts conveying building stone to a well-known resort black-listed by Cobbett as an incipient Wen. I wish I had more opportunity to listen to his stories about the district, which would have been well worth recording.

However it was apparent that a difference of approach lay between us, and the sight of the sweat-shirted young men and women, who by now were wielding mattocks to demolish the ruts caused by the farmer's tractor, seemed both to puzzle and displease him. He was prepared to concede, at least in theory, that there was a case for thinning some of the trees that were growing into each other, but he could not bring himself to agree on particular examples, since all were familiar landmarks to him. The sight of a young lady using a sledgehammer to put in stumps across the rutted track clearly had him divided between an urge to show her the correct method of doing so, and disapproval that an attractive blonde should be doing anything of the sort on his common. It was as well that a granddaughter appeared at that moment to lead him home to tea.

It was at about this time that I thought I ought to find out a bit more about the Giant Rhubarb. Nobby retreated to a safe distance while I used three or four different herbicides on selected patches, of which I made a sketch-plan. He was of the opinion that I would poison the kiddies, or the animals, starting with his dog, and forecast a holocaust. When I returned in a month or two it was difficult to identify the results, because either by accident or design he had trimmed back some of the plants I had treated. However enough remained to show that the knotweed was vulnerable, and that it would be effective to use a herbicide known to be harmless to kiddies, or other wildlife than plants.

Sure enough the Parish Council said soon afterwards that while they welcomed what the YNT had done in the restoration of the rutted track, which they had engaged the local rugger club to continue, what would please them above all else would be to be freed of the Giant Rhubarb. Accordingly, since it was now summer, and the stems were towering above us, I asked the YNT to cut it all at waist level, which they did, and we burnt up as much as we could until the fire was choked by the weight of the green stems, when we had to leave it until these had dried out. I had hoped that enough leaf would remain to absorb the chemical, together with the cut edges, and I sprayed the whole area with an ultra-low-volume sprayer. This was not very effective, and it was clear that not enough leaf was left on the lower stems to allow proper absorption and translocation. We therefore returned in the next winter, and cleared and burnt up all the stems down to ground level, as well as making passages into the blackthorn so that I could get closer to the plants that came up through it, and I waited until the new growth should appear in the next spring.

I used a patch of Japanese knotweed near my home as a guide, so when this was about a foot high, in mid April, I went to the common, but found that its congener had hardly begun to shoot yet. I sprayed all I could find with a watering can, which avoided my having to dress up in protective clothing, before going on to a conference in the Isle of Wight. I next visited the common in mid-May, to find that the plants I had treated were dying, but there was fresh and vigorous growth up to 4 feet high, and I had to use a ULV sprayer. I used about 2½ litres of mix, diluting the herbicide with twice its volume of water. Normally I would have expected to cover some 2 acres with this amount, but I had to go more slowly in this case because I wanted to make sure that the spray reached both the upper and under surfaces of the large leaves, so it took a couple of hours to do. Needless to say, my visit was not unperceived by Nobby; in fact I saw one of his friends and relations going into his cottage to tell him I was there. He duly appeared, and I had to give some time to his protests about danger to kiddies. He was astute enough to query why if the chemical was so harmless, I was dressed up so fully in protective clothing, but my explanation about working in a spray mist failed to allay his misgivings. We parted on fairly civil terms, and he engaged in displacement activity on the verges with his grasshook while I finished. I did however notice that by using the drive to the house with the donkeys I would not be so visible in my approach, and on calling at this house, I was given permission to do this by the owner, as well as an entreaty to spray the plants that had spread into his paddock too. So in future I included these.

On my next visit, on 7 June, on the first clear day after thundery weather, I was surprised to find new growth up to 10 feet high. This had all grown up freshly within a month, as the plants I had treated on 10 May were in various stages of collapse. I had to bend over the higher growth before spraying, but found that I could do this without breaking their stems. It took me an hour to spray the main group, using a stronger 1:1 solution, which was about as thick as the sprayer could manage. It did however then begin to play up, and I had to abandon it in favour of a watering can, which at least allowed me to remove some of my heavier clothing. I covered as much as I could, but I was due at a meeting in the afternoon, so I had to leave some of it, expecting to resume in the next week or so (*Photo 7*).

This however was not to be. Bad weather intervened, and it was a month before I returned on 7 July. Spraying weather is pretty uncertain and with a round trip to the common of 75 miles from my house, I wanted to be fairly sure of the day being suitable. This time I used the side approach, and managed to avoid interruption by Nobby. I used about 3 litres of mix with the ULV, giving a full coverage except where I could not reach without harming the blackthorn.

I was occupied elsewhere during August, and could not revisit the common until 17 September. Most of the knotweed appeared to be dead, but some new shoots had arisen, and some of these were flowering. I was not certain whether the plant can seed in our climate, but it seemed safest to cut off the flowering heads, before spraying all that remained. I did not have an opportunity to visit again that year.

My next visit was planned for the following May, but the weather was unsuitable until 27 May, by which time I expected the plant would be too high to deal with easily. I was relieved to see that it was not nearly so tall as I had feared, with some stems still only just through the soil, and none more than knee-high. A local resident had, no doubt with Nobby's permission, taken the trouble to dig up the main area I had sprayed, producing a formidable pile of thick roots. It must have taken him hours of labour to do this, but I was a little worried that in the process he might have broken off and left in the soil pieces that would produce new growth. I would have preferred to have left it longer for the herbicide to translocate. I expressed gratitude, and used 2 litres of mix on what was clearly still alive.

After the previous year's experience, I was careful to come back in June, but couldn't manage this until the 13th. However the plant had lost much of its intensity, and I was able to cover what growth there was with a watering can. Owing to an injury, followed by a holiday, I did not revisit until 22 July, but again a watering can was sufficient, and the same applied to my next visit on 19 August, though I had to refill it a second time.

I had an operation early in the next year, and it was some months before I could get about normally. When I went to the common on 17 July, I found the plant had regrown spasmodically, up to knee high, but so had a jungle of brambles and other herbage which had taken the opportunity to re-establish now that the knotweed had largely gone. I sprayed all I could see of the latter with a watering can, and on my next visit on 13 August, I did the same again, having to refill once. This was followed by a final visit on 1 October, when only half a can was sufficient, but I noticed that some more plants had come up, though in a form of low and bushy coppice growth with much smaller leaves of a different shape to the normal, which I had seen occur in patches of the Japanese knotweed that I had treated similarly. This coppice growth is possibly assumed under stress, and if left will ultimately produce a stem of the normal growth, but it is still susceptible to the herbicide.

This was my last official visit to the common, as my contract expired the following month. I did however happen to be in the area in the spring of the next year, in connection with other work I was doing, and while at the end of March the area of former dense growth of knotweed appeared to have been effectively colonized by grasses, bramble and young birches, a July visit showed that amongst the proliferation of flowering rosebay and ragwort, there were half a dozen or so of knotweed stems re-appearing that might increase and cause trouble in later years if they were not treated. I could only hope that the Parish Council would have learned from their experience, or that the local residents would remind them of the aggressive nature of the Giant Rhubarb, so that it would not be allowed to get into a state which would take another four years to control.

THREE

Altering the Slopes

Ivan rang, asking whether I would join him in looking over some land on the escarpment that had come to the National Trust by the recently introduced procedure of Treasury transfer. We walked along the steeply sloping chalk slopes, where hawthorn bushes were spreading, and he pointed out the place where red-backed shrikes had nested the year before, though they were becoming less regular visitors than formerly. An old carriage drive ran along the slope between occasional copses, and twisted round to make a zig-zag descent to the farm at the bottom. Beyond the farm it continued under the railway, past a large pond on the Gault clay, to join up with the main road that ran through the village a half mile to the south. This was one of several drives that had led to the big house at the top of the Downs, which was being demolished. I had been to the sale of its contents; it had been a large four-sided building of pretentious but ugly design; the bell system in the butler's pantry had resembled the control room of a battleship, and it must have needed almost as many people to run. This drive was the longest, though probably not the most convenient for visitors but it had clearly been the family's habit to drive out and plant evergreens along it – there were odd bushes of bay, portuguese laurel, juniper, holm oak, box and laurustinus as well as conifers, including redwood, with patches of equally evergreen groundcover of periwinkle, Rose of Sharon and the like. By Victorian standards it had probably ranked highly.

The copses were rounded, and enclosed by cast iron fence posts carrying thick strand wire. The posts had survived well; their sides had been cast separately, and put together with a solid finial at the top which seemed to be shaped in some family emblem. The strand wire was perishing, but could be replaced. The trees in the copses were Scots pine or beech, and there was spurge laurel growing under them. I found some earth-stars in one, and there were other fungi still remaining. It was a mild day, in early December, about thirty years ago.

We continued along the slope eastwards towards the town, to which another branch of the drive led. It was really just a walk round so that Ivan could familiarize himself with the land, and decide how he was going to manage it. It wasn't very accessible for the public, because the woods at the top had been given to the Forestry Commission, which at that time was keen on planting conifers everywhere, and inclined to discourage public access. The natural way onto the slopes would have been through these woods from where a very large rough car park lay between them and the minor road along the top of the Downs. This car park had been given to the Trust, but the woods cut it off from the slopes. Nor was there access from the site of the big house either, as this was still in private hands. The fields on the slopes had clearly suffered from lack of sufficient grazing; they must have been used for sheep in the past, and in the seventeenth and eighteenth centuries they were probably under the plough, as was much of the escarpment. But now there were no sheep around, and most of the local cattle were dairy herds, rather than beef.

Times were changing, however, and two years later when the County Naturalists' Trust was looking for a site with plenty of room for coaches, to hold a nature trail for schools, we were able to get permission to use this car park, and to set up a base-camp in the Forestry Commission woodland, from where we could take parties on a route that led to the slopes and back. We had great help from Rod, himself an expert botanist, who had by then become the Forestry Officer in charge of this area. Previous experience in running educational trails had shown us the need for a large car park, which could hold up to fifteen coaches at once. There are not many that can do this, but at this one they could all park side by side – quite impressive.

We had also learnt the need for six months preparation, so it was again in December when we visited the slopes and John, our Chairman, located enough leaves of bee orchids and other plants to plan a route. Rod co-operated by arranging for a new stile to be installed to give a circuit, and allowed a new track to be made through the conifers. There was quite a variety of these, including some old Silver Fir, and Douglas, while more recent planting included some Noble and Grand Fir, as well as Scots pine, Norway Spruce, and acres of the Western Red Cedar which was then in fashion. So there was some interest in the variety of these, as well as in the many kinds of broad-leaved trees present in the parts not yet given over to the conifers. Publicity in our annual report that spring asked for help in many ways over the seven days in July that the trail would run, as well as in the setting up and dismantling, and we needed the fifty members who responded, as well as the student teachers that John obtained from a Teacher Training College, who gave lecturettes while parties waited their turn to go round, and the night guard of scouts who protected the equipment from vandalism. Penelope and I took all the bookings, as usual, filling every space on the large chart we kept by the telephone, and though we had to refuse about 500 because of lack of space; in the event we probably could have fitted them in since there were gaps through parties arriving early or late, though one never knows when this will happen. The total number of people who came was about 8000, from 150 different schools, and other statistics included consumption of 2592 bottles of soft drinks (much less than if the weather had been warmer), 1824 packets of crisps, and 5528 of sweets. The sale of these was a necessity to cover the costs, since admission fees of £275 in total hardly covered the printing alone. The finances showed a modest profit, even allowing for the purchase of additional equipment such as small tents and trestle tables which would be useful on other occasions too, not only for nature trails but for shows and displays. You could get trestle tables then for about £4 from Gamages, and anyone spare helped to paint them green while the trail was going on.

While I looked after the logistics, John was responsible for the more important educational side: the preparation of the trail guide; the making of name plates to label the plants; the alterations and deviations needed as new plants came into flower, and the content of the talks and demonstrations. The Trust's Conservation Corps took charge of preparing and marking the route, removing snags, putting up posts and rope handrails, with frequent patrols to check and put right any vandalism or accidental breakages. My 30-year-old caravan was coaxed along the rutted track into position and disgorged its content of charts, postcard stands, fire extinguishers, latrine and fire buckets, and all the other items too bulky for a car, and was converted into its usual role of storeroom-warehouse-first aid centre and staff kitchen, as well as sleeping quarters. Tents were erected, notices positioned, and the basecamp area was delineated by ropes from which a variety of wildlife charts and posters were hung. Beyond this no child would be allowed to stray, and there was ample room inside for groups to sit and picnic. By the Sunday evening all was ready, and we had time to relax a bit over such drinks as were available. It was at that stage that a curious and all-pervading smell became noticeable which, after checking the calor-gas, paraffin, disinfectant, and all other things that might have leaked, was traced to the large colony of stinkhorns that surrounded us. Some choice specimens were selected for labelling, and the rest removed to a considerable distance. The arrival of the night guard allowed us to go home to prepare for the week to come.

Routine then followed. Each day we brought up a fresh load of Coca-cola and Fanta from the enormous stack that, on a sale or return basis, was housed in my garage, together with fresh supplies of crisps, sweets, guide leaflets, and goods for sale. We laboured up the hill in the old landrover, with the loaded trailer behind, checking the road signs on the way, and gave out supplies of leaflets, tickets, change and an updated list of schools coming to the Reception table. Fresh goods and change went to the Shop tent, new helpers were initiated, and the first school arrived (*Photo 8*). It was split up into groups of fifteen, which were given an initial briefing, and despatched at five-minute intervals round the trail. For about an hour things were quiet, and gave an opportunity to look for any chance daily additions, such as new flowers, or moths on the tree trunks, that might be indicated. Then parties started returning, new schools arrived, enquiries and minor crises kept us busy. At midday we ate our sandwiches in shifts, surrounded by several hundred children. Many had clearly never been in a wood before; to some to sit on the ground or fallen tree-trunks was a novelty. Particularly noisy groups complained of seeing no animals. Despite prominent litter bins, continuous clearing up was required. Finally the last party left, latrines were emptied, a list made of signs needing replacement before the next day, empties and litter sacks loaded, and the cash collected was taken home for counting and banking. Everyone was exhausted, but felt it had been worthwhile.

There were variations of course: the day one coach driver selected the wrong car park and decoyed others there; the day a party of boys opened the back of a tent and formed a chain to recirculate the empties and claim the threepences; the day when everyone started sliding and rolling down the chalk slope so that we had to rope the track continuously. We usually had both a tame badger cub and a fox-cub; most children knew which was which. Feeding the grass snake with young frogs was too popular, and had to be done out of sight. Occasionally parties saw roedeer, and sometimes rabbits, but birds kept well away from the disturbance and only the experienced realized there were crossbills overhead in the tree-tops. Butterflies were more obliging, whenever the sun allowed, while the cinnabar caterpillars on the ragwort were always visible, though they had to be relocated at intervals. We learnt how to tell on their first arrival which schools would be troublesome; this depended much more on the personality of the headteacher than on the district from which they came. We reinforced the parties that looked as if they might cause problems with some sturdy youths carrying sledgehammers, ostensibly to drive some of the posts in deeper. Some of the ESN schools clearly derived particular pleasure from the trail. Some of the nicest letters afterwards came from the schools which we thought had behaved worst.

Richard had taken advantage of the trail being arranged to carry out, as part of an M.Sc. (Conservation) course, some detailed studies into the effect of trampling on vegetation. This was topical then, as there was growing concern over the numbers of people who sought outdoor recreation in the countryside destroying unwittingly the very environment which they came to enjoy. Work was needed to establish what plants were resistant, what controls were needed, and so forth. This trail was a good opportunity, because many of the tracks were made freshly for it, and the numbers using these could be known precisely, both through woodland and on the chalk slopes. Even those omitting the latter by using a short cut through the woodland could be numbered by a photoelectric device. Measurements were taken in several ways: soil and vegetation samples were made at intervals; daily photographs recorded the increasing width of paths; tree stumps could be measured as they increasingly projected, and conversely the diminishing depth of soil to the clay or chalk below it could also be recorded; soil compaction and pore space could be measured by core samples. This work, and its subsequent analysis and publication, kept Richard busy all the time, and he became a familiar figure flitting between his chosen recording points. Subsequently this work of his, and those of others, led to the establishment of the Recreation Ecology Research Group, which soon became an important and active, if not particularly widely known, forum for discussion of such topics, and to whose various field meetings I was sometimes able to go, and always found useful and enjoyable.

Another by-product of this trail that affected me personally was a visit from the Conservator of the Forestry Commission for South-East England, which resulted in my being recruited as a member of the Regional Advisory Committee for the Conservancy. Although I knew nothing of this body before, twenty years of subsequent service on it were to be of considerable interest, particularly since they covered a period of great change in the Commission's attitude towards other organizations and individuals who value its large areas of woodland for reasons not always directly concerned with the production of cellulose.

This trail was such a success that we subsequently used the same general area for further trails, alternating the location of the camp site and the direction of the route followed, sometimes to bring the parties out on the chalk slopes owned by the National Trust, and sometimes, with the owner's permission, on to basically similar, but in detail very different, slopes to the west of the woodlands. We still used the same large car park, with the popularity of these trails increasing so that we found schools applying to come on them from well outside our own county. We never quite reached a total of 10 000 visitors during the week, but we came very close to it. However increasing vandalism and the need for a more permanent base led us to look for somewhere we could purchase and adapt for such usage. The opportunity to do this arose some ten years later, and we took it, though with mixed feelings whether we were making the right decision. In retrospect it was inevitable, as the strain on those involved in running such large events on a purely voluntary basis was beginning to show, and the alternative of employing a whole-time staff member, assisted by volunteer teaching assistants, on our own ground, was becoming increasingly attractive. In the event, this coincided with the abolition of the large car park by the National Trust in favour of a more circumscribed and tidier area that could not have accommodated the coaches in the numbers we needed.

Some years later, however, and in a different capacity, as Regional Conservation Officer for the National Trust, it fell to me to get to know more intimately the slopes over which I had first walked with Ivan that December. Ten years of seral succession had allowed the hawthorn and other scrub to spread further, but basically the slopes retained their interest for botanists and entomologists, and had been made a SSSI. Grazing by beef cattle and horses had prevented their domination by scrub, though this had proliferated within the fenced-in line of the old carriage drive, from which it was seeding out into the nearest sections of the fields. There was a need for a good deal of detailed recording of what was still present, and where, and for a large amount of manual work in controlling and reversing the spread of the scrub. Farming methods were changing, and the many herds of dairy cows grazing in the fields below the escarpment, that we had been able to point out during the trails to school parties as being the origin of their daily bottled milk supplies (a suggestion often received with incredulity), were no longer in evidence. Sheep were beginning to be talked about again, and it was even being suggested that they could be used, under suitable restrictions of timing and numbers, to graze public open spaces, without them necessarily interfering with the enjoyment of the public, or being immediately torn to pieces by dogs. A neighbouring County Council had pioneered this on land with which I was not unfamiliar, so I went to learn of their experiences. These had turned out to be not entirely straightforward, though the experiment had been considered a success. Dogs did not seem to have been much of a problem but there had been several casualties from the sheep eating yew seedlings. It had been necessary to reposition fences so as to exclude areas of these, as well as the parent trees, and to remove any others. However the excluded ground served as a control in showing the utility of the grazing.

The slopes with which I was concerned covered about 250 acres. They ran along the east-west line of the escarpment for over 1½ miles, though the depth of the property from north to south was only a quarter of a mile. The ground fell from over 600 ft height along the ridge of the Downs to the north, to 300 ft at the base of the escarpment, with the railway line, running along the Gault, forming the southern boundary. The copses formed some 10 per cent of the area, and the rest had been fields of varying sizes, of which the boundary lines were clear enough, whether as wire fences in various stages of disintegration, or as former hedge lines. It seemed best to keep to these former divisions. The arms of the carriage drive ran east and west, about half-way down the slope, rather above the 400 ft contour where they joined the approach to the former mansion in the middle, and rather below this contour as they extended to the sides. They had been made for carriages to use, so were fairly level, giving a most useful approach for vehicles carrying tools and equipment, as well as for parties walking, thus saving a great deal of toiling up and down the slopes.

In general there was one line of fields above the driveway, and another below it, with a third line along the flatter ground at the foot of the slope. This third line was still arable, or had recently been so, and had thus become of little value for conservation. The two higher lines however were of prime importance, and it was of some urgency to limit the spread of the scrub on them. The drive itself was also of importance, both because if cleared it would afford a sheltered and insolated flying route, and because the absence of grazing along the length of its verges had led to the survival of patches of kidney vetch, which supported colonies of the small blue, not otherwise present.

Management at the time of the slopes, apart from the copses was through a part-time warden who did such necessary maintenance as the repair of broken fences and stiles. An attempt to clear a small picnic area at the eastern end had resulted in unfortunate consequences, since the site chosen had been one used by a colony of the chalk race of the five-spot burnet moth, and the timing of the operation had also been unfortunate in regard to this species. This had aroused the wrath of a number of entomologists, since this species (the earliest of the three burnets present here) was becoming scarcer. The incident showed the sensitivity of the site, and the need for authoritative information. Burnets are day-flying moths, with aposematic coloration of red spots. Uncommonly, the red is replaced by yellow (*Photo 13*).

I was able to obtain this readily as far as the flora was concerned, since the county botanical society, of which I was a member, pro-

1 ◁

2 ▷

3 ▽

4 ▷

PLATE 1 *Stepping up Box Hill (1)*

1 8 March 1975. BTCV putting the first line of stakes across the head of a gully. The retaining wall, with spray-paint camouflaging, shows on the left, running along the downhill side of the Gun Road.

2 November 1975. Brian put a series of spruce revetments, filling up with chalk to the original slope, and later putting earth on top. The chalk was fairly thick, so it suppressed the plant growth underneath.

3 Some of the Acorn Camp putting in the left-hand flight of steps in May 1978.

4 The right-hand flight was extended by a team from a Midlands firm in May 1979.

PLATE 2 *Stepping up Box Hill (2)*   5 △

5 The upper photo, taken in 1966, shows the erosion scars on the side of the Zig-Zag valley at
Box Hill, above and below the Gun Road. The photo was taken from above the Zig-Zag road,
of which one can just see the approach to the first 'zig' down below. One is looking southwards,
with the Lower Greensand country beyond Dorking visible over the ridge. The ridge track lies
just over the brow, and the yews whose tops project beyond it are at the top of the steep river-
cliff of the Whites.

6 The lower photo taken in 1985, shows much the same view. The right-hand flight of steps is
clear enough, with the path leading from their foot to the former small car park at the first zig,
near where the columnar (Dawyck) beech can be seen rather more easily, and with 20 years
more growth, than in the first picture. The left-hand steps are more difficult to make out, but if
you look just to the left of the tip of this beech, you can see where they finish between two
clumps of shrubs. From there you can trace them diagonally up to the left, where they reach the
Gun Road between clumps of yew. The erosion gullies have largely disappeared from sight as a
result of the restoration, but some are still visible above the Gun Road.

                                                                                      6 ▽

7 △

PLATE 3

7 *The Giant Rhubarb*. 18 June 1982. The giant knotweed showing various stages of collapse after a recent spraying on 7 June, and earlier in April and May. Fresh shoots had appeared by 7 July, when I next sprayed, and again by 17 September, when some had flowered. However after the five sprayings in that year it had peaked, and only three each were needed in '83 and '84. The highest stems reached to nearly 10 feet.

8 *Altering the Slopes (1)*. A County Wildlife Trust nature trail in July, manned by volunteers, attracted nearly 10000 visitors during the week it was open. Schools were divided into smaller groups for going round the trail.

8 ▽

9 △

11 △

12 △

PLATE 4 *Altering the Slopes (2)*   13 △   14 △

9 A YHA group clearing the banks of the carriage drive.

11 Ringlet butterfly, *Aphantopus hyperantus ab. lanceolata.*

13 Five-spot burnet moth, *Zygaena trifolii f. lutescens.*

Starfruit (*Damasonium alisma*).

10 The first stirring-up. 22 March 1973.

12 A minute plant of 1986.

14 A floating form in 1990.

vided all the information needed, and was always ready to supplement this with tours on the ground if required. Insects were more difficult, except for the butterflies, for which Ken was able to produce, from long study of the area, detailed plans of a nature seldom available in land management. Not only did he provide large-scale maps showing the parts of the individual fields that were used as breeding sites by critical species, over ten years of records, but he was able to supplement this with the reasons why they were so used, and consequently a guide to how these areas might best be conserved and if possible extended. Moths were less well-known, except to the specialists, but over a period I was able to gain the confidence of these people and discover where their interests lay. It took several years to accumulate the information, and there may be species for which I did not sufficiently allow, particularly in the microlepidoptera, but it was evident from the start that all agreed that scrub clearance was a prime necessity. The extent to which it should be carried out became later a matter of argument between those chiefly interested in the butterflies, the moths, the birds or other fauna.

Beginning in 1973, it took nearly ten years to clear the scrub from the fields, At first the only money available was to purchase a few hand tools that volunteer parties could use, either here or on the many other National Trust sites in the Region. The stock of these tools had to be kept in my office at the Regional headquarters, but some of the ladies who worked there did not like to see me continually carrying them in and out, as it made them think of the French Revolution, so I was allotted a shed outside. Here I was able to sharpen them after hours, and paint them a distinctive colour, with numbers on them to keep a check, though my doing this menial task was also the subject of criticism. Gradually however the supply increased, so that the original thirty or so slashers and saws grew into many hundreds. Meanwhile the availability of volunteer parties also increased. At first it was limited to a very few local groups, or those staying at a Youth Hostel within walking distance of the slopes, where Graham, himself a keen conservationist who had helped at our nature trails, was not slow to advertise the availability of active conservation work in the neighbourhood as one of the attractions of his hostel (*Photo 9*). Almost all this work necessarily took place at weekends, and being without other help in those days, it was necessary for me to arrange dates carefully so that I could be there to equip, explain, and look after the parties who were prepared to give of their time. Explanation meant not only what was required of the participants, and especially what was not, but also to those passers-by who saw occasion to remonstrate or question the activities, though these could often be satisfied by an explanatory notice, and some even were prepared to commend the work they saw in progress. Occasional references in the local papers also brought offers of fresh groups, Venture Scouts, or other organizations, and the variety of those offering help increased. A few years later, as the National Trust itself realized the need for greater volunteeer involvement in the immense task of managing its open-space properties, a base-camp to house such parties for a week at a time was set up not far distant, with the object of carrying out work on this and other Trust land in the vicinity, which in all totalled some 5000 acres within a half-hour journey of the van with which the camp was equipped. John was installed as its first Warden, so that thereafter I was able to hand over the work on these slopes largely to him, and concentrate more on places further afield where such help was not so available.

Gradually the amount of work that could be undertaken increased. In 1973, the total number of volunteer days that I could arrange for work on these slopes had been only 60 out of a total of 2000 in the Region, so I had largely to concentrate on the clearance of the sides of the carriage drive. In 1974 this increased to 180 and further increases followed. By 1980 it had risen to 500 in the year out of 10000 days of such work in the Region. By then the intention of clearing such chalk slopes for sheep-grazing was a formulated policy, and had already been implemented for several years on the fields that had already been cleared, which with grant-aid from the NCC were both perimeter fenced and subdivided where necessary with moveable electric fencing. Fortunately there was in the neighbourhood a farmer who became extremely interested and helpful in co-operating with us in the reclamation, both for grazing and for the conservation of the flowers and insects. Nigel had by then taken over the Wardenship of the base camp, with John moving to a wider sphere, though later he was to come back to one that included this area.

We all got to learn about the good effect of winter sheepgrazing on the conservation of downland, both from our own experiences and those of others, particularly the NCC, who were then using it as a management method on several National Nature Reserves. ITE was also extremely helpful in more technical advice. Indeed it is now so well-tried a method that I have heard people, mainly recent students, speak as if it was a panacea – you just have to get some sheep in, and stand back. It was never as easy as that; there are many different breeds of sheep, and they behave differently. The same applies to farmers. Also to butterflies. To take the sheep first, some will eat yew without harm, even standing on hind legs to reach it, while others curl up even if it is fresh, and more do if it is cut and wilting. Some breeds can be very good at eating down the grass tussocks, but equally some can make a real mess of juniper, and most kinds are fond of sallow, to name only two of the plants one normally wants to retain as caterpillar food plants. Sheep adopt a pattern too, sometimes grazing from one end to another, sometimes starting in the middle and eating both ways outwards. Often if you pass at the same time each day, the sheep are in the same place, so one may not realize this daily movement. The varieties of farmers I will not go into, except to say they all have their likes and dislikes, of methods, equipment, and everything else. Some will refuse to adopt methods that have worked elsewhere, and it isn't any use trying to force them, though one can control the all-important timing and numbers, provided one can explain what is needed so that they don't think that 500 sheep days means 500 on one day, or one on 500 days. But for control, one needs a licence, not a lease, and this means not being able to get ADAS grants. The variation of requirements of the butterfly species were a puzzle to us at first, but Jeremy did a lot of work on it, and we got to know which species needed short turf, which shorter still, and which preferred long grasses, and of what type. Even so, it wasn't easy, as some species that need short turf for their caterpillars also need long grass to roost on, and if you think you have left enough of this for them alongside hedges, that is where the birds roost and pick them off in the morning. Obviously one needs a mosaic, and indeed it is hard to get anything else, but it must be a mosaic in the right place.

I tried to observe whether there was any pattern in the area where blue butterflies congregate to roost, and was inclined to think that it was usually close to some landmark such as a bush or tree, or a place where tracks cross, but it must also be influenced by wind and shelter – the same as for pigeons, but they are easier to watch! Rather more is known now of the times at which caterpillars feed, which we didn't then have much information about. Though I am still not clear whether when a grazing sheep meets a grazing caterpillar it eats it with relish, or avoids it, or just doesn't notice it is there. This probably varies with the kinds too, both of sheep and caterpillars. There was also difficulty arising when the winter grazing was too prolonged so that there was hardly any litter layer left in which insects could shelter from wind-chill, and we ran into criticism in some years because of this. While for conservation one normally wants to keep sheep on to eat tussocks down beyond the point at which a farmer would take them off if he was thinking purely of fattening them, this can be overdone, or there can be problems over the shepherd being ill, or the lorry broken down, when they should be moved. So like many other things, it is not as simple as textbooks can make out.

However it was sufficiently successful to be shown off to parties of invited Councillors and others on early summer days when there were plenty of orchids and other plants in flower, with the object of impressing them with the need for financial support to extend this treatment to other downland areas. Such an area had already been obtained, under a long lease, in the shape of a chain of former fields on private land to the west, part of which we had used on some of the nature trails. This too had become invaded with scrub, but clearance by volunteer parties had started in 1981, from the western end, and was going well although it would take five to ten years to complete. There isn't really an alternative to hand clearance on these slopes, which are too steep for machines to work on, and though I have tried winching bushes out with a tractor at the bottom, and long lengths of steel wire rope, sometimes with leads to several bushes at a time, it takes so long to set up, and there is so much standing around waiting for the big pull to happen, which isn't always successful in the event, that it really seems quicker to do it by hand. At least everyone is busy then, either cutting or putting herbicide on the stumps, or burning up, not waiting round and getting cold and wet. Adders are frequent on these slopes, in fact I have seen them far more often there on a sunny spring day than one does on heathland or in woodland, but as long as people are warned not to put their hands down holes, the adders soon hear them coming and keep away. The other hazard one needs to warn people about is the wild parsnip, the only yellow-flowered umbellifer there, which can take off the protective coating of the skin, and allow sunlight to give a rash or burn – we had several casualties from this, but none from adders.

The additional land to the west, and some that we also obtained a few miles to the east, meant that we were working on over ten miles of the south-facing escarpment of the North Downs, which is like a backstop to the Weald, in the sense that any migrant bird or insect is bound to come up against it, and very probably settle there for a while, if it is in a condition to satisfy their needs. So there is always a chance of seeing migrants there, such as humming-bird hawk moths, or the Queen of Spain fritillary, in addition to resident butterfly fauna, which is itself fairly rich for England. 40 species of butterfly have been recorded from these slopes in recent years and about the same number of day-flying moths, if you include the pyrals and plume-moths. On a walk round leading a BBCS party on 1 June once, we saw fourteen kinds of butterflies including the first brood of the Adonis blue in good numbers; two weeks later there might have been twenty, with new species out, but some of those we saw would by then be over. More important perhaps than numbers of species is the recurrence on these slopes of particular variations in some species, some of them striking in altering the wing colours, others less noticeable in giving additional or fewer or differently shaped spots, or combinations of spots on the wing patterns (*Photo 11*). Such variations are possibly the first attempts in evolving new races, but are usually absorbed in the normal pattern before they can spread far. However it has been calculated that a character that gives a selective advantage of only 0.1 per cent will establish itself in 50 per cent of the population within 5000 generations; a long time to us, but not to insects with two or more generations a year.

One tends to notice the butterflies more than other insects, but there are many of these, and of molluscs too, including the big Roman snail. The Downs escarpment has the fascination of a shoreline, which it once was, and despite 30 years acquaintance with these slopes in varying capacities, I still find them full of interest.

FOUR

Starfruit

Soon after moving to this village, some forty years ago, I was asked to join the Committee that managed the local common. A year or two later, in the way that things happen in villages, as people move in and out and vacancies have to be filled in what are deemed to be essential functions in the corporate life, I found myself appointed to the secretaryship of this committee. Effectively this meant that I became estate manager for the Chairman, whose many interests on a national level limited his personal supervision of all of the schemes he initiated for the benefit of the 500 acres of heath and downland that formed the view from his house, and of which the upkeep was the Committee's concern. Gradually I acquired familiarity with the terrain, which had surprising variety and wildness for a common within 20 miles of the centre of London, and also with the bird and insect fauna with which it was so richly endowed. Its flora was less varied, since most of the common was acid heathland, though the west side fell away to a series of valleys and intervening spurs, where the soil was chalk. Although this area comprised under a tenth part of the common, it contained at least ten times the variety of plants and insects, and consequently I occupied much of my spare time in its study.

This was probably a mistake, because although the much larger extent of heathland appeared less varied, it was exposed to greater threat, both from the natural spread of birch, bracken, and other invaders of its original heather, and since it extended outward from the car park, from the increasing activities of visitors in their various manifestations. The many walkers and riders did not affect it unduly, though the tracks became increasingly churned up, but the large numbers of dogs they exercised caused the gradual diminution of ground-nesting birds such as nightjars, and the fires which vandals amongst them persisted in lighting burnt out many of the insects, including the grayling butterflies that had been a welcome feature as they flitted along the heathland paths.

There was, however, another habitat present on the common which I neglected for far too long. This was formed by the few remaining survivors of the ponds, which must in commoning times have been a valuable attribute, and no doubt were then much trodden round and fouled by the livestock. Maps of the last century showed some ten of these on the commonland or manor waste, but only two or three survived as ponds, though the sites of a few of the others could still be identified. Only one of them, however, was what most people would expect of a pond on a common, and though not large it retained a reasonable extent of open water, fringed with rush and willow except on the margin adjoining a bridle-path from which it was still used by occasional horses to refresh themselves, assuming that their riders allowed, or were unable to prevent it. Its aquatic life included newts, dragonflies, and some fish, which when it was found necessary to evacuate them during a period of drought, appeared from their ornamental fins to have once been goldfish. Needless to say the vegetation had also been embellished by well-wishers from time to time, and included a patch of red water-lilies, also, more surprisingly, the greater spearwort.

This pond lay well out on the common, and of another formerly near it only a muddy patch remained. It seemed probable that all the ponds had been natural in the sense that while they were no doubt excavated and enlarged by human hand, they were not puddled or embanked, but had been dug out in places which were naturally damp through the vagaries of the soil and surface drainage. Indeed there appeared to me to be several other places on the common where the presence of rushes or marsh thistles indicated that similar conditions obtained, and I was able to persuade the Committee to let me hire a machine to make two more, which were successful, as well as trying to revitalize one that was shown on the maps, which was not a success. These new ponds, which have later been enlarged, were made in places where there was no evidence of a pond before, which is what makes me think that the ones on the old maps had originally also just been excavations where there appeared to be a wet patch. Whether their original makers could equally well have dug in the places where I later did, I do not know, since the war-time use of this common for training operators of earth-moving machinery may have altered the drainage pattern.

Many of the old ponds had lain much closer to the village than any of these, and seemed to have been made not so much for the watering of livestock, as for the draining away from the cottages of the surface run-off which would otherwise have rendered them damp. Most of these ponds had since been filled in, but a few still remained. They did not appear to the casual observer to have much interest, though some had newts in them, as well as tadpoles in their season, and occasionally pairs of mallard attempted to raise a brood in them, which usually fell victim to foxes. However they came under scrutiny from botanists, and in the early 1970s a case was made to me regarding the need for conservation of a plant which had occurred in one of these formerly, but had not been seen for some years.

I had heard of the existence of this plant from time to time, but being then comparatively ignorant of botanical matters, had not paid much attention, because it appeared from reports to be somewhat insignificant and its name of Thrum-wort did not sound terribly exciting. Its scientific name was *Damasonium alisma*. It was said to have small white flowers, and to be recognizable only to botanists. I had thought it was therefore best to leave it alone. The pond lay just in front of a large house on the edge of the common, and it seemed likely that any activity there might meet with objections. However the case as made to me was that the nature of the plant was such that its preferred habitat was on the edges of ponds used for watering livestock, and that if the pond edges were no longer stirred up by such activities, it tended to die out. Seed, however, was still likely to be lying dormant, and if a section of the edge could be stirred up, then it might possibly re-appear. It was now some seven years since it had last been recorded there, and this had been almost its last recorded station in Britain, apart from one other site, where it was also of doubtful status. In fact my leaving of the pond untouched for whatever amenities it provided to the adjacent houses, was likely to hasten its decline.

This of course put a different complexion on the matter, and I consequently obtained the Committee's permission to carry out a small and local disturbance of the pond's perimeter when occasion offered. At that time we were making intermittent use of machines of the bulldozer type both in extending our network of fire-rides and of riding tracks, and in connection with a new policy I had instituted, of rehabilitation after heath fires. We had by then learnt that these unfortunately frequent calamities could be turned to positive use by clearing all the resulting debris, levelling, and controlling the regrowth by swiping to get heather back, rather than, as we were frequently advised "leaving it to nature". If one did that, one merely got a recrudescence of birch, gorse and bracken, and very little heather. So after such fires, we used the large numbers of Boy Scout, school and other parties who were willing to volunteer their services, to remove all the remaining charred vegetation, and burn it up. We then hired a machine of the Drott type, to extract all the roots that would form an impediment to the passage of the warden's tractor and swipe, levelling the surface roughly in the process. This allowed the warden to control the regrowth, and by successive passages of the swipe, he was able to eliminate the bracken and the various other forms of vegetation that would have shaded out the heather, until this could re-establish itself, and slowly form the expanse of purple that our visitors clearly preferred to other forms of surface covering. The process was in fact a little more complicated than that, because it was usually necessary to reduce competition from gorse, either by laborious hand-cutting with secateurs, or in later years, by applying a selective herbicide, but it was successful in getting us back a large acreage of heather, which was considered a good thing both by the conservationists who had thoughts of sand-wasps and the like, and by less informed visitors who may have been inspired by recollections of chocolate-box covers, or romantic fiction. From either view-point it was beneficial, and it depended on the essential stage of hiring a machine, usually for two or three days at a time, to get out the roots, which were then either burnt up, or buried in a sort of mass grave.

So next time we had such a machine, I asked Dave to stir up the pond edge a bit. Dave was a man of stature, and when astride his machine, seemed somehow to dwarf it, even though it was itself quite sizeable. He also worked with furious energy, gripping each root with the jaws of the bucket, pulling it out bodily, banging it on the forefront of the machine to loosen the soil from it, and tracking rapidly with it to wherever he was dumping the growing pile of roots. Although he did not usually say much, it was somehow easy to explain to him what was wanted, and on this occasion there was no difficulty. He ran his machine down so that the bucket was opened out in the margin of the pond, pushed it forwards and back so that the mud ran over it, and the job was all done in five minutes. This was on 22 March 1973, and the first plant was visible in June, flowering in July (*Photo 10*).

It was not such a bad plant really. The leaves looked a bit like those of the pondweed also present, but were on long stems, rather like the sort of spoon which one is advised to use if one has to sup with the Devil. The flowers are small and white, which helped me understand its attractions to botanists, who tend to go for small white flowers, just as ornithologists like small brown birds. An interesting feature of this plant to me was its development of plentiful seed-heads formed like small knobkerries, which has led to its present name of Star-fruit, replacing the Thrum-wort of earlier books, and which is more understandable and evocative. I had never been quite clear what a thrum is or was, though it must have been more familiar to earlier generations since it also occurs in the classic description of the two shapes of primroses, pin and thrum. But the way these seed-heads were formed in such quantity, and held apart from each other by their stems at all angles, seemed to indicate that the plant was doing its best to produce much more seed than one would expect to be necessary. I therefore thought that this must be an adaptation to enable it to survive in the face of odds, and that the odds against it must be considerable for it to need such a degree of insurance.

There were several plants that year, but the water levels fell in August, leaving them stranded, though bearing large heads of seeds, top-heavy, but still mostly keeping above the mud. There were some plants again in 1974, and one or two in 1975, but we seemed to be running out of steam, so the next January, when I had a JCB working on the common, I got the operator to stir up quite a section of both ends of the pond. This gave us plants in 1976 and the next three years, but again they got fewer. In 1977, which was a plentiful year for it, I thought we really ought to be spreading the risks a bit, so I got the botanists' permission and on 2 November '77 put some plastic buckets in the landrover, and inserted a shovel under the first plant. Nothing could have been easier: it came up roots and all in one piece and fitted nicely into a bucket. I took two plants out of the dozen I could see, with the intention of putting them in the new ponds I had made 5 years before – call them A and B. A looked the most likely, and already had a flora of a sort, introduced by someone when the warden wasn't looking, or possibly the reverse. I had been asked not to let this happen, but to let them colonize naturally, but you can't do much about it when someone has already tipped in quite an assortment. I put both in B, which was always being stirred up by dogs or children wading in, but was more gravel and sand than mud. Next year, 1978, we again had a good crop in the original pond, and on 15 July I again took some buckets, and moved 5 plants, putting one in B, and three in A, choosing different parts of the pond, but with the water depth they had come from. The other, which was small, I put in a small water-filled scrape rather hidden away, but this was a failure. I will come back to A and B later, but I ought first to say something of what sort of hazardous life the plant seems to have.

Firstly some books give the impression that it is a spring plant. I suppose this is so in a sense, as it comes into flower about June, and most of my photos of it in flower were taken in June or July. But the fruiting goes on a long while, certainly to September, even November. There was healthy-looking fruit on the ones I moved to B on 2 November '77, and it went on looking healthy for some time afterwards, as I saw when I revisited them. There is no stream on the common, so the ponds can only be fed by the run-off from rain, and their water levels, in our English climate, consequently go up and down like a yo-yo. If the level goes up in late summer, and this is not infrequent as one can remember from wet summer holidays, the flowers get drowned, and I don't think they can then set seed. But the plant does have a trick up its sleeve, because it seems to be able to extend its flowering spike, and produce another set of flowers higher up. It can only do this however if it has time, and if the water level rises too quickly, following a downpour, then it's had it. But this trick does give it a bit more chance, and I have seen such extension spikes in flower still in September.

If the level goes the other way, and the pond dries out, then the plant seems to dessicate, and the seed-heads are shrivelled thin and dry. I think they may still be fertile, but another danger arrives because in such a condition people and animals walk all over the pond, and anything brittle is likely to be trampled out. So by and large, I don't suppose it is very often, perhaps one year in five, or less, that water levels behave to suit it. Then there are all the other possible factors; competition from other plants, increase of shading, alteration of pH, and interference, though I have not noticed any evidence of browsing or pecking.

1978 was the best year we had had for these plants, and I see I described them at the time as 'plentiful' in the original pond. But it was not until September, by which time the water level had gone up and down, that I was asked to send some seed to Cambridge University Botanic Garden for their rare plant project. I was doubtful of its viability, as I thought it had been drowned and dried out again, but I sent a few seed heads from which CUBG managed to raise quite a stock, which they still keep going. I am told that their experience has been that it is not affected by frost, so that is one hazard from which it doesn't suffer. They also found that individual plants could live and flower over at least two years. Germination occurred principally in autumn, when the seedlings over-wintered, or in early spring (February-April), but could occur at other times. It only occurred below water-level. The water used at CUBG was tap water with a high pH.

In July 1979 there were only two small plants in the original pond, but there were 3 fruiting in A, though none in B. By September A was largely dry, and trampling was a risk. I was particularly worried on the occasion of a visit of a large party of mycologists, but luckily one of their number was the botanical recorder for a northern county, and she and another girl undertook to keep watch over the site. However it was looking unhappy then, and dried up still more later, becoming a sort of adventure playground for boys – I even saw a party with bicycles on the island.

We did not see any plants in 1980 or '81, so in November '81, I tried to stir things up again. Unfortunately the machine I had working then was too large, and not really suitable. In fact it made rather a mess of the banks. We had already that September tried to reduce competition by hand-weeding the bur-reed and bur-marigolds that had been spreading, and I had intended to follow this up by spraying the floating sweet-grass, but did not get an opportunity to do this before heavy rain brought the water level right up again.

Meanwhile I had received from CUBG a supply of seed grown from what I had sent them in 1978, and I started to try to sow this. Attempts to dig it in under water were ineffective, so I made up pellets, wrapping grains of seed in clay from the common, and casting them into the waters of all the ponds. One could do this with some accuracy, but it proved over the succeeding years to be totally unfruitful. I also tried raking in seed during lower water-level periods, in places where it would be submerged when the level rose. This too was ineffective.

In 1983 a plant appeared in pond B, on the site of where I had put one in 1978. Although this pond is much used by the public and their dogs, it survived and fruited that September continuing into October. No other plants appeared on the common that year. On 4 October 1983 I took advantage of low water levels and the absence of the plant at the original pond, to spray all the floating sweet-grass there with dalapon, using a two-gallon watering-can with a spray bar attachment. I used 5 gallons of tap water from a container, filling the can three times not quite full, and using 3 oz of dalapon powder in each. I used this method because I have not found it effective to spray dalapon from an ultra-low-volume sprayer. No plants appeared on the common (or elsewhere in Britain) in 1984 or 1985.

On 6 September 1985 the pond was visited by a member of the Chief Scientist's Department of the Nature Conservancy Council, on a warm sunny afternoon. She noticed overgrowth by bur-reed, and shading by large willows and oaks. The pH of the water seemed very high at 8.1, which she thought possibly due to algae. The water was about ¼m deep with over ½m brown organic mud containing half-rotted plant debris. The surface of the mud had patches of filamentous alga, also decaying. She made a sketch of the areas occupied by the various plant species, the small patch of white water-lily in the centre, the considerable area of bur-reed which had spread again since the weeding in 1981, the still reduced patch of bur-marigold, the pond weed, lesser spearwort, soft rush, and other species including the floating sweet-grass, still present at both ends, though much reduced following my spraying of it with dalapon two years before, when it had covered almost the whole of the pond. All the southern half of the pond was suffering from shading. She recommended drastic action in cleaning out the mud and vegetation from half the pond (east or west) to regain a gravelly and less organic substrate, with the removal of the shading trees. She thought present conditions of the site were obviously unsuitable for the plant.

The Committee agreed to drastic action, subject to expense, and combination with other work on the common. Ro came over to discuss details, and, looking at the record, we thought February or March probably the best time to do the deed. I put in for an NCC grant to cover the cost of a Hymac for two days, including transport, which was about £300. Most of the tree clearance could be done by the Warden, or with the help of volunteer parties. We thought at first that we could pile the mud in the centre to make a better island, and to preserve any seed still latent, but on reconsideration NCC suggested the mud was so suspect that it would be better removed altogether. Ro thought there was the possibility that long-viable seed from previous good years might be lurking closer to the bottom unable to germinate because of the more recent gunge on top. Removal of the overshadowing trees would expose an area on which nothing but ivy remained, and we decided to put the mud there. A letter to local residents evoked some sorrow at the loss of a large sallow, which had been spared from earlier attempts at reducing shading because of the increase of purple emperor butterflies in recent years, but following many years of avoidance of including sallows in scrub clearance, and despite the depredations of visitors seeking pussy willow branches, there were by now quite a number of sallows on the common. So we thought one could be spared in the interests of a still rarer species.

In February 1986 Tim started on the shade removal, and I arranged for the machine to come on Monday 24th, to work first on pond A, because Ro couldn't be present until the Tuesday. She rang me on the Friday to ask if it was still on, in the very cold conditions, but we thought we had better keep to the date. The local residents had been warned and some had arranged to go abroad then. Also the frozen ground would not be churned up by the machine's tracks. The machine, a JCB 805 Excavator, not unlike a Hymac in appearance, arrived on the Monday morning, and we tried it out on pond A. I had at first demurred at the scoop which the operator clearly preferred, thinking a toothed bucket would be needed in the hard ground, so we took that over as well. Actually the scoop worked well enough, though being simply a slightly curved blade without sides, it could not retain the sheets of ice, except by balancing them like in an egg and spoon race. The ice was nearly 4″ thick, but it broke up easily enough, and we didn't think the machine should venture into it in case it got stuck. Our object at pond A was to make up the banks at one end and deepen the other so that water levels stayed more equal throughout, instead of one end drying out always. We also needed to make the islands rather less accessible to boys with or without bicycles. Again we had to lose some sallows, but though I had seen a purple emperor on these some years earlier, I thought they were still too young as breeding sites, and there were older bushes nearby. The excavation work was soon done, but the transferring of the material from one end to the other in a series of swings and fresh piles in a leap frog manner took a long time. We didn't finish it that day, though we did before the machine left on the Wednesday.

Tuesday morning we started on the main pond, where we had decided to clean out the eastern half only. The machine scooped out the roots of the large willow, and after a tussle, those of the oaks. It then got right into the pond and started transferring the mud from the north side to the south. The ice had broken up in that half by now, and the machine was up to the top of its tracks in a mixture of water, ice, and debris. Tim and I meanwhile cut away the lower boughs of trees behind, so that it could later swing the mud it had piled up on the south bank well clear of the pond onto the ivy-covered ground beneath the trees. The mud was scraped from all this end of the pond, in some areas exposing the bright orange substrate, though some mud was bound to be re-deposited when disturbance ceased. Hopefully this might contain dormant fruits, but in general as much mud and leaf litter as possible were taken right out of the pond. The margins were scraped to give more shallowly sloping banks. Ro thought we should try to get out the floating debris of *Sparganum* leaves and Tim and his wife Ruth improvised an arrangement of two ropes to a floating timber. Standing on the still firm ice of the western end, they were able to drag this towards them, but with the blocks of ice still floating we couldn't manouvre it up clear of the water. This was therefore left till a thaw. Ro measured the pH at 6.5, suggesting that the very high September reading was indeed due to algae.

Ro thought that any germination in 1986 would depend on a warm growing season, and we ought to wait until 1987 before considering work on the western end, or re-introduction of plants from CUBG. Meanwhile we should try to prevent over-growth by floating sweet-grass, or other competitors, though without using herbicides until we knew more about what would happen naturally. I revisited the pond on 12 March, when it was all frozen over again, with some of the ice blocks up-ended like floes. The ice didn't all go until a week after that, and one could then see the changes. The pond looked considerably larger, more open, and a bit devastated, but the frost had prevented the ground from being churned up, and it looked as if it would settle down well. We arranged to put something in the newsletter of the County Flora Committee, which was then due to go out, to warn botanists in case any thought that some vandals had been at work. We didn't think any other publicity was advisable.

So we waited to see whether 1986 would produce a flourish of starfruits, or none at all. What happened was quite unexpected, in that when I looked at the pond in June, I could see no plants, but Ro visited on 15 July, when I was abroad, and counted twenty-six. I looked again, on my return, less casually, and at each square yard of the drying mud, in which bur-marigold and bur-reed seedlings were appearing. The star-fruit was indeed there, some in flower, and some already wielding their knobkerries, but they were all minute plants, with not more than one or two seed heads on each. They seemed to have reverted to the form I had been told about twenty years before, in which only a botanist's eye could detect them. Not all botanists either, as Esther, in her garden over the wall, heard several cries of frustration (*Photo 12*).

In 1987 the bur-reed was so thickly dominant that even if a star-fruit had appeared, I doubt whether it would have been visible. By now the pond was in a ringed area within the re-notified SSSI under the direct control of the NCC, so that I could not do anything to clear it without reference, and permission was only received after any working party was available. Meanwhile I had a letter from Chris, on his appointment as NCC Plant Conservator at CUBG, who had been looking up the files, and asked for further information. This led to a visit in February 1988 when he took the pH of this pond, then 5.35 to 5.56 in the water and 4.0 in the mud, and of five other ponds on the common, with ranges from 4.85 (pond B) up to 6.18 (pond A). He made various suggestions, including introducing seed at one of these, which I will call pond C, and this was agreed and carried out in October 1988. Meanwhile he had brought a party of four botanists on 25 September 1988, and in five hours pulled out all the stems of bur-reed present in the original pond, though inevitably some of the rhizomes were left. The churning up in this operation hopefully may have brought starfruit seeds to the surface. At that time there was hardly any water in the pond, and levels continued low through the winter, so that there was only water over a quarter of the pond in late January 1989, though the bur-reed seemed to be sprouting again rather ominously.

Record rainfall in March 1989 only increased the water area to about three quarters of the pond, and dry spells in May and June lowered it again. The bur-reeds grew thickly, and on 8 June I wrote rather despondently to Chris that no starfruit was in sight. On 21 June I was taking Carol, the new Conservation Officer of the County Wildlife Trust round on a tour, and thought I should at least show her the site. I noticed one small flower of Starfruit, with its familiar three white petals, at the edge of the water, and Carol spotted another plant already with three seed-heads. I rang Joyce, and next day Ken came to check, finding nine plants in all. They were all small and feeble, though possibly slightly larger than in 1986, and some had already been trodden or had bent down into the mud between the many plants of bur-reed. I looked again at intervals, seeing at least one seed-head up to 26 June, when it rained heavily and the level of the water rose a bit, but this didn't last long, and on 9 July there were four plants still visible when I looked with Frank, all with seed-heads, though none with more than two or three. It was difficult to imagine that the plants I had moved ten or so years before had been large enough to fill a plastic bucket. On 22 June, I had taken Ken round all the other ponds too, including A, B and C, but we had seen no plants at any of them, nor did I see any in them later in 1989, though I looked if I happened to be passing them. So despite all the theories advanced, we still did not seem to have discovered the way to increase the plant in a natural situation.

Yet it continued to appear during 1989 at the original pond, where Chris recorded 14 plants on 17 July, mostly with single seed-heads, though two had six and nine respectively. One of these was still visible into mid-August, when the pond had dried out. Later I was to hear that star-fruit re-appeared in 1989 at two of its former stations elsewhere in the UK.

In the autumn of 1989 the pond was again weeded by a party of botanists, but by the following spring the bur-reed was so thick that I did not think the star-fruit would find any space left. However we were encouraged by its appearance in pond C, more or less in the position in which it had been planted in 1988, having failed to appear there in 1989. Water levels were falling with the dry summer, and it was soon exposed, though protected from trampling by a fence.

A fortnight later, on 20 June 1990, a detailed survey found it was also present in the original pond. Two plants on the south side were of rather better size than in recent years, though still much smaller than those of the late 1970s. A new development (*Photo 14*) was the appearance of several plants of what seemed to be a floating form. One of these, close to the northern bank, was quite a complex assemblage, and was much photographed. I would not have been aware of the presence of one photographer when I drove past, as he was crouched motionless behind his tripod under the cover of the bank, if I had not stopped to investigate his apparently abandoned bicycle. These floating plants seemed to go to ground as the water level fell, but they still had seed-heads, and indeed even into September 1990, one could see at least two plants still each carrying a branch of four seed-heads, though these appeared desiccated. By then there was still eight inches of water in the centre of this pond, more in places, though all the other ponds on the common had dried up. The botanists again came and weeded the pond, and when I next saw it in mid-October, it was dry.

Starfruit is listed in Schedule 8 of the *Wildlife and Countryside Act* of 1981, and protected under Section 13 of the Act. One can't say that it is the rarest plant in Britain, though I have seen it so described, because unfortunately there are quite a few other species of plant or animal of which only a single site or specimen is known to survive. Having these rare seed banks is a tremendous help, because often one feels that the species is dying out in the field through changed conditions, and one can only get them back to what one thinks they should be, by taking some drastic action. While this may be right, one hesitates to do it without having a reserve on which one can draw if it proves the opposite. With animals the position is rather different, since any replacement stock, if it is still available, may have to come from a different country, or a zoo, and it may not be justifiable to deplete such a stock in a reintroduction to a situation that seems unfavourable.

Such seed-banks allow a series of methods to be tried out until one is found that allows the plant to re-establish in the wild. They also permit trials to be made at other sites, where rather different combinations of environment or competition may obtain. This has been done in the case of this plant, not entirely without success, but so far such trials have not produced a convincing explanation of why this formerly widespread plant should have come into the intensive care category. It would seem that some influence or accompaniment to its growth may have been lost in recent times, and awaits rediscovery.

FIVE

The Threat to the Valley

The valley ran northwards from the coast into the Downs. It was a dead end in the sense that you couldn't reach it by car over the Downs, but you had to go round and come up from the south. This meant joining the road that had once run behind the original villages and small towns along the coast, but now had been engulfed in their spread, so that it was built up on both sides, and crowded with traffic. You could join it a few miles either to the east or to the west, and you then had to go along it hoping to recognize one of the turnings off it that would take you northwards into the valley. There were several of these turnings, none very obvious, but after a short way they united, like the arms of a delta, into single wider road that ran up the valley floor. There were some roadsigns but it wasn't easy to see them with all the shop fronts and advertisements, the traffic lights and pedestrian crossings, the delivery vans and lorries. The first time I went there, I overshot it badly, and had to come back, checking the street names in turn, until I reached one that must lead into the valley, but it wasn't until I had gone some way up it that I was certain that I really was on the main artery that served all the population of the valley. For the valley too was heavily built up, with houses on its slopes.

It would have been pleasant to have come over the hills from the north, as you could if you rode or walked, following any of the several old tracks that led either straight over the crest of the Downs, or meandered through their dry coombs. All united at the head of the valley, where the metalled road from the south ended by the pub, turning into a gravelled track which continued only as far as the farm beyond. Probably one could have driven over the hills, but there were frequent gates and other deterrents, and it wouldn't have been popular. So one always had to go round through the traffic.

If you looked at the street-plan, or even a large-scale map, you could imagine how the development had spread. Fortunes had been made as blocks of farmland had been sold one by one, and filled up with houses in turn. The streets that served these houses were crescent-shaped, following the curves of the slopes, and the houses along them looked over the roofs of those to the south. The new houses in each of these crescents would have had access northwards onto the Downs, until a few years later another crescent was built above them, overlooking them, and in turn cutting off their access to the downland, except for an occasional alleyway between them where a footpath had been. You could trace successive stages, five or six deep, with crescent rising above crescent, concretionary like the growth of a gall, until it had reached a point where it suddenly had stopped, and solidified. The spreading tide had then halted, and instead of proceeding further, had concentrated on filling up all the gaps where former greens or large gardens had resisted the pressures for a while, but now became criss-crossed by a closer network of streets and meaner houses. The few open spaces that remained on the map were marked with clues to the reasons for their survival, school playing fields mostly; sometimes a golf-course or a cemetery; a recreation ground, or allotments, or more obscurely 'Works'.

The reason for the halt of the tide of building was not clear, though the informed might have been able to work it out from the growth in the powers available to the local planning office. Even so, one would question whether such a tide could really be curbed by edict alone. Possibly it was a result of a combination of the direct and the indirect; the shops would have been easier to control than the dwellings, and the distance over which people were prepared to carry their daily purchases uphill to their homes would have had a limiting effect in itself, until the planners' powers became sufficiently draconian to perpetuate the situation in a sort of plagioclimax – lasting only while the political will to contain growth was stronger than the pressure to expand. One wondered for how long.

An observer from another planet might well have thought that the reason for the sudden stop of the rising tide of building was quite different – that it had reached a level above which the human race could not live, due to shortage of oxygen; distance from the coast; freezing of pipes in winter; or perpetual sea-mist caused by the effect of the inshore winds meeting the insolated chalk hillsides. All sorts of theories might have been advanced and discarded in turn. Comparison with other inhabited coasts would have led to the rejection of theories based on the physical, since many such coasts show that mankind is perfectly capable of covering all seaward-facing hillsides with an unending series of villas, rising above each other as high as the hills allow, and only stopping in the occasional situations where there is a more or less permanent cloud layer at about 1500 metres. Such an observer might have concluded that the reason for the abrupt ending of the spread of development at a very much lower altitude here could only be attributed to some numinous factor. Possibly planning regulations should be considered in such a light. They are after all only an enshrinement of the current consensus of opinion! Even so, it would have seemed extremely puzzling that the particular area that I was visiting should not have been built over, since it was clearly within the acceptable altitude limits for development, as evinced by the opposite side of the valley, which was thickly covered with houses, except for the central block of a large school with its playing fields around it. The explanation would never have occurred – that it had been given to the National Trust some thirty years before, when only the two lowest lines of houses had been built, with the less tangible assistance of a constituency boundary that was only much later to become the dividing line between two full counties.

I went along the street that served these houses, and sure enough between the two whose numbers I had been told, there was a narrow passage leading uphill. Going up this, between the palings that protected their back gardens on either side, I came out onto the downland turf. The first thing that struck me was the exceptional number of electricity pylons, from which no less than three parallel rows of wires ran over my head. The next was the considerable quantity of round-headed rampions in flower, not in clumps but spread widely in twos and threes, even between the bases of the pylons. I then followed my usual routine on visiting a property new to me, of going clockwise round the boundary, or close to it, with occasional forays into the centre when particular features caught my eye, and making notes on a standard check-list of the various species of plants and animals. I soon reached a higher point, from where I could see, though hardly admire, the power station on the coast to the south to which the three lines of pylons led, and in the other direction could trace their course over the Downs, until they gradually diverged from each other and disappeared over the horizon. This southern end was clearly a much-used approach route, with several footpaths leading to it from the conurbation to the south, which lay out of sight below, though only the width of a ploughed field away. There were a number of people present on this August day, and they seemed to be enjoying themselves, having picnics or strolling about. I knew there was no resident warden as the 150 acres were not large enough to warrant one, or to cover the expense of his employment. A local resident kept an eye, particularly at weekends, on an arrangement that included a small retainer. The gates and stiles seemed to be in reasonable order. One stile had recently been completely rebuilt, indicating that the vandalism to be expected in such a situation was not unknown. Children had built a 'house' in some of the bushes, and it all seemed to be fulfilling its function as a pleasant place for the local people to use, and get away from the houses below and across the valley. Rather monotonous fields lay beyond, which like far too much of the South Downs were still intensively farmed.

The upper part of the property was covered with drifts of gorse and bramble, in which blackthorn, hawthorn and elder were mixed. There were some clearings in it towards this southern end, and in the shelter of which there was a variety of rather taller flowers, such as ragwort and musk thistle, mostly bearing testimony to recent disturbance. I knew that there lately had been fresh searching for war-time bombs, and I saw where recent rides had been made through the scrub to give access for this search, though it was evident that their distance apart must have made this rather cursory. One such ride had revealed a concrete trigonometric point, which indicated more open conditions had once existed. However there was little temptation for anyone to stray into the thickets, certainly not in the summer clothes that most were wearing, and the likelihood of an explosion seemed remote.

Going northwards along the crest, the belts of scrub became thicker, though still with irregular clearings at intervals, joined up by rather muddy trackways. I had not long before been sent a list of birds seen on this property over the last six years by a local resident whose name was familiar to me, though I had not met him. The list comprised 65 species, plus some occasionals, which he had marked according to whether they were breeding, migrants, winter visitors or regularly seen throughout the year. There were no particular surprises, but the almost complete list of the warblers and other small migrants to Britain showed the importance of these belts of thickets so close to the sea as a landfall for birds coming in over the Channel. The need for such cover for birds as a temporary refuge, especially in bad weather, after their flight and before they subsequently move on, is sometimes forgotten in a desire to extend as much as possible the area of open chalk downland. Nor are birds the only creatures that migrate, and need shelter on their first arrival – if circumstances had allowed, it would have been an interesting place to run a moth-trap.

The list of birds was the only previous information I had, and the plants and insects remained to be noted from what I could see myself, or the reports of others. I knew I was unlikely to be able to visit the property very often, and it would be impossible for me to walk over every part of it at the various times of the year needed to make a complete list. One could only hope to observe or deduce the presence of those species that were the more important in conservation terms. This was the sort of place that seemed fairly stabilized, and unlikely to change much. It was already under considerable pressure, but a reasonable, though not outstanding, range of plants was evidently surviving nonetheless, and it had a good deal of interest. There was work that could usefully be done by volunteers in widening the muddy defiles between the glades, but this would be relatively simple to explain and organize if volunteer parties became available. It was the sort of place where one could happily spend a couple of hours, at different times of the year, going over it, noting the improvement that could be brought about, and checking the plants and insects, but these were unlikely to alter much, and it did not seem an urgent task, in the absence of obvious threats to their survival. The main handicap was the time needed to get to it, which meant taking up a whole day, which could otherwise be spent on looking over two or three other properties where work was more urgently needed.

Over the next eight years I visited it half a dozen times, working up a species list of about 100 easily recognizable plants, which meant that a botanist would find at least twice as many, since I lumped many species of the same genus together, and left out the grasses entirely. It was, as expected, strong on chalk turf plants – cowslips, fairy flax, fleawort, vetches including horseshoe and kidney, marjoram, dropwort, mignonette, mulleins, common spotted, fragrant and pyramid orchids, tway-blade, round-headed rampion, salad burnet, field and small scabious, squin-ancywort, thyme, toadflax, yellow rattle and yellow-wort. There were six common kinds of thistle, several with white forms, and other taller plants providing nectar sources included hemp agri-mony, fleabane, woundwort and others. The thickets of thorn, bramble and gorse also contained privet, honeysuckle, and occa-sional holm-oak, cherry and crabapple, while the field edges had heartsease, poppies and scarlet pimpernel. I noted about 20 but-terfly species, but there would undoubtedly have been some ten others to be seen, particularly if I had gone there in spring, which I never managed to do. Again all these were species one would expect to find on a chalk hillside; there were dark-green fritill-aries but I never saw marbled whites, and the only noteworthy discovery was made when Glynn and I were walking round with a visiting Trust warden from Northumberland who spotted a colony of small blues on the furthest edge, these being less com-mon in Sussex than in Surrey. All in all it was, like the plants, quite a good range of species for a much-visited National Trust property, and pleasing to see, I hope for many besides myself. But in a Sussex context it was average, not outstanding, and unlikely to qualify for SSSI rating. I was not surprised that it was omitted from the list of sites that the NCC thought worth includ-ing in a downland survey they later commissioned, and it was only just in the edge of the Green Belt.

Its strong point was that it had kept its interest despite thirty years of public access, and it looked as if it would happily con-tinue to do so. Most of the people who used it admittedly kept to the southern part, as was evident both from observation and the more worn, but not eroded, state of the turf there. This southern part was like a rectangle on the western slope of the valley, with houses along the lower edge and on the eastern slope, and not far from the main urban area to the south. But inset to the north-west was a further rectangle, rather larger and much less used, though again with clearings in the thickets, between which passages were kept open by bullocks as well as walkers. Its lower part was fairly open, though dotted with thorn bushes, and had longer grass – it must have formerly been cultivated. In the valley floor below this was a ploughed field, intensively farmed despite the three pylon lines running through it. There was also a rifle range, to reach which involved walking through the property, and no doubt some of those who used this may have explored the further rectangle in the hope of finding a rabbit or two on which to use their marksmanship more rewardingly. There was little chalk turf in this section, but there were more of the taller plants, especially along the field edge. You could walk along this, past the rifle butts, and round the far end of the field, where there was a sloping strip of land with a mixture of shrubs and open patches with a good range of plants, and return by the track along the valley floor. It made quite a varied walk, and it was useful having progressed through the thickets northwards, with usually a good many diversions to look at things on the way, to have such a quick and easy return route if one was getting short of time. Beyond to the north, arable fields extended up the dipslope of the Chalk to the horizon, large squares bordered by wire fences, not hedges; pleasant rolling country but without trees or bushes except for a very few places where the sides of old lynchets were too steep for machinery and had been left uncultivated for rough grazing. So the thickets of this property were important in their oasis quality.

One tends to suppose that both these thickets and the arable fields, were relatively recent, deriving from the decision to plough up the South Downs in the interests of the war-time economy. Before then one imagines it had all been sheep-grazed, but with the shift to cereals in the war the steeper slopes became unwanted. They were then used for target practice, after which they would be still less wanted for farming, and would be left to grow scrub. I do not think that this supposition is wholly correct. Certainly the South Downs suffered major devastation in the war-time ploughing, and this was prolonged after the war to a quite unwarranted extent, perhaps for longer than any other cherished landscape of England – in fact it still continues. Yet parts of it were previously arable. W.H. Hudson's *Nature of Downland*, published in 1923, mentioned the teams of black oxen, and the extent of grazing land brought under the plough for a few years in the early 1800s when wheat prices escalated. He writes that this was still identifiable over a century later (though I suspect there may have been later cultivations too) and that it had not yet reverted to turf, though turf plants had colonized. To that extent it was different from land ploughed up in the previous twenty years, which was still barren, thirsty and weedy. Then there are the old lynchets that one can see even in the heart of the Downs – these must have derived from ploughing. So perhaps there have always been periodic attempts at cultivation, and the war-time ploughing was only different in being much more widespread, extending the arable land from its previous nuclei in the coombs where the old farmhouses have lain snugly for centuries, and running it up to the flatter crests. One hopes that this expansion will recede, but it will be generations before the turf rebuilds, and who knows what further threats may arise in that time.

One such threat became a major anxiety some ten years after I had first known the property, though there had been rumours of it before. The need for a better east-west road was clear enough, but it was not so clear why it had to go through the middle of this property. There seemed to be other possible routes it could take, and a good many arguments for or against each of them. One suspected that this was a further case of a faulty decision taken a generation earlier, to enlarge a road already destined to be overtaken by development, and that any new road now built to parallel it would become overtaken in turn, with the onus of dealing with the consequences being thrust on the next generation. The arguments were skilfully presented, though one wondered whether the basic reasoning was sound in running a new major artery close to the coast rather than through the centre of the county. It is always difficult for those in the middle, when they are told that both ends are firmly fixed, and they can only make the best bargain they can of it. Two options were offered. In both cases the road would slant through the heavily used southern part of the property in a large cutting, destroying the area used by the majority of visitors to the property, which was also the main area of chalk turf with its horseshoe vetch and other plants (*Photo 16*). Both options offered a cut-and-cover tunnel at the crest of the hill, the difference between them being purely in the height at which this tunnel would lie. The choice of a lower level for the tunnel would involve more ground being lost to a deeper cutting, though there would be more of the surface restored afterwards. The higher level would however involve the loss of a great deal of ground that would need to be covered by an embankment to bring the road up to that level. It was not a choice of options, but of disasters, and either would ruin the property physically. It would also destroy the atmosphere of peace and quiet enjoyed by the users of the property, since the noise from a motorway carries most strongly uphill. Experience of the Trust's properties along the central sections of the North Downs after the construction of M25 to their south, had made this shatteringly clear. The views northwards to the Downs, and southwards to the sea, already had to contend with the pylon lines and the power station. A motorway would complete their destruction (*See Photo 15*).

The National Trust was given powers as early as 1907 to declare its land inalienable, and this had been done in this case. This meant that in effect the Trust could not take any decision to dispose of the land or accede to its destruction, and must refer to Parliament. There had been cases where this had been done, not always resulting in a decision in the Trust's favour, but sufficiently often so to ensure hesitation on the part of the protagonist, to whom the costs and delay were also bound to be factors. A warning was given that the Trust was considering invoking this procedure.

The main objection was to the idea of a cut-and-cover tunnel, combined with the loss of land to an embankment and cutting. Cut-and-cover would mean the removal of the turf, which could only doubtfully be kept alive if it was laid out somewhere and kept watered, while the cutting was made, the sides and roof of the tunnel installed, and the soil replaced on top to bring up the level to the original height, when the turf could be relaid. It seemed hardly likely that this could be done, and no precedents for its success as an operation were quoted. Without the turf, the land would lose its character as well as much of its wildlife.

During this time my visits were more frequent, often with senior members of the Trust, or representatives of the Nature Conservancy Council or other bodies. It was necessary to convince people of the extent of harm that would be done, and one could really only do that by showing them on the ground how much would be lost. By now the wardening situation had become much better, and with the growth of the conservation volunteer movement, a number of working parties were helping in the practical amelioration of the property both for visitors and wild-life. Notable amongst these had been parties from the large school on the opposite side of the valley. The property not only still retained so much of its former values, but seemed likely to improve on them. It was four years after my last visit to it, and my retirement from the Trust, during which time no doubt many more meetings and negotiations had ensured, that I was relieved to see from a press cutting that it had been decided to put the road in twin-bored tunnels 400 yards long at a much lower level, rather than instal a cut-and-cover tunnel less than a third of that length. When this road is made, I will visit the property again to see what is left. I fear that it will not be a pleasant visit, but it will be a lot better than it would have been if the Trust had not appreciated that a cut-and-cover tunnel, though it might seem adequate to a planner in preserving the sky-line, would really destroy the chalk turf and thus the character and wildlife of the property, and that it was necessary to fight such a proposal with every means in its power.

SIX

Frensham Moats

John and I hung about most of the Friday, waiting for the Hymac to come. That February of 1977 was not as cold as some, but it was maddening having to wait, as we wanted to get started before the weekend. We rang the depot, and found the machine was on its way, but the transporter had broken down on the road. Finally it arrived about 3 pm, and the driver (another John, so I will call him JD) got it unloaded and ready to go. We only had a couple of hours before dusk, so I quickly explained what we wanted him to do, and we started in the middle of the first moat.

JD got the idea pretty quickly, though the lakeside was a bit unlike his usual working sites. In the two hours he dug out about 10 metres of the moat, which had to be 4m wide and two deep. He put the top soil, which was discoloured by leaching down to about ½m, on one side, and the pure yellow-orange of the rest he heaped inshore of the moat. By starting in the middle we avoided water coming in, and even after the weekend surprisingly little had seeped through. More importantly we were able to establish that the Folkestone Beds sand was uniform, and there wasn't a hard layer of iron pan concealed underneath. We left the machine on site, roped everything off, put up warning notices, and arranged to resume on the Monday (*see Photo 17*).

Frensham Little Pond had been bequeathed to the National Trust a few years before, on the death of Mr F.S.D. Atherton, who had spent many years in restoring it from the state in which wartime draining and use for army exercises had left it. He had established a bird sanctuary in the south-east corner, where the feeder stream comes in. He had fenced this off from the main part of the pond, of 15 hectares, by a barricade of poles driven in through holes made in the thick ice of the hard winter of 1963. Upstream to the south, this feeder runs in several channels through a marshy area, now becoming wooded, but still wet enough and wide enough to prevent people crossing it, so this gives a further protection to the bird sanctuary. The stream itself originates from the Bargate Beds, so is alkaline, giving a pH of well over 7 to the pond, though the actual level of the water at any time is controlled not by this feeder stream, or by the penstock at the northern end, so much as by seepage from the water table. The high pH allows a good range of plants to have developed along the margins, and formerly for this pond to have been a habitat for the natterjack toad. It also produces big fish, and I have seen some very large carp and pike caught there, though not often. It is not a deep pond, but wide and shallow, and though I have taken soundings all over it I have never found depth of as much as 2 metres, in fact 1½ metres is the norm. To swim in it, even on a hot day, is not particularly pleasant, as it is rather like swimming in tepid clear soup, and the centre, when you stand up, has a growth of furry water weed round one's feet. It is more enjoyable to skate on in winter, and it doesn't get littered with stones like most ponds do, because there aren't any stones handy to throw on it.

However it is water, and therefore an attraction to a lot of people in a hot summer, with dry heathland all round. Mostly they come in family groups, but it is on the beat of some schools, and there are also visiting parties from the ILEA place north of Hindhead. At one time, before it was National Trust property, it got a reputation as a rendezvous for motorbikers, and for the sort of parties that go on all night, with bonfires, swimming and a lot of noise. The Trust blocked off the access to the further side, and put a warden in the cottage, so after a bit it quietened down. But there are still a lot of people who come there in summer, and Waverley District Council put in a big car park for them, sited so that they had to walk past the warden's cottage to get to the beach.

In winter it looks pretty deserted, but there are still a good many visitors. If you stay at one place any length of time you may only have one party, usually dogwalking, in sight, but when they have gone past you, another comes along, also with dogs, and so on. Round the edges there are reed-beds, varying in width, and not continuous, and these reed-beds suit a lot of birds for nesting, grebes, coots and moorhens of course, but also small birds, reed warblers and the like, and there are occasional visits by bearded

tits, bitterns, and other less common birds. Gilbert White mentions it frequently, and there are a lot of later records, in fact the
bird list for the two Frensham Ponds includes most of the European species and quite a section of the North American.

In 1974 I was asked by the Trust's Agent to make a plan to
protect these reed-beds. As people walked along the shore, their
children sometimes, and their dogs always, went out into them,
which wasn't good for the nesting birds. The idea at first was
some sort of fencing, with notices, but it was apparent from former relics scattered around that fencing didn't last long in that
area, and the lifespan of notices would be shorter still. Anyhow
there wasn't the money at that time, but I was asked to make a
plan for when there was.

The first thing was to find out just what needed protecting. We
knew about the birds, but what else was there? Waverley got a
map drawn out from airphotos, and I asked a botanist friend,
who knew it well, to fill it in. This he did, and a pattern became
evident. The reed-beds were mostly *Phragmites*, but there were
some patches of *Typha*, usually further out, with more *T. latifolia*
than *T. angustifolia*. Inshore of the *Phragmites*, there was a belt,
sometimes more of a line, of sedges. The main kind was *Carex
paniculata*, the Greater Tussock Sedge, but there were about six
kinds in all. This sedge belt ran along inland of all the larger reed-
beds, and both seemed to have increased in size in recent times.
In the old days this probably didn't happen, since the pond was
drained every five years or so to get the fish. But it was now over
30 years since it had been re-established in 1948 (*see Figure 1*).

The interesting thing was that most of the more attractive
plants, like marsh cinquefoil, skullcap, yellow iris, and many
others, grew in the zone between the sedge-belt and the reed-
beds. So these were clearly getting hammered every time anyone
went through them to get to the reed-beds. There were also records of other species, now 'lost', which would probably have
grown in this zone. It seemed therefore that any protection must
include the sedge-belt, together with the plants between this and
the reed-beds, as well as the reed-beds themselves.

Inshore of the sedge-belt, between this and the lakeside path,
there were scattered bushes and small trees in a sort of fringe.
Mostly these were sallow or birch, though some oaks had managed to establish themselves. None of them was large, perhaps

5 △

16 △

PLATE 5 *The Threat to the Valley*

15 May 1975. Looking back from the north to the much visited southern end of the Down. The road will run this side of the houses and follow a tunnel under the ridge.

16 June 1982. Plants of the downland; field fleawort and horse-shoe vetch.

PLATE 6 *Frensham Moats*   17 △

17 We dug 'dry' as much as possible to minimize the fractures that kept occurring when water washed out the grease of the joints of the jib-arm of the Hymac.

18 The first loop after completion. By the time we left, grebes were nesting in the reeds of the new island, now cut off and protected by the moat.

18 ▽

PLATE 7 *The Field (1)*

19 The entrance to the rough field, with the steep bluff on the right, and the hillside slopes on the left. The central growth shows the line of the small stream.

20 One of the three Alpine cows.

PLATE 8 *The Field (2)*   21 △

21 The Dryad, *Minois dryas*, is an attractive satyrid of late summer found locally in woodland edge habitats of Central Europe.

The Peculiar Common

22 Bill's photograph of the brown hairstreak, *Thecla betulae*, that kept us entranced for an hour

22 ▽

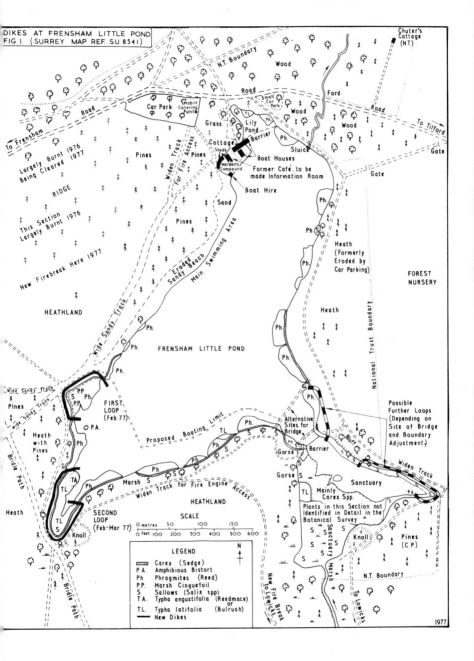

DIKES AT FRENSHAM LITTLE POND
FIG.I. (SURREY MAP REF. SU 8541)

N.T. Boundary

Wood

To Chuter's Cottage (N.T.)

Road

Ford

Road

Car Park

Mobile Catering Point

Small Car Park

Wood

To Tilford

To Frensham

Grass

Lily Pond

Barrier

Wood

Gate

Largely Burnt 1976
Being Cleared 1977

Pines

Cottage

Sheds

Boat Houses

Sluice

RIDGE

Wide Sandy Track
For Fire Access

Pines

Warden's Compound

Former Cafe, to be made Information Room

Gate

This Section
Largely Burnt 1976

Boat Hire

Sand

New Firebreak Here 1977

Pines

Ph.

Heath
(Formerly
Eroded by
Car Parking)

Ph S

FOREST
NURSERY

HEATHLAND

Eroded Sandy Beach

Main Swimming Area

Heath

Wide Sandy Track

Ph.

Ph.

Ph.

Wide Sandy Track

FRENSHAM LITTLE POND

Ph.

Ph.

National Trust Boundary

Ph.

Pines

PP
S PP

FIRST LOOP
(Feb.77)

Ph.

Ph.

Possible
Further Loops
(Depending on
Site of Bridge
and Boundary
Adjustment)

Bridle Path

Heath
with
Pines

O.P.A.

Ph

Proposed Boating Limit

TL

Ph S

Alternative
Sites for
Bridge

Ph
Gorse S

Barrier

Widen Track

PS

Heath

TA

Ph

Marsh S

Ph S

P.A.

Gorse S

Sanctuary

TL

SECOND
LOOP
(Feb-Mar 77)

TL

S

Knoll

Widen Track for Fire Engine Access

HEATHLAND

SCALE

Mainly
Carex Spp.

Plants in this Section not
Identified in Detail in the
Botanical Survey

Knoll

Pines
(C.P.)

0 Metres   50   100   150
0 Feet 100   200   300   400   500   600

LEGEND

N

Carex (Sedge)
P.A. Amphibious Bistort
Ph   Phragmites (Reed)
P.P. Marsh Cinquefoil
S   Sallows (Salix spp)
T.A. Typha angustifolia (Reedmace) or
T.L. Typha latifolia (Bulrush)
—— New Dikes

New Fire Break To Lowicks

N.T. Boundary

To Lowicks

Sanctuary Marsh

S

1977

up to 20 years old, and they were in the wrong place growing there, because as well as interrupting the views from the path over the lake, they were tending to dry out the sedge-belt, and they were also channelling erosion of the banks where people could get between them. This fringe of young trees therefore seemed a less useful feature.

On the landward side of the lakeside path, the heathland took over, with heather, gorse, and scattered pine and birch. This had its own fauna, which included Dartford warbler and sand-lizard. This heathland stretched some distance, up to the Kings Ridge, and down the other side to the Great Pond, though to the north and south it was bordered with pine woodland.

Looking for a pleasanter alternative to fencing, I thought of substituting a wide ditch or moat round sections of the reed-beds. I didn't think it should be continuous all round the pond, because there were visual objections, and people would want sometimes to be able to get to the water's edge. But a number of loops would protect the more important sections, and these could be dug where the fringe of trees ran, so that they would not detract from either the zones of the waterside plant community or of the heathland. The soil could be heaped up on the present path, raising it, and giving better views over the pond. Some could be lorried along the beach to the north to form islands just offshore that would be an attraction for the boys, and distract them from wading into the reed-beds.

I wasn't sure how wide or deep they should be. They would need to be large enough to stop any attempt to jump over them, and the depth would have to be enough to prevent wading across, plus a bit to allow for some silting. I began to take measurements of the sort of ditch that deterred people. The 1976 summer was very dry, and the water-level in the Little Pond fell by nearly a metre. All sorts of tracks were made cutting into the reed-beds and across the inlet at the south-west corner where a small valley ran into the pond, though with no visible water in it. It happened that summer that I joined a botanical party that went to Amberley Wildbrooks for the day, which because it was tidal, was one of the few places that still had its usual amount of water. I was able to measure the size of ditch that deterred the most enthusiastic and agile botanists from even attempting to cross it. I decided that a width of 4m was needed at the top, but the bottom width could be less, say 2m, which would give a reasonable slope, though there would be bound to be some slumping in the sandy soil of Frensham. A depth of 2m would however allow for this to happen to an acceptable extent, and the sides of a moat would anyway be protected from wave-action, so the most likely causes of any slumping would be progressive trampling. This could be reduced if the path were set slightly back from the moat (*see Figure 2*).

The work would therefore be within the capacity of a Hymac working from one side, and costing this out, I found that making such a moat would really not cost so much more than putting up a fence with similar deterrent capabilities. Over say a ten-year life, it would probably be cheaper if one considered the amount of maintenance a fence would need. I therefore put forward a plan that involved four sections of the reed-beds being surrounded by such moats, with a total length of about 1200m. Two of these were on the western side of the pond, and two on the eastern. In the case of the latter however, to put a moat in the required position would involve some boundary adjustments that were not likely to be immediately negotiable.

There was also the question of a bridge over the mouth of the Sanctuary. The advantage of a bridge was that it would allow people to walk around the pond which, when they first saw it, they usually thought they could do. When they tried, they found they couldn't do this, because the Sanctuary itself and the marsh

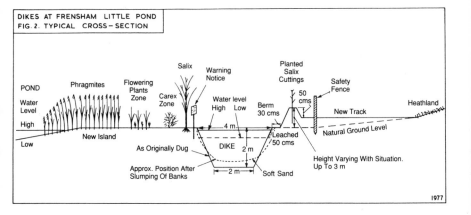

DIKES AT FRENSHAM LITTLE POND
FIG. 2. TYPICAL CROSS–SECTION

to its south, were still uncrossable. Some of them tried very hard. This marsh is wooded now, and it is no longer somewhere where snipe can breed, but all the same such efforts can cause a lot of disturbance. Really to walk all round the pond people had to strike across the heathland and use the ford at Lowicks to the south, and come back along the eastern side through land that is in private hands, though there is a footpath. This way is about twice as long as they expected, if they ever find it. So a bridge would stop a lot of battering of the sanctuary marsh.

The disadvantages of a bridge would be firstly its cost, and then the danger that it would really bring more people, and there would be disturbance to the Sanctuary. There was also the maintenance question, and the danger of vandalism. Then there were the aesthetic questions. If a bridge were made just on the pond side of the barrier to the Sanctuary, it would be shorter in length, and less visible, but disturbance to the Sanctuary was more likely. If it was taken further north, this last would be reduced, but it would be twice as long, and much more visible from all round the pond. A well-designed bridge, perhaps of the suspension type, might be acceptable, but would cost more than the sort of scaffolding and timber bridge that could be put up more cheaply, and would be easier to maintain.

The position of the proposed moats is shown on Figure 1, though this plan was drawn for another purpose, and refers to them as dikes. I believe 'dikes' to be technically more correct, but as they have become locally known as 'moats', I have used that term in this narrative. Figure 1 also shows the alternative positions considered at that time for a bridge, but the need for this has subsequently lapsed since after lengthy negotiations the Trust was able to acquire a greater width of land round the eastern side of the Sanctuary. The tree growth in the former Sanctuary marsh had meanwhile increased, and in 1988 a sleeper causeway was installed across this marsh, just north of the NT boundary, with culverts allowing the various branches of the feeder stream to flow under it, the whole being hidden by this tree growth from the water area of the Sanctuary itself. When I saw this causeway in July 1989, it seemed to be a happy resolution of the problem of giving a route for walkers all round the pond, or at least it would become so when it was better known and sign-posted, though already the added pressure on the tracks leading to it was evident. There remains the need to guide visitors well to the east of the Sanctuary itself, to avoid disturbance to the birds using it, and possibly my suggestion of moats on that side may later be adopted.

All this was well into the future when I put forward my proposals in 1975, and nothing could then be done on the eastern side until the negotiations were concluded some ten years later. The two western moats were however accepted in principle, and when a legacy to the Trust became suddenly available for the purpose in 1976 I was asked to start on these. This involved firstly a great deal of consultation with interested parties, of which there seemed a large number. There was Waverley District Council, which manages the National Trust land of Frensham Common, on which we would be working, as a Country Park. The NCC needed consulting since it is an SSSI. Various societies concerned with different aspects of the flora and fauna gave their views. The Surrey Flora Committee helped to peg out the edges of the zone to be protected – this was of great value in explaining the proposals to others – and though the pegs tended to disappear, they were replaced often enough to show the line. Finally we thought we had sufficient agreement to start work, so the Warden, Steve, started on clearing some of the birch, pine and small oaks which would be in the line of the moat, or interfere with the swing of the machine.

We had, inevitably, left out one society in our consultations, and could only apologize in reply to its pained letters, but it was based some miles away, and we had not known of its interest. We also put up notices to say what we were doing; and the work was done by Trust staff who could explain the purpose. The work could in fact be justified in terms of this line of trees tending to dry out the marshy edge, and shade out the ground plants, but this did not prevent a number of critical comments, mainly concerning the perching needs of reed buntings, a relatively common but attractive bird. So we were glad when the excavation could start, and people could see what was really happening.

When we resumed this work on the Monday, all went well with the digging, but the attempt to transport some of the material to form an island to the north was a disaster. The lorry when loaded could just about traverse the loose sand of the foreshore, but when it shot its load, its wheels spun, and it had to be dragged out by the Hymac. This was done by the latter inserting one tooth of its bucket in the ring of a chain attached to the front of the lorry, like leading a bull by the nose-ring. Although an engaging sight, this was unproductive, and after the second such rescue, the lorry was dismissed. The watching fitter's comment, about drivers and screwdrivers, was possibly unjust, since the sand here is very deceptive, as we were to find ourselves later on. So we decided instead to see how troublesome the now formid- able piles of soil would be to level off and consolidate into a raised path. The Tuesday was largely spent on this, and we also incorporated a low bank of ½m between this consolidated path and the edge of the slope down to the moat, on which we could put a light safety fence. This seemed to work well, and after spreading the top soil, it toned in satisfactorily. As this was a section where soil disposal had been expected to be a particular problem, we decided to continue in the same way, since further on there was more room and the cut and fill would balance out.

February fill-dike was now with us, and the pond level was up by some 20cm, flooding the sedge-belt. The depressions made by tracks across this caused runnels to drain back into the moat we were digging. We blocked these, to avoid an inrush, by having the Hymac deposit soil on their mouths, but we tried not to do this too much in case it affected the flora. The machine was now digging in water, discoloured by the sand, and had to feel its way. We checked the depths at intervals with a calibrated stick.

This working in water led to recurrent breakdowns, sometimes two or three a day, because the grease applied each morning to the transverse bolts on the machine's joints washed out, causing overheating and fracture of their retaining pins. These, the equivalent of a split-pin on a smaller machine, were about a centimetre in diameter, and had to be replaced each time by cutting a length of reinforcing bar, and hammering the ends side- ways in a Z shape with a club-hammer. This took about 20 min- utes each time, or more if the bolt had slid partly out and needed re-positioning. The operator, JD, could do this single-handed, but it was a lot quicker if one of us helped, since it usually meant having to ground the bucket and moving the forearm to get the apertures level. Later we found coach-bolts were quicker, but the fractures still kept occurring.

So we continued, day after day, with John and me taking

alternate days to watch and help, with the other off on other work. It wasn't really monotonous, as there were always things to do, clearing ahead, or tidying up and cutting off projecting roots. For February the weather wasn't too bad, though with frequent showers, which often led to rainbows forming over the pond. JD was warm enough in his cab, and we could bring a car close enough to the site to shelter if needed and yet see if things went wrong. One can't afford to leave these machines unsupervised for long as they can do a lot of damage very quickly, and though JD had soon got the idea, there were often minor variations wanted because of particular plants or other features. There were occasional passers-by, and it was amusing see how frustrated the dogs were at being unable to have their usual hunt in the reed-beds, though their owners were unanimous in approval of the work. There were birds too; we could hear the grebes chuckling in the reed-beds; there were always coots and moorhens, ducks on the pond, herons, and sometimes less usual birds, though we didn't see anything very rare. Occasionally an early brimstone fluttered by. There was always litter to collect, especially from what was rapidly becoming an island, and would soon be cut off.

Before we had finished this first loop, which would enclose and protect the main colony of marsh-cinquefoil, we had a more serious breakage. This was a fracture of the metal sleeves lining the aperture in which lay the main connecting-bolt between the jib and the forearm. No replacement machine was available, and we were anxious not to wait until one was, because the nesting season was getting near. Fortunately there was an alternative position for this bolt, and by making a ramp and laying the whole of the arm out flat on this, the fitters managed to transfer it to that. It meant a slight loss of reach, but not an undue lowering of performance, and we decided to carry on, though we had lost half a day's work.

At last we came to the point where the moat would re-connect with the lake, and this required some thought. A Hymac can work in about a metre's depth of water. We needed to extend the depth of the moat into the lake until it evened out, but with working in disturbed and cloudy water, we had to improvise a system of back-markers to keep the line. The disposal of the soil needed consideration, as an accessible sand-bar would attract people, so it was better to make it on the island. We also had always to leave an escape route for the machine in case of break-down. Communciation was difficult, because JD couldn't hear us when his engine was going, and he wasn't always working at an angle from which he could see our signals. However the connec-tion was completed, and JD then decided on a short cruise, which to our horror took him towards a rather fine floating clump of amphibious bistort, not so easily seen in February as it is in flower in late summer. Luckily he missed it and it still remains.

Meanwhile we had had to put up some form of safety fence, of three lines of light wire stapled to pine thinnings that were avail-able. Later we found this was so often broken by parties standing on the lowest wire, that we had to replace it with 14 gauge. We reinforced this by taking cuttings of sallow boughs, long enough to reach down to the water level, and putting them along the fence line. This was not uniformly successful; some of us clearly having greener fingers than others. But even those that didn't take gave the idea of a screen. We also put up notices on the island before it was cut off, though these naturally became a target for bottles, which we then had to collect up. Possibly the notices were a mistake, but at least one small boy thanked us for them, saying that now he could read that the moat was six feet deep, he wouldn't need to jump into it to find out how deep it was.

This first loop, of 250 m length, was completed on Monday 21 February, the seventh day of work, including breakdowns (*Photo 18*). It seemed unlikely that the second loop, round the south-west inlet, would be finished in the month, as it was 100m longer, and also looked more difficult. We had to decide whether to run on into March, or to have a second machine, which was now available, either another Hymac, or a Drott to do the spreading and levelling, while the Hymac dug. Two machines would have made it quicker but would greatly increase the disturbance. We decided to carry on for a trial section, and see what conditions were like.

In this inlet, the sedge belt was still present almost continu-ously, but the *Phragmites* was replaced by *Typha*. Trilling from the middle of this indicated the presence of dabchicks, while great-crested grebes were using the *Phragmites* bed to its east. We would have liked to have continued the moat beyond this point too, but this would have brought it out in a small section known as the marsh, where there were plants such as marsh-lousewort and shoreweed, which we didn't want to disturb. There was also a feature we called the knoll, where sand-lizards were believed to exist, though we thought it probable that they would prefer its sunnier side, away from the inlet. We decided to bring the moat out between the *Typha* and the *Phragmites*, and time it for the late afternoon, so that the grebes could re-settle at night. We also decided to go between the knoll and the inlet, even though this would give a much higher bank than elsewhere, but this could be staked or covered with pegged-down brashings to prevent children sliding down it. It might even become acceptable to kingfishers as a nesting site.

Again we started in the middle, so as to allow dry working for as long as possible. The soil was much siltier here, but this decreased rather surprisingly as we neared the point of the inlet, and though we started by stacking it separately, it didn't seem worthwhile. The dabchicks did not mind the machine working round them, perhaps because the noise stayed more or less in one place, so we decided against using another machine. This loop went quicker, though still with annoying breakdowns, including one of the tracks coming off on one occasion, and the bucket splitting on another. Because of these delays, which each lasted several hours, we concentrated on the excavation, and left the levelling of the spoil until later. We made the connection back to the pond at right angles, in the late afternoon, and though it only took an hour, each bucket load contained growing plants, underwater at first, as we were digging backwards, then by stages back to the bank flora. Each had to be rapidly identified, and its positioning indicated by hand to JD. Finally the remaining surplus spoil was deposited in a heap on the *Typha*, where it has proved an interesting area of colonization. The dabchicks had taken off as the machine advanced towards them, but were back by next morning.

The last three days were spent on levelling, burying the roots in the process, and keeping to the same general design as the first loop, though in this case at a rather higher level, which gave even better views over the pond. We left a gap at the point of the inlet to avoid flooding the bridlepath which came by there; later pipes were put in. There was a lot of tidying of broken branches needed, and a rather stouter fence was installed, with ratchet tighteners. We finished at midday on 9 March, after 27 days in all, including weekends, or 19 working days for the machine, of which a sixth were lost in breakdown time, which was not charged for. The machinery bill came to £910 including VAT, well within my limit agreed with David of £1000. The materials used, such as for warning notices, were not costly, and even if one added staff travel costs, the total would have come to under £1.75 per metre, probably about a third more than a fence, but giving much less of an eyesore.

All along we had been expecting to come across some human artefact. After all we were digging along a shoreline that had existed for nearly 750 years – the pond was made in 1246. This only happened once however, towards the end. JD sensed he had struck something metallic, and we probed the contents of the bucket gingerly, expecting a mortar bomb or sten gun. It was a horse-shoe, of cart horse proportions. JD picked it up and, in prescribed manner, threw it backwards over his shoulder, to bring luck. This it brought, in that I was facing him at the time, and could see it had fallen in the machine's tracks, from which I retrieved it before it caused a further breakdown.

On the last day, the weather had improved, and it was possible to take some photographs for the record. The first orange under-wings were flying, and spring was in the air. The dabchicks and great-crested grebes were still nesting in the second loop, and others had by now occupied the first one. Coots were foraging in the new moats. Visitors were increasing, and usefully compacting the new paths. It was time for us to leave.

The warden continued weekly checks, tightening up the wires, or replacing broken ones. The danger signs needed frequent re-placement at first. Gradually natural vegetation colonized, aided by some grass-seeding. No really warm weather occurred until July, by when the banks were fairly well consolidated. Amphibi-ous bistort had by then colonized and was flowering on the water in the moats, and yellow iris and purple loosestrife were visibly increasing on the protected islands. We hadn't noticed much of the latter before, so presumably it had always been picked.

August was hot, and the chance was taken of giving a nearby National Trust Acorn Camp a relief from their usual task of clear-ing scrub, in asking them to drive in posts at the mouths of the moats to carry notices deterring their navigation by canoes and inflatable craft, which was beginning to be a problem. The largest six of the fourteen young men and women available were asked to help John and me with the heaviest post-driver we could find, crowding round in bathing suits as we heaved it up and down, but it was very hard to get the posts in as deep into the sand as we needed, even though we dug holes for them first. We were glad to refresh ourselves by wading along the moats to check how much slumping had occurred, and found that even with the water level then 30cm below normal, or some 50cm below what it was at the time of construction, there was still a metre's depth of water and some 20cm of soft mud below that, even in the shallowest parts. Meanwhile the less tall members of the party had been asked to clear an adjoining area of seedling pines, which they did largely on hands and knees. In the process they found three sand-lizards, which reinforced my belief that they are more locally widespread than sometimes supposed, as this was not a part of the common where the herpetologists had told us they were known to occur.

These notices had some effect, but it wasn't easy for the Warden to see whether a boat had in fact got into the moats. The previous owner had let out dinghies and canoes, but the Trust soon banned the dinghies because people got them into the reedbeds, and the oars caused a lot of disturbance. Canoes were better, and the system was changed so they they weren't put on hire until July each year. But quite a few visitors brought their own inflatable boats, and although this was against the by-laws, it wasn't easy to stop them. In the end we put an arc of buoys round the southern half of the pond, so any boat going beyond these could be seen easily. So the reed-beds then were protected from the pond side as well as the land, and since then they have been pretty well undisturbed.

Birds clearly enjoyed their protection from the start, and kingfishers were frequently seen. So too were grass-snakes, which basked on the track and slipped into the moats as footsteps approached. Botanical evaluation was left until 1979, when a Surrey Flora Committee party was transported to the islands in the warden's workboat. The marsh-cinquefoil colony, the largest known in Surrey, and previously decreasing, was now expanding strongly, and several species thought lost from the Frensham list, such as bog pimpernel, were found to be alive and well.

Public acceptance of the moats was favourable, and even the natural history society that had unfortunately been omitted from the list of those originally consulted, began to give grudging acceptance of the *fait accompli*. The dogs, whose enjoyment of hunting in the reed-beds had been so curtailed, possibly had other views, but it was surprising that none of them seemed to try to swim across the moats, which would have presented no obstacle to a trained water-spaniel. Fortunately they were mostly of other breeds.

Now, over ten years later, the moats have become part of the scene. Attempts to thatch them with pine branches held in place by wires were probably unnecessary and certainly unsightly, though intended to prevent slumping of the banks caused by incursion. The planted sallow cuttings form too much of a screen; their roots are useful in holding the banks together, but their tops should be coppiced irregularly, not like a hedge. The reed-growth on the islands is almost too luxuriant, and some periodic check may be needed, possibly by controlled firing in winter, if weather allows. Re-excavation will be necessary at some stage, but at present it looks as if this may not be required for a while, and the life of such moats may be more than the ten years originally estimated. When it has to be done, this would be likely to be much easier than the original excavation, since there is now a path from which the machine could work, whereas if we had put up a fence, there would have been a lot of dismantling of the remains to be done, before a replacement could be put up instead.

SEVEN

The Field

We were engaged in the not infrequent marital argument that arises from the need to find somewhere suitable for stopping to eat our picnic lunch. One place is too overlooked by a house, another too unsheltered, yet another would have been ideal if the driver had seen it in time, and there hadn't been a Mercedes immediately behind us just then. This provokes further discussion on whether it is worth turning round, and if so, where to do so. I have known this process to go on for some twenty or thirty kilometres, ending sometimes in an *autoroute* lay-by, many of which have pleasantly accessible woods or meadows behind, or sometimes even in a village sqaure, where the benches under the plane trees afford room to spread things out, while observing the comings and goings of the village, and hearing the clicks from the game of *pétanque* that is occupying the attention of its menfolk. On this occasion, in one of the wealthier parts of the southern Alps, we knew from the map that having left the villas of the previous settlement, it would not be far before we reached those of the next, where again many of the old cottages would be renovated and the village dotted with modern villas, housing commuters, or forming second homes. So when we came round a corner of the hillside road to see that the next bend had a wide gravel verge, no doubt a legacy from former road-widening, we would probably have stopped anyhow. The choice was confirmed by the glimpse of a secluded meadow behind the gap where a stream came out to trickle in a culvert under the road (*Photo 19*).

We set up the picnic table and folding chairs beside a clump of the big yellow Salvia, that for some reason has the English name of Jupiter's distaff, and while Penelope laid out the food and drink, I had a quick wander into the field. The buddleia bushes overhanging its entrance were covered with silver-washed fritillaries, including many of the dark silvery-green form of the females, while further in there were smaller fritillaries and whites flying around the low clumps of dyer's greenweed and soapwort. The stream that trickled from the marshy central depression of the meadow was fringed with mint and devils-bit scabious. The September sky was clear and blue, and we ate our lunch to the polite greeting of 'buon appetito' from each occasional passer-by. After lunch we locked the car, and walked through the gap into the field.

It sloped up from us to a fringe of birch, sallow and aspen, interspersed with buddleia in flower, behind which the slope increased; the rocks there were too frequent for it to have been worth clearing for pasture, and it had been left to such woodland, mainly oak and sweet chestnut, as could establish itself in a country where, at that height, a metre of snow would lie in winter. On our right a large bluff rose in a sheer cliff and formed the reason for the corner in the road. Beyond this the edge of the field ended in a drop to a terrace, and a view down the valley up which we had come from the *autostrada* along the shore of the lake below. The field was not much over a hectare in size, sheltered on three sides; its short turf of herbs and grasses had been grazed, though not recently and there were no cattle present at the time. We walked round it slowly, noting the Adonis and Idas blues, the occasional skippers, grey and brown, the heath and Queen of Spain fritillaries, the sooty coppers, pearly and small heaths, and meadow browns. Two large green lizards scurried for cover, and we also disturbed a large green bush-cricket. A praying mantis twisted its triangular head, keeping me in binocular vision whichever way I moved – one cannot help feeling that it must be the most intelligent of our European insects. Clumps of thyme and birdsfoot trefoil were an attraction for the smaller butterflies, while flitting among the silver-washed fritillaries on the buddleias were painted ladies, red admirals, Scotch arguses, and the large dark satyrid, with big blue eye-spots on its wavy-edged wings, *dryas* that the French call *Le Grand Nègre des Bois* (*Photo* 21). The whites all seemed to be the southern summer form of the green-veined white, with little evidence of the green veins. A clump of brambles in one corner housed Jersey tigermoths; lying crouched as triangles of black and white streaks, until they took off with a flash of scarlet underwings. We walked round the field slowly twice, and I counted sixteen species of butterflies, none particularly uncommon there, or at least not yet uncommon, but we feared that it would not be long before the spread of villas reduced them.

We were relieved to see on a visit the next summer that the field remained unused, except by the three placid dun-coloured Alpine cows that were grazing it. This was in late June, so marbled whites were a feature, and we also saw large and wood whites as well as the green-veined. A worn green hair-streak remained from the spring, and a single high brown fritillary, still drying its wings after emergence, was the precursor of its silver-washed cousins we had seen the year before. The flowers included a tall purple orchid with spotted leaves, and a number of the large true broomrape battening on the roots of the broom along the terrace below the field. Exploring this terrace, we found that it led to what must once have been a cart-track to a higher level of the hillside, now too overgrown to follow. A small burnet moth with streaky red-spotted wings was new to us, though we were later to see others, as well as a commoner larger kind.

These southern Alpine valleys have a number of species which have penetrated from the lowlands of Lombardy to the south, and which add to the interest and variety of the flora and fauna, but they also have a varied pattern of weather in the summer. Thunderstorms are frequent, about one a week, lasting perhaps one or two days or nights, after which the air is clear and fresh, allowing the distant peaks of the main Alpine chain to become clearly visible, snow-covered, to the north. Gradually the valleys heat up again, becoming misty and oppressive, with the views decreasing until the next week's storm renews the process. One needs to plan one's activities accordingly; there are some days when it is safe to drive the two hours of motorway up into the high Alps; there are rather more when a less ambitious visit in the foothills is indicated, and there are a few when the only course is to drive into the large towns and take refuge in the department stores and arcades.

We did not go that way until two summers late, when we hardly dared to re-visit the field for fear of finding it built over. However it was still intact, with the only alteration the addition of a water pipe bringing clear water from further up the hillside to a drinking trough for the cows. It was early August, with the buddleia and mint in flower, contrasting with the yellow of the dyer's greenweed, and the patches of marjoram. Clumps of hemp agrimony were round the edge. The field was alive with insects, and we again walked slowly round it, then had our lunch, and walked round it again. This time I listed twenty-three species of butterfly, not all the same as on previous visits, but increasing the total numbers we had seen there to above thirty. There were also two further species of burnet present, as well as other moths, while other insects included the large black bee, and several kinds of dragonfly.

Thirty species of butterfly is a good total for a small field even over three summer months, and there may well have been others we didn't notice since I have counted about sixty in the district as a whole, and almost all of them could have occurred in that attractive field. The gradation from the longer growth along the marshy course of the stream through the grazed herb-rich turf on both its sides to the dry edge of rocks gave plenty of variation of habitat, while the low clumps in the field itself and the bushes and trees round its edges afforded a wide choice of food plants. If one had deliberately set out to form a butterfly garden with an abundance of nectar plants, one would have been pleased with a result only half as good as existed here. There were really very few plants present that do not occur, native or naturalized, in the wild in Southern England, and these few were incidental to the attractions. But the likelihood of replicating such a field here at home is small, because it depends so much on both the intensity of the summer light, and the severity of the winters there, which restrict growth so that changes are slower. Here such a field would soon grow out of control and require constant attention to maintain the balance, which in those conditions can be controlled by three Alpine cows.

One of the butterflies that reaches that area, is the Southern glider (*Neptis rivularis*). The first time I saw this species flying, I mistook it for one of the white admirals, and it was only when I looked more closely to see which white admiral it was, that I realized that it was something different. When you see it sitting still, which is not often, unlike the white admirals, then the difference is clear enough, as the wings are much more rounded, and squatter than our white admiral, while the Mediterranean admiral has more pointed wings than our species. But on the wing, there is considerable similarity in appearance, though the flight is different, seeming to consist of an unremitting and indefatigable search for something it can't find. Possibly this is due to the fact that one usually notices it in gardens or the edges of meadows, whereas its food plant, goatsbeard spiraea, common throughout the sweet chestnut woodlands as an understorey plant, though only developing its full height in clearings after coppicing, is sufficiently mundane to be considered unworthy of cultivation. Both white admirals feed on honeysuckle, also widespread there, but although that district is within the range of both species, the few I have seen there have been of the same species that occurs in Britain.

Another attractive species was the chequered blue, *orion*, which feeds on stonecrops, and is one of the many species of blue butterflies that require the partnership of ants in its development. In this district it assumes a large and striking form, with the black spots on the underside of the wings, normally in blues rather small and delicate, being bold and coarse, as if they had been put on with a gem-marker. The upperside of the wings is very dark, indigo to black, but the white chequered fringe gives contrast. Usually we have found this blue as singletons or couples, widespread, but not many in one place.

The most conspicuous family in the field however, were the fritillaries, because of their size and numbers. The silver-washed, when they were out, were particularly attracted to the buddleia bushes, round which they fluttered incessantly. With their strong wings they had no difficulty in flicking away smaller species, or even normal-sized bees from their chosen flower, but had to quit rapidly when one of the big shining black bees came along. The dark form of the female, *valesina*, which seemed to equal if not outnumber the brown form, was particularly striking in its silver and green livery when seen from below as it drank from the swaying sprays high up in the bush. High brown fritillaries, and dark greens too, were present, though more usually on the brambles. Of the smaller kinds, the heath fritillary was the most numerous, using the lower plants in the meadow, while the Queen of Spain was more frequently sunning its wings on the barer parts of the turf. We saw *phoebe*, the knapweed fritillary, once or twice, and both of the pearl-bordereds, the smaller *selene* more often than the larger *euphrosyne*, though both are much the

same size there. The names of these are taken from classical origi-
nals, goddesses or nymphs in the case of the fritillaries, and in
that country the people, too, still retain classical names, mostly
polysyllabic. In some ways it seems more dignified to be introduced to an Orestes or a Leonardo, whereas our equivalents,
derived from biblical sources, such as Abraham or Jonathan,
would be inelegantly shortened to Abe or Jon. I have not yet met
a lady christened Euphrosyne, but I am sure there must be one
around in that district, and that she is called so in full, not by
some shortened form.

A question that arises is what did the silver-washed fritillaries
do before the buddleia came, to flower conveniently at the time of
their emergence; were they always so numerous, or have they
increased as a result? And if previously they fed on the nectar
from other flowers, and in doing so assisted in their pollination,
have these flowers decreased correspondingly? In our woodlands bramble blossoms seem their staple diet, with marsh and
other thistles, scabious, knapweeds, hawkweeds and other com-
posites. All these were present in that field, and had plenty of
other insect visitors, so are unlikely to have declined in numbers
for that reason. Wheeler's *Butterflies of Switzerland and the Alps of
Central Europe*, answers the first question, also negatively, since
he describes *paphia* as "everywhere in lower valleys, generally
common, often abundant". As this book is dated 1903, and the
buddleia we know was only discovered in China towards the end
of the last century, this seems convincing evidence. I should possibly write it Buddleia, since the genus (though this species was
then still unknown) was named by Linnaeus in honour of the
Rev. Adam Buddle, who wrote an English Flora in 1708. The
specific name, Davidii, also indicates the frequent interest in bot-
any by men of the cloth, since it commemorates the French mis-
sionary, Père Armand David (1826–1900) as does the Père
David's deer, and other species of plants also, though none of
these have achieved such success as the Buddleia in colonization.

However I remember once seeing quantities of it in a dry river
valley in the Pyrenees, where it was deserted by butterflies in
favour of almost everything else. It must, like other plants, have
its daily peaks of producing nectar, and I may only have seen it at
times when the nectar had been drunk dry, but it still seemed
curious that it was so devoid of insects, and I wish that I had

made further observations at the time. Though later I have seen it relatively unfavoured by insects in other southern situations, and can only speculate whether it needs less heat, or a damper root-hold to bring out its full attractions. It is not a plant of which I can claim much success in handling, since when I once embarked on a modest outlay to acquire as many different colour forms as local garden centres could provide, with the intention of growing them at the further end of my lawn so as to see if there was any colour preference shown by their insect visitors, they all succumbed to a spring frost. Nor when I found a dozen or so had seeded themselves in my woodland, to do which the seeds must have travelled at least a quarter of a mile, was I successful when I tried to transplant some of them to what I considered, but they clearly did not, was a more appropriate and unshaded situation. Next time it happens, I would do better to consider moving the trees instead.

But to return to the field, as indeed I hope to do when I am again in that district, though the likelihood of finding it still un-spoilt must reduce each year as the villas increase. The total area shown on the large-scale map as unwooded is perhaps a tenth of the whole, and much of this is taken up by the settlements and the villas around them and along the roads. The chances of there being other fields there as good as this one must therefore be small, though they may well exist. When one has found such a place, one tends to return to it, rather than to search for others, and in the ten days or so that is all one can manage for a visit to such a district, first priority is given, if weather allows, to an expedition to the higher Alps. Sadly economic forces dictate that these lower valleys will become more residential and less farmed, and imported foodstuffs will supply the villas. One conjectures that the small farm is even now only kept going by the older members of some family whose children have long since adapted to the plastic society, though one hopes that in their old age they too will revert to the solace of a traditional regime, and continue to maintain the field with three Alpine cows (*Photo 20*).

EIGHT

Rules for Wardens

1) Always carry a small tool such as a billhook or spanner. This shows that you are working.

2) Never wear a badge or armband. This avoids people asking pointless questions about your property which will waste your time.

3) Your duty is to get on with your work, not to disturb visitors by proffering information. If they want to know anything, they can ring up the Office.

4) Never answer your telephone. If your Supervisor wants to talk to you, he knows where you work, and can come to find you. What is urgent to him is not necessarily urgent to you.

5) Never volunteer information about what is happening on or around your property. If your Supervisor doesn't know it already, it is not your business to teach him his job.

6) Do not go around looking for bits of land that could be added to your property. You already have enough to look after.

7) When you visit the Office to see the pay clerk, do not let anyone else know you are there, as this will delay your return.

8) Arrange your holiday for when there are likely to be most visitors to your property. That is when you will need one most.

9) Always have an urgent job ready in a distant part of the property for when there are too many visitors to allow you to work properly in the main area.

10) Never offer local groups a conducted tour. Public relations are a specialized subject and should be left to the Publicity staff, who are trained for the purpose.

11) Complaints from the public require no action from you. The office staff are experienced in dealing with these.

12) It is an important feature of countryside management that it should carry on traditional practices, and as an experienced warden you know how these outlast passing changes of fashion. You may sometimes have to explain to junior staff that they should ignore new methods and ideas.

13) The garage accommodation provided is for you to keep your private vehicles in. Official cars are sufficiently robust to stand outside.

14) If you should meet a member of Council, remember that such people are always glad to have special information, particularly of the way money is being frittered away on unnecesary projects. Impress on him or her the inadequate conditions in which you work, and how greatly you could improve the property if you had more help and support from the Office.

NINE

A Peculiar Common

There are some plants which one tends to treat as indicating that it is worth exploring a new locality further, in the expectation of finding greater riches beyond. I think this is true of insects also, and possibly of birds, but plants are there for more of the year, and many are visible all through it. One can be misled, but it is surprising how often such indicators do prove correct. I remember once in Northern France stopping beside the main road where it ran past a wood, for purposes of nature as the phrase goes, and being led by the sight of, I think butcher's broom, or possibly it was spurge-laurel, both not uncommon such indicators, into penetrating further through the hazels and other shrubs that grew under the partial shade of the oak standards. I soon came on to a track alongside which was a greater butterfly orchid, and this track led me to a wider one, where I found a whole colony of lady orchids in flower. I would have liked to investigate farther, but the need to catch the ferry at Dieppe restrained me, so I followed the wider track along which discarded lady orchids indicated that it probably returned to the road, as in fact it did at a corner of the wood, not far from where we had parked, though the absence of any space to park where it came out suggested that the despoilers of the orchids were children from the nearby village, rather than visitors such as ourselves. I marked the wood on my map, for future visiting, but by the time we next were in that area, some years later, that map had been superseded, in the way that maps are, by a later edition, to which I had not transferred my note, and anyway it was much further on in the year. Though I expect other woods in the area might have been worth a visit just as much, if one was able to allow the time that one should for stopping in the north of France, rather than pressing on to reach the hotel one has booked ahead before the curfew hour when telephoned bookings are cancelled.

Recent experiences of driving across France have led us unjustly to assume that nothing much is left this side of Dijon, which is only true in part, and the second day's drive is always such hell anyway, that we tend to neglect the opportunities afforded by northern Normandy, thinking it is close enough to make a visit some other time, and anyway it is not so very different from our own countryside. This is only partly true also.

That incident, however, reinforced my faith in some species being indicators, so that much later when on the other side of the Channel I found my way to a small Y-shaped common that I had traced from written sources as being the property of the organization for which I was then working, and again on entering it I noticed plants of butcher's broom, and also tutsan, it was with a feeling of expectation and the morning before me, that I went deeper into the wood. The circumstances this time were rather different, because it was not such a dense wood, and there was quite a choice of tracks. It was small too, not much over 20 acres for the whole common, of which the woodland only formed the surrounding fringes to a central space where the arms of the Y met, and there still were vestiges of heather, but now almost overcome by bracken. So it was not long before I came out to the further edge of the wood, where a bank and hedge separated it from the surrounding fields and orchards. There were a number of orchids flowering along the edge, again including a greater butterfly, though I could not expect, in this part of the Weald, to find lady orchids too. There were also a number of trees and other plants of interest as I explored the rest of the common, and I thought it well worth another visit.

It had a number of pits or small ponds round the edges and along the stalk of the Y. The central area formed the meeting place of several tracks leading in all directions. It was clearly also a meeting place of the local hunt, since all of these were churned up by horses, except for the one gravelled track by which I had driven in, and which led to a farm beyond it. There was a rather attractive cottage in the fork of the Y, to one side of this track, which appeared empty at the time, though I was later to meet the occupants, a retired doctor and his wife, and learn from them that its idyllic situation had considerable drawbacks, not least in the frequent breakages to the old metal pipe that carried its water supply for the quarter mile from the main road. He was too deaf to appreciate, as his wife did, the compensations of the several pairs of nightingales that regularly took up their summer residence on the common, and I had noted on my first visit as a further inducement to return again.

This happened a month or so later, when Penelope was with me, as we were on our way to some family occasion, and had time in hand enough to deviate to visit the common. Being in tidy clothes we kept to the gravel track, listening to the nightingales, when I suddenly noticed that a white butterfly that was flying along the edge of the track was not a female orange-tip, as I had thought at first glance, but a wood white. As we watched, we saw that there were a number of these, flying intermittently but steadily along the tracks, and we had some difficulty in finding one that settled long enough to photograph; even then the picture was not good, though adequate for confirmation. This was another plus for the common, as we were well outside the usually accepted area for these butterflies, though I had known their range was tending to spread.

This small common probably had an interesting history, though I found no source that could tell me more about it. All I knew was that it was one of a handful of pieces of manor waste in that area, that had somehow become linked to a large property quite a distance away on the Downs. This large property, which included a village, had for some centuries been an 'Archbishop's peculiar', meaning that the Cantuar of the time could stay there, on his own ground, when on tour of the dioceses – a sort of second home, and no doubt he had others too. This arrangement presumably saved any embarrassment that might have arisen if he had had to stay with the bishop whom he was visiting, should there have been any matters of difference of doctrine or otherwise, and no doubt also afforded a base for the collection of information at other times. But I do not know how these very outlying pieces of manor waste became attached to this Peculiar, though one can imagine all sorts of reasons, from the pious to the disciplinary, that might have led to it.

How it, and the others, had become manor waste, was rather easier to guess, because there was very little in any of them that would have been of use for agriculture, or the fruit-growing of the neighbourhood. Most were too damp for cultivation, and some were merely strips along the wide verges of what had presumably once been drove-roads. All afforded some conservation interest, whether of individual plants, or marshy habitats that had remained undisturbed and unreclaimed over the centuries, and some, like this one, included patches of old woodland. The pits around its edges had presumably been excavated by the surrounding landowners, perhaps for clay for bricks, or some other purpose, and no doubt they had helped themselves to timber from it too, but there had been insufficient inducement to include it in the fields, which would have involved a great deal of levelling and draining. So it had remained simply manor waste. I followed up the muddy track that formed one of the branches of the Y to see if it reached the streak of large Paludina that the geological map indicated not far along it, but of course it did not – Sussex marble would have been too valuable to leave in manor waste. The other branch of the Y did not extend so far, with its track petering out in some very fine large bushes of blackthorn, in which young ash was beginning to get a hold. A small paddock had been made to one side, again with plants of interest in it, and I later found that the ownership of this went with the cottage.

I had noted several things that needed doing to maintain the conservation interests, but at that time there were insufficient resources available apart from what I could do myself, such as cutting out some of the ash from the blackthorn, and treating the stumps. I suggested it next year as a suitable site for a visit from a botanical society of which I was a member, and quite a number of knowledgeable botanists came and found enough of interest to fill a morning, before we went on to another common in the afternoon. Of the orchid family we found common spotted, early purple, greater butterfly, and violet helleborine, which last isn't so common in that county as in some others, and in the marshy areas there was marsh cinquefoil, devil's-bit scabious, sneezewort, water mint, brooklime, yellow iris, typha, bur-reed and yellow loosestrife. The woodland ground flora included dogs mercury, bluebell, wood anemone, wood-ruff, wood sorrel, wood sage, sanicle, ground ivy, herb bennet, and primrose, with a surprising number of false oxlip plants, though we did not see any cowslips for their other parent, though these are possibly present in the orchard. There were fragrant agrimony as well as the common one, betony, cuckoo flower, both currants, gooseberry, red bartsia, dyer's greenweed, six species of willowherb, and a number of common wayside plants. I was particularly struck by the number of butterfly foodplants, including honeysuckle, hop, sallow, devil's-bit scabious, cow-wheat, blackthorn, nettle, holly, ivy, violets, hedge garlic and vetches, while nectar plants included hemp agrimony, and marsh thistles, as well as others.

There were incidentals, such as some clumps of white-flowered herb robert, and the ferns included male, lady, buckler and hartstongue. The trees were beech, pedunculate and a few Turkey oak, birch, cherry and ash, with among the smaller trees and bushes, crabapple, cherry plum, elder, hawthorn, hazel, holly, field maple, wild service, rowan, willow, yew and the intrusive snowberry. There were 5 species of rush, and 23 of grasses. For so small an area it was quite a good list, and I was very grateful to the experts for coming so far, while they themselves seemed to have enjoyed the visit, with general agreement that sections at least were undoubtedly ancient woodland.

I was never able to make as satisfactory a list of the butterflies, because I did not have time to visit it very often, and I never discovered whether there were purple emperors as well as the white admirals and silver-washed fritilaries that I did happen to see. Purple hairstreaks were much in evidence, and later that year I took Bill and Ceres to see whether we could find a brown hairstreak there. It was some time before we spotted one, but after an hour of searching Ceres did so, and it then, a female, behaved so beautifully that we did not look for others. Coming down to eye level it perched on a young oak near the cottage, dividing its time between sitting on its leaves and on the flower of a neighbouring marsh thistle, while Bill photographed it carefully and expertly, and I snapped away with my ancient camera, though I could only guess the 3 foot distance which was its shortest focus. So I was very pleased when he kindly gave me one of his slides (*Photo 22*), and allowed me, since he was one of the generation that used the old 4" square kind, to cut it down to fit a 35mm frame. Bill sadly died only a few years later, so this is a memento to me of a charming and very competent all-round naturalist, with whom it was always a pleasure to be out, though unfortunately I did not meet him often, as we lived two counties apart. I believe he wrote a book on Asian birds, though I have never seen it, but his knowledge of all forms of wildlife was very great. I have been fortunate in meeting a large number of naturalists of his generation, mostly friends of my father's, and though the names of several of them are still well-known, I would put Bill high among them. I am always tempted to judge the competence of naturalists by the amount of equipment they do *not* find it necessary to carry in the field, but it is perhaps unfair to dismiss as useless someone who carries as many gadgets strung round him or her as the White Knight in Alice, since if such paraphernalia had been available to earlier generations in its present light-weight form, they might well have put it to excellent use. As it was, they did without it, and managed very well.

The brown hairstreak is one of the loveliest European butterflies, despite its sombre name, and his slide shows it sitting on marsh thistle in the sun, so that the tangerine of the underside of the wings, with their red antemarginal stripe, contrasts with the brilliant white of the body, the thin irregular stripes on the wings, and their fringes. One of mine shows the wings partly open to disclose the orange patches both on the brown of the forewings, and also on the part of the underside of the forewing that is covered by the underwing when it is sitting still. I suspect that much of this contrast fades after death, as I have not seen it appear so striking in set specimens. This was the nearest I had been to a brown hairstreak since, ten years before, one had fluttered down like an autumn leaf and sat on my wife's yellow jersey, when we had stopped on a roadside in the Massif Centrale, though in most winters I had found the conspicuous white eggs on the blackthorn, which is its food plant despite its misleading scientific name of *betulae*. Sadly the use of mechanical hedgecutters, and the urge to cut back clumps of blackthorn as they grow outwards, is reducing its numbers, since the eggs are often laid on the outermost sprays. It would be less damaging to it for whole bushes to be taken out at a time, rather than all being clipped, if it is really necessary to reduce blackthorn despite it being such an attractive shrub.

Although this common seemed to be off the beaten track, it did not have much protection, since it was not even marked with the name of the organization that owned it, nor did it seem advisable to so advertise it. I did however think it should be put in for SSSI status, and my suggestion was accepted by the NCC. I was also able to arrange for it to become part of the area of a warden who covered several properties not too far away to pay an occasional

visit. The cottage changed hands a few years later, and the pur-
chasers were a younger couple who were willing to keep an eye
out, once we had got to know them, and explained some of the
interests. They put in a plastic water pipe, whose route we were
able to influence so that the excavation did not spell the demise of
the marsh plants, and we came to an agreement on how far back
the bushes could be cut from in front of the cottage in the interests of protecting their children from the numerous adders that
lived in them, and sunned themselves round their edges. As
volunteer working parties increased over the years we were able
to start on some of the overdue conservation work needed; coppicing along the edge by the orchards to give more light to the
orchids, and cutting back flight paths for the butterflies. A few of
the ponds were cleaned out too, and the marshy areas increased
by cutting back invading scrub. I sprayed some of the bracken in
the centre, where the cottage owners had asked if they could
tether an old horse they had, and we had a further go at clearing
out the ash from those excellent blackthorn thickets. But on the
whole we left it very much as it was, a small oasis for wildlife,
that had survived through the centuries largely by accident, and
one hopes that in the hidden recesses of the Weald there are
others as good too.

TEN

The Orchid Bank

The dry valley that runs south-westwards from below our house to where, after a couple of miles, it joins the river gap through the Downs, does not run straight, but takes a dog-leg course between shoulders of the harder strata of the Upper Chalk. The first such shoulder is half a mile below us, and just within the boundary of the nature reserve. It is made by a bluff crowned by a large but now stricken beech tree, and the chalk of the steep bank contains large numbers of flints, which is no doubt what caused the deflection of the former stream that in postglacial times eroded out the valley. Each year I pick up the flints that have become detached at the foot of the bank, and the next year I find some more. They are not angular, or round like the sea-urchin casts that we often find when digging post holes, but knobbly and irregular, though usually flat rather than chunky, and some can be a foot or more across. We can use them for repairing walls, but more often as hardcore for cesspits or tracks; there is always a need for hardcore for some purpose.

After this first deflection the valley swings more westward, until it meets the next resistance point some 300 yards further on. From this 300 yards therefore the bank above it faces due south, and I remember it in the 1930s as open downland, free of trees and bushes. When my father and his friends used to shoot there, the guns stood along the bank, and the wood above was driven towards them. People motoring along the valley road used to stop and watch, and I remember one pheasant falling between the bonnet and mudguard of a car, which the driver was courteous enough to hand back, instead of driving on with it lodged there as he could well have done. However since then it became covered first with a mixture of scrub – dogwood, blackthorn, hawthorn, spindle, guelder-rose, wayfaring tree, and other species – and then as the trees seeded in, it was overgrown with birch, ash, beech, oak and the occasional yew and crabapple, up to some 30 ft high, and the sunny downland bank was no more. There remained only a less overgrown patch towards the upper end, where the flints were thickest (*Photo 23*).

It was Lavender who first pointed out the number of orchids there and as it was by then a County Trust nature reserve, we decided to clear it further until we had an open patch about 50 yards square running up the bank. We poisoned the stumps, and tried to keep it open, by handcutting and by using a small flail-mower which the NCC helped us to buy. We had trouble with the dogwood, but after we had discovered how to use Krenite, this problem could be overcome. The orchids responded well, and most summers we had 500 or more spikes. The majority were fragrant orchids, but there were some common spotted, and a few bee orchids, with pyramid orchids later in the summer. So we called it the Orchid Bank, and decided that when time and numbers allowed, we ought to clear most of the rest of the 300 yards, down to where, at the lower end, there was a small quarry, round the floor of which we had found a colony of fly orchids.

Between the bank and the road there was then a long narrow field, which the farmer often used for growing silage crops in alternation with another small field across the valley road. When he had lucerne there, it was alive with butterflies, with many kinds of blues. After the first cut for silage, the lucerne grew up again and sometimes flowered before the second cut. Later the cows were brought in, with the electric fences being moved along, so there was usually a further flowering before they reached the far end. There were common blues, brown arguses, chalkhill and Adonis blues then, but I never saw any small blues there. Then unfortunately the farmer gave up the lucerne in favour of a kind of rye-grass which gave five cuts a year, and this strip field was planted with that instead. So we lost many of our blue butterflies.

However along the upper edge of this strip field, where the bank began, there was a narrow belt that was not ploughed so deeply, because of the flints, and this always carried a good flora. Mignonette and viper's bugloss were particularly conspicuous, and several times I had people coming to the house, having seen the latter across this narrow field, asking if they could have a closer look as they thought they'd seen meadow clary. We have never had meadow clary there, though there are a few plants on part of the escarpment not far away, so it is in the books as occurring in the neighbourhood. Also along this belt, and now spreading out into the bank we had cleared, was some kidney vetch. It was a surprise however, only a few years after we had cleared the bank, to find that we had acquired a colony of small blues, although we hadn't known of anywhere close from which this rather sedentary species could easily have come. However there it was, and it increased, so that in some early summers I have counted fifty or more. I have never seen an autumn brood here, though it is bivoltine in some of its habitats in southern England. On a sunny June day you find them all along the bank, but in dull weather they congregate more in the long grass above, where the Norway spruces give some protection.

So this was an example of where we had improved the habitat with particular plants, the orchids, in mind, and been rewarded with a colony of a butterfly that we did not have in the reserve before. However this wasn't the end of the story, because several years later Sheila and I found at the top of this bank, where we had cleared, a few flowers of the autumn lady's-tresses, again new to the reserve. There were four the first year, and sometimes we found up to a dozen in later years, and sometimes none. It is a plant which has good years and bad. The next summer we found a plant of the knapweed broomrape on the bank, and this now occurs in most years.

I don't know whether the flints underneath had some effect that made it good for orchids, either in drainage or temperature or some other way. It has however proved a good area for them, as is the wood above, where there are usually early purples, and occasionally we have found great butterfly and birds' nest orchids there too. When the farm changed hands, the new tenant found the strip field uneconomic to farm with his larger machinery, so we took it out of his lease and included it in the reserve. About four years later we found that bee orchids were coming up in it at the end below the small quarry. There were four the first year, all strong plants, and they gradually increased each year for 5 years, until we had well over a hundred, all in an area not more than thirty yards square. The following year there were none at all, but it seemed a bad year for bee orchids everywhere round us. I can't really tie up the pattern of the flowering of orchids with the weather; the summer before had been wet, but one possibly should be looking at what it was like seven or so years previously, when the parent plants seeded.

Meanwhile we did manage to clear the rest of the 300 yards of the bank (*Photo 24*), apart from two or three patches, including the best crabapple, that we left so as to break up any transverse wind. It had gone quite a long way in transition to woodland, so it will be some years before we get it back to downland turf. We had the usual flushes; violets the first year, then biennials, and it will take time for it to settle down. Most of it was cleared by volunteer parties, followed by a local training group for MSC leaders, and some of it still needs sorting out where they cut the stumps too high. Usually I like to go over them afterwards as low down as possible with a chain saw, and then put a herbicide on, mixed in old paint, immediately afterwards. But we have to take our voluntary working parties as they come, and some of these came on a weekday when I couldn't be there.

Even without the orchids, this bank and what had been the strip field below it, had become one of the most attractive parts of the reserve, so we put in another entrance from the lane that could be used by visiting members of the County Trust. They could leave their cars there and walk along the 300 yards of the bank, without having to climb the hill into the rest of the reserve. There are plenty of plants of interest, bugle, milkworts, including chalk milkwort, and cowslip in the spring. Later there is marjoram in sheets, and all the other summer flowers, ending with the clustered bell flowers and felwort of the autumn. One member photographed a purple emperor that he saw on several days flying over from the other side of the valley. Immediately after it had come out of the farm tenancy, while it was still in an arable state, I got a contractor to rotovate a strip close to the road, and plant lucerne, but this died out after three years, and it should probably be done yearly, as the old farmer used to do it. However there was some still left when we last had a clouded yellow invasion, and it was a pleasure to see the numbers it attracted in 1983, and again in 1990.

We also decided to improve the access to the small quarry, so that people could walk around close to its face, and perhaps see some of the smaller sea urchin *micraster* that occur there. We made some steps at each end, and a fairly level track round just below the face, so that people could see it close up, at eye level. The steps were made of sawn and tanalised timber, and we fixed them with 2" square pegs. It looked rather neat and tidy when we had finished, and I was amused to see that the next week a cock pheasant had adopted it as a display area. But we have to clear it each spring of the chalk fragments that the winter brings down from the face.

So that part of the reserve has, with a bit of work, become very interesting for visitors, as they can see something of the geology, as well as the orchids and other plants, even if it isn't a sunny enough day for the many butterflies. It has been a lesson in how one thing can lead to another, including welcome additions that were not expected. But we still have a lot to learn, and particularly how long it will take for the parts of the bank that had pretty well turned into woodland to revert to chalk turf, and whether we will need to help this process along in some way.

The wood above, which is an old wood, has still kept its own margin, though it was the shrubs from this that had since colonized the bank. There always remained a slight gap between the two, which was used as a path by animals as well as people. In this margin there are still primroses, which sometimes cross with the cowslips below to produce plants of the false oxlips. The cowslips themselves are fairly small plants here, on this exposed bank, not nearly as large as some we have along edges in more sheltered parts of the reserve. A few years ago, I found a particularly good clump of false oxlip, of which I took a photograph, and meant to take another, but had run out of film. I came back a week later to find it had been destroyed, and I could not make out what agency had been responsible for this. I thought it was probably deer browsing, as it did not seem to have been picked, as by a human hand, but all the blooms had been torn out in an irregular manner. The cowslips flowering close beside it were untouched. It did occur to me that some botanical purist had been so enraged by the sight of a hybrid that he had torn out the centre of the plant in fury, but this seemed unlikely as it was not in view from below, and you could only see it if you happened to climb the bank just there. Also if such a person had been so minded, surely he would have pulled up the root, instead of leaving it to flower again the next year, which it did unscathed. It remained a mystery, with deer the most likely explanation.

With this in mind, I kept a bit of an eye out for other plants of this hybrid in subsequent years. We had had rather a good example in another part of the reserve, and we had put a small cage round it. This plant flowered for nearly 20 years. I noticed that small plants of the hybrid tended to disappear if not protected, so thought that possibly they were browsed, being more conspicuous than cowslips. However some of the cowslips, particularly the short-stemmed plants low down in the chalk bank were subject to a rather different form of attack, in that one sometimes found patches where the flowering heads had been nipped off and left, uneaten and apparently undamaged on the ground. I thought this might have been done by a bird, in the same way that early yellow crocuses are attacked by sparrows, but this is purely conjecture, and it may be the work of insects, or of some other creature. The stems of the individual flowers are cut off a little below the calyx. I think it happens in the early mornings, or overnight, and I have only seen it where the cowslips are short, within 3 or 4 inches of the ground, so even a small bird could reach them. Sally tells me that roe are responsible, but I don't know why they should do this.

I have seen this elsewhere round the edge of the reserve occasionally too, but not in its centre where most of the cowslips are. I expect there are quite simple explanations for all these minor mysteries, but meanwhile they are intriguing. So is the variation in colour of the orchids, with the pyramids showing the widest range from deep red to pale pink, but while the reds and deep reds are widespread, the pink is exceptional, perhaps one in a hundred. The bee orchids too are nearly all alike, and then one finds an odd one that has a somewhat different coloured pouch, or slighty different markings on it. So too with the small copper butterflies which are frequent here, and have a fairly high proportion showing the blue spots inside the red margin of the hindwings. The female common blues are also variable, usually a dingy brown, but occasionally towards the end of the year in particular, with patches of vivid blue on their forewings, contrasting with the red marginal spots of the darker wing edges with their white fringes.

All in all, the orchid bank has become rather a fascinating place.

ELEVEN

Wind and Tide

It was a pleasant afternoon at the seaside in the late July of 1975. The tide was half-way in, and the many family parties spread along the beach in front of us, as we looked northwards along the spit, had retreated to the strip of sand that remained below the shingle ridge of the head of the beach. They had an hour or two to go before the tide would reach them, and were making the most of the sunshine as they lay on camp beds and lilos in their shorts and swim-suits. Some had used the remains of the battered breakwaters we had erected several years before on which to hang clothes and towels, as protection from such wind as there was, but those lying on the strip of sand were protected by the shelter given by the shingle ridge, which stepped down steeply. It was this step that was the problem (*Photo 26*).

Sidney pointed out to us how it had been moving inshore during the summer. The winds had been the wrong way consistently, and the beach was being eroded, not built up. It had not far to go now before it would eat through the rest of the shingle ridge, and then there was nothing that would stop it cutting through the neck of the spit. The line of dunes that ran along the centre of the spit were only soft sand, and could easily be breached. There was no back-bone; nothing solid that would hold against the force of the waves with the wind behind them. If the spit were cut through at the neck, the saltings it protected would be washed out, and their high importance for plants and birds would be lost. It was clear that something must be done before the winter storms.

The threat had been developing gradually, but in the way these things happen, had been largely ignored until now when it had reached the stage of quick and obvious deterioration day by day. Sidney had built up the head of the spit so successfully with the sandtraps he had devised that it had almost doubled in size.

Twelve years of struggle had gone into it, with many parties of volunteers making windbreaks of chestnut paling and brush-wood fences to break the force of the winds, and cause them to drop the sand they were carrying to form new dunes. Marram had been planted to stabilize these, sea couch had spread, sea rocket had grown up, and the original core of old dunes was now reinforced by a wide belt of new ones, forming a habitat for other plants; centaury, Portland spurge, sea bindweed, and evening primrose. The strips of shingle remaining between them were used for nesting by ringed plovers, and the little tern colony was spreading to them from the low islands in the main harbour to the north. This habitat would still remain , even if the neck was cut, and the spit became an island. It would be a loss to the public, who would no longer be able to roam around the spit from the mainland; some of them on a daily jog, or walk with their dogs, all through the year, others just on a pleasant summer visit to picnic or sunbathe in the dunes. There would be diffi-culties in wardening, or maintaining the sandtraps. It would be a pity, but acceptable if necessary.

The potential loss of the saltings was a different matter entirely. If the spit was cut, the channels would alter and they would soon be scoured out. The acres of sea lavender would go, the fringes of sea heath, and the complicated network of creeks and channels with *Spartina* and *Zostera* that harboured the shelducks, teal, mallard, and the winter-visiting brent geese, would all be lost. Such saltings are amongst the richest and most prolific natural habitats, and one of the few which humans seldom penetrate and disturb.

What we could do was largely dependent on resources – financial chiefly, but in materials and equipment too. We had very little of any of these. It is a curious fact that as you approach the coast the number of organizations that have a say in matters increases, and though there may be needless consultation and arguments between them, it is still possible that in time, and allowing for a disaster or two in the meanwhile, something effec-tive will ultimately be done. But here we were not on the coast, at least not on the legal coast, because we were technically inside the harbour. The large groynes that had been made all along the coast, and round the turn into the harbour, stopped just south of where we stood. Indeed it was them that were causing the trouble, because they were the chief agents in stopping the shingle coming round the corner to build up the beach. They also caused scour in their shelter, which diminished the beach. If they had not been there, the shingle would, with the westerly long-shore drift in that section, have been washed round the corner. But with their substantial timbers running far out, they stopped this. Off-shore in the Channel itself, we could see a dredger working, taking up marine gravel for sale, and this too was helping to starve our beach. Many organizations were willing to give sympathy and advice, and particular assistance was given by the County Water Authority, but none was empowered to give practical help, and it soon became clear that if we did not act ourselves, nobody else would.

The history of the spit was well known. Its position from many old charts had been plotted on a composite map. Two hundred years earlier it had projected halfway across the mouth of the harbour, in continuation of the coastline then. A century later it had moved some 400 yards back inshore, as the whole coastline was gradually worn away, but it still projected north-west across the harbour mouth. It had then begun to pivot, on the part we called the Hinge. By 1910 it was projecting almost due north, and fifty years later it had swung round to point north-east. In 1963 a storm had breached its centre, and we had airphotos taken then that showed it almost inundated, with a gap in the middle of the dune ridge, through which the waves could flow, though the saltings were still protected by the remains of the ridge. The County Council had carried out stabilization works, using earth-moving machinery, and installing gabions. When the breach was restored, they had given the spit to the National Trust. Sidney had been appointed the Trust's Honorary Warden, and it was due to his energy and enthusiasm that so much had been done since.

He had written a booklet based on extensive research of tidal records, which the Trust had published. This analysed the building-up effect of the flatter summer waves, compared to the more destructive steeper waves, experienced often in winter, whose powerful backwash carried more to sea than they brought in. For a long time the dominant wind, most effective in building up the beach, had been from the South-West, but in recent years the periods of north-east wind had increased, and these tended to blow the sand back into the sea. This led to a study of the tides and tidal streams of the area, which showed patterns of both 4 and 18 years periodically. When the two peaks combined, high tides could be particularly dangerous, especially if there were strong winds increasing their heights. With this knowledge, the sandtrap programme had been designed to extend the protection on the harbour side of the main dune ridge, so that they were now shielded by a much greater width of new dunes, and a recurrence of the 1963 breach had become unlikely. However all depended on the Hinge remaining firm, and it was this that was now threatened.

Sidney's successful use of permeable structures to trap the sand suggested an analogous method of meeting the present crisis. It was decided to instal a row of 'soldiers'; these being individual posts with gaps betwen them placed in a row along the beach as if they were facing the enemy. These break the force of the incoming waves, causing them to drop their content of sand and shingle, which is then partly obstructed from returning by the posts themselves. Suitable timber was available from Trust woodlands in the form of thinnings from Douglas fir plantations within twenty miles, and some hundreds could be assembled.

They had to be of a size that could be man-handled, and a length of 10 feet was selected. Their thickness averaged about 8″. Some discussion arose over whether the thick or the thin end should be pointed; there were arguments for each, but in the end it was decided to point the thinner end, so as to allow a greater surface on which the rammer could operate. They were therefore cut and pointed, and brought down to the coast. A tractor-mounted rammer was hired, and the first batch were driven in on 1 October 1975. A publicity sheet was produced to inform people of what was intended.

Three decisions were needed; how far down on the beach to make the line; how far apart to put the individual posts, and to what depth to ram them in. The answers were to some extent dictated by the situation and the equipment. The rammer was mounted on the side of the tractor behind the rear wheels, and operated by the tractor's hydraulics. The heavy head of the ram was hauled up and then descended vertically in a groove on the same principle as a guillotine. Consequently the tractor needed to be on ground that was both fairly level and also firm. The stretch of sand immediately below the shingle ridge gave a suitable site, and the soldiers were put in along this, just about where the sand met the shingle, with the row being slightly curved to follow this line.

The distance between the posts caused much discussion, and the decision to space them twice their diameters apart was largely taken on the experience of Basil, of the Water Authority. It was also decided to drive them in to a depth of 4' 6" inches, on the argument that this would allow them to stand even if there was an initial loss of material, so they would project 5' 6" above the present beach. A measuring rod was quickly made to check this.

Driving posts in sand is very hard work, as I have found on other occasions, and even the powerful rammer had considerable difficulty. With later batches, by which time the success of the method was evident, the depth was reduced to 4', since the last 6" took an undue amount of time. The method adopted was for the two Trust woodmen, both called Denis, who had cut them, to man-handle each timber into position, then hold it upright between them with ropes, while the tractor lined itself up and ramming commenced. Sometimes an underground boulder made it necessary to pull more one way than the other, but in general the operation was not unduly difficult. Later we found it helped considerably if the hole was first softened by using a tractor-mounted auger (*Photo 25*).

It took three days to get in the first 170 posts, with the weather co-operating in providing fresh but generally sunny days – good anorak weather for working. On 4 October I paint-sprayed numbers on every tenth post, and measured their projection above the level of the beach. I continued this as more posts were installed in November and December, to a total line of 300 posts, and even from the start the effects were evident. The end posts did not show so much gain as the centre ones but, to take an example, the hundredth post from where we had started, and which projected 50" on 4 October, showed only 40" as early as 15 October, 34" in November and December, then fluctuated slightly during the winter months, but a year later only 20" projected. By December 1976 this was reduced to 18", and this gain of 32" in beach height was about the average, the maximum gain shown then being 40" at the 170th post, roughly the centre of the completed line of 300 posts.

The projections were rather uneven northwards of that, partly because the later posts were only driven in to 4' depth, and partly because the rise in the beach level meant that for the tractor to operate on smooth ground the line could not be continued absolutely straight. Aesthetically it could have been better, and there was some discussion a year later whether the posts should not be sawn off to improve appearances. However it was decided that they were better left to continue to do their work, and a chance event in 1977 led to them being buried to their full depth. This occurred through a breach in the major groynes to the south, at the corner of the harbour mouth, allowing ample supplies of shingle to be swept round onto the Hinge, so that the protection here increased rapidly to an extent in which it seemed unbelievable that there had ever been a threat of a breakthrough. This certainly showed that these main groynes had been, as we had suspected, instrumental in starving our beach, both by their position and the scour they caused in their eddy (*Photo 27*).

These groynes are part of the coastal protection however, so in due course, about five years later, there were plans made for their repair, and enlargement. Representations of the likely effect on the Hinge of such work were largely dismissed, and the work was carried out. Though some protection was given such as by installing a series of gabions to the north of the last groyne, by 1984 a fresh incursion was evident, with the shingle being drawn northwards and not being replaced. Again a pronounced step worked inshore, and though the soldiers still remained in position, they were in 1985 and 1986 slowly being uncovered, with two feet or so of their tops projecting.

So the cycle began again, as with so many other forms of erosion, and repair of erosion. One wishes for some better overall coordination of environmental protection, so that the actions of one body should not adversely affect the efforts of another. However, though matters are now in the hands of others in this instance, it was fascinating to have had the opportunity over a decade to have taken part in such an exercise, and to experience at first hand how much can be done in relatively simple ways to harness, at least for a time, the forces of wind and tide. It can only be for a time, since as any geologist knows, the sea always wins in the end.

TWELVE

The Fate of a Wood

It would have been reckoned a large wood anywhere and so close to the suburbs it seemed immense. Great flocks of birds flew over it, or into it; one could not tell. They disappeared from sight over the horizon of trees. Animals came out of it, or were seen standing at the edge before going back in again; foxes usually, sometimes roe deer or badgers, standing for a moment in the sunlight before they disappeared again into the shadows. Some days there was shooting in the woods, and clouds of pigeons hurtled up out of the trees, wheeling round over the hill and settling again further off. Poachers perhaps, or perhaps the shooting tenant; though he lived the other side of the hill and few knew who he was.

So the wood remained. Most people in the village had been there sometime in their lives, just out of curiosity, to see what it was like. But without paths, it was no use for an evening stroll. Boys sometimes ventured into it; some to fish in a pond, though accounts differed over how many ponds there were in the wood. One was said to have perch, and another goldfish, glinting as they surfaced out of the darkness. But bramble covered the ground, and bracken came up high in summer, so it was difficult even for boys to find their way.

In the old days it had been different. When the Family lived at the Court had been its heyday. Then, the ponds had been looked after, and the avenue of rhododendrons planted as a vista, running up the slope to the crest of the ridge. There had been picnic excursions then, carriages and footmen.

Later, after the wars, there were woodmen working in the winter. You could hear axes, the hammering of wedges, and occasionally a tree crashing down. Men were busy with tractors and wire rope, and the ground was churned up and muddy. But after a few years these activities ceased too. Perhaps they became unprofitable, or the men found easier occupations.

So for a further twenty years the wood remained almost unvisited, except by the occasional naturalist. Even the crowds of visitors to the downs and heathland did not stop as they passed it – there was nowhere to park a car and it did not look inviting to them. The old oaks and Spanish chestnuts spread further, the pigeons fed on the fallen acorns, and the duck came to the ponds. Woodcock bred there undisturbed, and flew out on their roding flights over the village. Sparrowhawks nested, and woodpeckers made their holes in the trees. Life went on as usual in the wood.

But suddenly one September day there were large boards round it advertising an auction. A catalogue gave the date and time of the sale, five weeks later, and described the 112 acres as "a valuable block of woodland and an excellent capital investment". There was a map showing how many ponds there really were. The number of timber trees was listed, oak, beech, chestnut, ash and others, over 1600 in all, and there was a current felling licence covering 63 acres, subject to replanting with conifers. The catalogue said the wood was open for inspection, and inspected it was. Never had there been been so many people looking at it. Tracks became trampled open with their passage. Timber contractors came from far and near. Local people came to see it again. They suddenly realized that the wood might not be there much longer and were worried.

The County Naturalists' Trust had special reasons for wanting to preserve it. The wood was part of an almost unique area of contrasting habitats from chalkland to heath, woodland and meadows. It would be a suitable location to hold our annual nature trails, with less of the vandalism that had been so annoying when we had held them on public land. We could even put up permanent features instead of having to erect and dismantle them each time. John, who was then Chairman, and I knew the wood fairly well, and there was certainly enough there to make it of interest to the school parties who were likely to come. The catchment area for these, on the edge of London, was enormous. We decided to put it to the Trust's Council.

John could speak of the natural history interests, and the educational opportunities, but the financial implications fell to me as Treasurer. I had already found out that our bank would advance £10 000 at 2 per cent over bank rate (then 5 per cent) if we mortgaged the wood to them, and that three neighbouring landowners would form a syndicate with us to buy parts of the wood totalling some 60 acres, and adjoining their properties, to protect their skylines. This would leave the central area, with the hilltop and all the ponds, for the Trust. But we did not know what the price was likely to be, and estimates differed widely. The best advice we could obtain suggested over £25 000. The mortgage would cost £2000 a year for 7 years to pay off, and though we could run an appeal, there was no time to mount one before the auction. Our own members might be generous, but on a national level a suburban wood was likely to rank low on the scale compared to the Hebridean islands, Yorkshire moorlands and Ouse washes then on the market. The County Council had been sympathetic, but could not promise immediate grant aid, though they would consider a loan.

They had however advised me to approach an individual, referred to as the anonymous benefactor, and I was able to tell Council that I had taken him for a walk in the wood that afternoon. We hadn't gone very far, because he was a busy man running a large business as well as a considerable charitable foundation, but we had seen enough of the wood for him to savour its character. We had gone as far as the top pond, which was the largest, and he had looked across its still water at the reflection of the trees beyond. "I will give you £3000", he had said, in a quiet voice, so quiet that I had to ask him whether he had said two or three thousand. "Three", he had replied, and we had gone back to his car.

Our Conservation Officer had also been busy canvassing for support, and he had already found three or four members who would be prepared to give us temporary loans of £250 each. Council was hesitant at first, but gradually became enthusiastic. It particularly weighed with the Council members that this was the first time that the anonymous benefactor, who was known to support the National Trust very considerably, had taken an interest in the Naturalists' Trust. They decided that we should try to buy the wood, and our Honorary Surveyor (another John) who had seen and been impressed, not least by its photographic opportunities, agreed to bid for us. We worked out that £26 000 was the maximum we could go to and I privately gave him £500 discretion on top.

On the day of the auction the hall was crowded with timber contractors and their professional advisers. Local people too had come to see what happened to the wood. The bidding started at £10 000 and went up quickly £1000 at a time. Six or seven timber merchants were bidding keenly; they knew exactly what the timber was worth at so much a Hoppus foot for each kind of tree. Quickly it rose to £20 000 and still the bids came fast. At £22 000 the auctioneer paused; he was over his reserve price now, and he wanted the best he could get. He looked round to see who was still in the market. Then on again went the bidding, now £500 at a time. Now it was £25 000, and he was taking £100 at a time. The bidders had dropped to two or three, eyeing each other, and waiting till the last moment before raising the price. At the back of the hall stood our Surveyor, who had not yet bid. He had been at many sales in this hall, and taken many auctions there himself too. He knew it would be best come in at the time when the others were flagging, and the sight of a fresh buyer would have the most impact. But he was getting worried. He was near his limit, and he had to make certain too that the auctioneer would catch his eye. Now it was £25 500, and a grudging bid had just raised it again. This was the critical moment and he acted. At £25 700 the auctioneer took his bid. He looked round, but there were no more bids to come. 'Going, going, gone', said the auctioneer, and the Naturalists' Trust had bought the wood. The date was 4 November 1971. This was the Trust's ninth reserve, but only the third, and largest, of which it owned the freehold.

I was running a firm then and that day was one on which I could not be away from the City. I had thought I had better not be present anyhow since my connection with the Trust was known, and we had decided that if we were succesful we would not give the Trust's name as the purchaser until we could combine it with a press announcement. I was surprised at first to hear from our anonymous benefactor that he had been there, and had sat anxiously as the bidding increased. Later, when I knew him better, I got to know that he always took a personal interest in anything he decided to support, though insisting on strict anonymity, as well as on the business efficiency of the arrangements. He continued this interest and helped us in other ways too, until after his wife's death he moved out of the county.

Our next need was to find the money for the purchase price. We had undoubtedly been very lucky in buying the wood for about £250 an acre, as only a year or two later other Trusts were having to pay considerably more for woodland. In fact we ourselves were soon offered a profit on it, but by that time our plans were far too far advanced for us to have second thoughts. We had decided to concentrate on the 'woodcock' theme, as a bird everyone had heard of, yet was not commonplace. We ran a series of advertisements in the glossy monthlies, on the lines of 'How much is a woodcock worth to a London school child?' and we were fortunate in recruiting Norman, a retired Chartered Accountant, as Appeal Treasurer. As well as keeping the accounts in an exemplary and most legible manner, he allowed his initials to be altered according to the magazine in which the advertisement appeared to give a coding system. Keith kindly gave us a drawing of a woodcock that we used as a logo, both on the advertisements, stationery, and the ties and brooches that we gave to donors of over £25, as well as the car stickers that were sent to all. We set up a management committee for the wood, of which the former shooting tenant agreed to be chairman, to carry out tasks immediately needed, such as checking the boundary fences, investigating the interconnections between the ponds, and their safety for visitors. A large number of Trust members offered help in their various specialities, and a great deal of work was undertaken. I can only summarize this later, as I was not so directly involved in it, as in the finances.

The Trust had paid the initial deposit of £2570, and its balance of £13 230 plus its share of fees was due to be paid on 3 December. Even with the promised donations, we would need to draw the full extent of the facility offered by our bank, but we hoped that we could before long replace this by cheaper loans from conservation sources, or interest-free loans from our members. We had decided on a minimum of £100 for interest-free loans, with 10 per cent repayments over 10 years, to minimize accounting complications. We could not circulate members until our early February newsletter, when Pat made a press release simultaneously, but they then responded nobly, so that by the end of the month Norman had received £4000 in interest-free loans, and nearly as much again in donations into the separate account we had opened for this purchase. As our professionally-produced appeal leaflet (which Nigel arranged) and advertisements became more widely seen, these totals increased, and by the end of June both donations and interest-free loans had reached £12 000. Although our rather sudden purchase had not initially been well received in conservation circles, these now began to rally in support, and following a front-page article in the Spring number of *Conservation Review*, we began to receive grant-aid from the World Wildlife Fund and other conservation charities. We had however upset a number of schedules, including that of a prominent member of the County Club, who had previously told us that he intended, in a few years time, to head a major appeal for the Trust though County channels, and now felt that he must cancel this, since we had 'jumped the gun', though he nobly still offered his own intended four-figure contribution. Charities such as ours have difficulty in keeping within an orderly sequence of appeals, because sudden opportunities for land purchase are bound to arise, whereas the continuing struggle faced by medical or educational charities may allow them to accept a place in the queue, and keep to it.

To continue the financial history, donations grew steadily following repeated advertisements, and wider dissemination of our leaflets, which were revised and updated as required. Wherever possible we tried to combine the advertisements with an article in the magazine concerned. Many individuals and groups sent donations, and many also ran events in our aid. Youth groups were particularly helpful in this, but they included a number of office whip-rounds and one from a pub called The Woodcock thirty miles away. By the time we came to wind up the appeal, four years later, and take the balances into our main accounts, we had received 1126 contributions, totalling over £20 000.

It was possible to repay 50 per cent of the interest-free loans after a year, and a further 10 per cent in each of the next three years, leaving 20 per cent to be repaid over the next two. Each time we made a repayment a number of the lenders asked us to convert the residue into a donation, but a core still remained. However by then the Trust had decided to commit itself to further expenditure at the wood. It had been bought for use as an educational reserve, and a car park large enough for use by coaches was essential. We had started negotiations on this with the County Highways Department within a month of our original press release, and a fairly level site had been agreed with access from a B road. Sight-line requirements however involved the removal of two mature beeches from an avenue, planted about

1870, which was a local feature. Admittedly these two beeches were almost the end ones of the avenue, but the requirement caused some heart-burning and threats of resignation from some prominent Trust members if it was carried out. An alternative plan considered would reduce the loss to only one tree, but involve a lease of land from an adjoining golf-course, which would insist on provisions to prevent unauthorised entry to the latter, difficult in practice to fulfil. On further investigation it transpired that a restrictive clause in the golf-clubs's title deeds would prevent such a use. Another alternative approach from a different side of the wood meant using a lengthy stretch of private road that might well change hands, and in fact was later to do so. The Highways Department was obdurate, on safety grounds, and we finally decided to agree – no resignations seemed to result. To cover the cost of over £3000, it was however necessary to write to a number of donors asking if they would allow their donation to the purchase price to be diverted to this work. All agreed, and some sent further donations.

John, our Honorary Surveyor, who had conducted the negotiations with the Highways Department as well as doing much else for the wood, now arranged with Ken for our volunteer conservation corps to make trial borings over the proposed car park area, to establish the best means of surfacing. He drew up a plan which would allow for parking 15 coaches (the maximum number that we had had at any one time at our previous nature trails) as well as about 40 cars, giving a splayed entrance and room for screen planting as required by the District Council. Various contractors were approached, and application for grant aid was made to the Countryside Commission. This last was refused, since they had requested applications from County Trusts to be channelled through SPNR, and on re-applying through that body, we were confronted with a formidable questionnaire about the likely extent of use by members of the public, as opposed to schoolchildren (who appeared not be considered as members of the public), and our application was rejected as not primarily for general public access. They drew a distinction between our proposals, and those of a neighbouring Trust which they had supported, where the site was open to the public on four afternoons a week and Sundays for six months of the year. However our anonymous benefactor, who considered this rejection rather petty, kindly sent a further £500 towards the cost. We also had a similar gift from a lady member and further aid from the World Wildlife Fund.

We were now held up for formal planning consent because the local Council had written in a condition that the car park was to be used for public access. The County had returned this as unacceptable, and the file had been mislaid. When it was found, we had to wait for a further Committee meeting. The car park was at last installed in 1973 and I was able to get a couple of heavy farm gates adapted so that they kissed, with a hinged flap to join them together, which could be secured with a padlock and chain. I also ordered a cast metal sign for the entrance, on the same post as our standard reserve sign, to record the £20 000 raised by donations, including that of the World Wildlife Fund. The latter sent us one of their own plaques, and as we had decided on the need for a notice explaining from which households in the neighbourhood members could obtain keys, we ended with rather a plethora of signs. Some of these were later consolidated into a more comprehensive panel, on the lines of an information board, kindly constructed and painted by a member. The car park area had turned out to be on chalk, so we had decided that a more expensive sealed surface would not be necessary, as an unsealed one would drain down satisfactorily. The underlying chalk in fact gave this area a different flora to the rest of the wood, and while we embellished it with cowslips, the bee-orchids and other chalk-loving plants that came up in it were natural. Buddleia also seeded in, and the butterflies it attracted added to the interest, so it soon became rather an inviting place to go to from a school. The screening from the road was more of a problem, and the District Council became insistent, having apparently visualized laurel or other evergreens. We compromised with holm-oak, and added a small collection of native sorbus species, that I was able to get from a specialized nursery, as well as some variations of other native plants, such as a double wild pear. In time the screen became accepted. The car park was first used for an open day in August 1973, and stood up satisfactorily despite wet weather.

Simultaneously with the car park negotiations, the continuing success of the appeal had allowed us to do some financial sorting-out. We first repaid the temporary loans made to help tide us over the immediate purchase, and we next paid off the bank loan, substituting the longer-term interest-free loan money for both. The three adjoining landowners who had formed the syndicate with us, had all paid their shares, and had all given their permission for the Trust to make use of their parts of the wood for teaching as and when required. In the case of two of these, the areas were somewhat remote from the centre of the wood, so this facility was not likely to be used often. We sold outright to one of them an outlying arm of the wood that lay in the view from his house, and which had little of value to us in it. The third section, which my own family had bought, was rather closer to the main interests, and as my family had given the Trust an option over three years to buy it at the original cost price, the 16 acres it comprised were now bought by the Trust. This increased the Trust's own holding to a solid block of 81 acres covering the hilltop, the north and south slopes and all the five ponds. The car park had been made at the south-western corner, which was the only part that had a reasonable road-frontage, though much of the southern slope fronted onto a bridlepath, which was technically a vehicular track, though seepage from the springs in the Thanet Sand made it unusable as such. It did however need fencing, as did other sections of the boundary, particularly where a neighbouring farmer had adopted part of the wood as the shortest way between two of his fields. Arrangements also had to be made concerning a cabin-like hut, now deteriorating, that had clearly been the pride and joy of the Scout troop that had made it, but it seemed some years since they had last used it, and it took some time to find out which troop was concerned. The dene-holes along the northern edge had been used for dumping by generations of farmers, and it took a long time to extricate all the hardware in them. When this was done, they turned out to be of considerable interest because not only could one see the water percolating down into the underlying chalk, but they illustrated an unconformity between the chalk and the Thanet sand. One geologist dug his trowel into it and said significantly to me, "There's thirteen million years missing here". At least I think he said thirteen, but it may have been more, or less, and I had not argued.

Enquiries of local historians had given some information of the past history of the wood, including its mention in about AD1300, so it seemed safe to assume that it had always been woodland of a sort. Indeed its configuration and geology would have made it almost unusable for any other activity. Later we were to find two mentions in Domesday. The hilltop was pock-marked with small excavations, but we could not determine their individual ages. Lying within a bowshot of a main Roman road they could have been made at any time over 2000 years, including by the Home Guard in the last war. Rather more could be discovered about the five ponds, most of which were artificial, and fed from a grid of drainage ditches criss-crossing the hilltop, as well as from the underlying Reading Beds and Thanet Sand. These ponds had once formed a sequence, with the largest not far below the hilltop and its overflow supplying the others, though in many cases the connections were broken or diverted. Information was also received from the family who had owned the land for the last two hundred years, and gradually a picture emerged that showed that one pond had been made to supply water to a farm a few miles off, which explained a reference in the sale particulars that had puzzled us, and then progressively had been taken over, adapted, and enlarged to serve the needs of a large house, and its garden, that had been the residence of the founder of a firm of silversmiths that is still a household name. Other ponds were made or used in connection with the Court, one for the stables and garden, another for drinking water, while the largest pond which mainly fed the others, had been enlarged to supply a projected golf course further afield, a plan that the 1914–18 war had prevented from realization. It was interesting to hear from a member of the family that the dene-holes, which he considered natural, though we had suspected they originated from marl-pits, had got noticeably deeper within his memory, and that his family had considered that the small colony of martagon lilies, of which they had kept the exact location secret, was native. Lavender and I had little difficulty in finding it from his directions, but I was surprised when later Eila showed me another in quite a different part of the wood. Later we had another letter taking us to task for some passages in our appeal leaflet which the previous owner felt indicated intended preservation of the wood for short-term purposes, over a few decades, rather than the creative activity over a time-span of centuries, which his family had tried to follow, and had sold the wood in the hope that it would be continued by others. I hope I was able to reassure him on some of his anxieties, but there is always a danger, when such appeal leaflets are drafted by a professional, or even by an in-house publicity department, that some phrase may appear to criticize previous management, and that this may come to the notice of those who were responsible for it, with unpleasant results.

The first meeting of the Local Management Committee for the wood had been held in June 1972, and they met quarterly thereafter. At first there seemed to be everything to do, and there were only too many people wanting to develop particular interests, so some tactful control was essential. The Management Committee was a useful forum for discussion of priorities. Clearly a large-scale gridded map was needed for many purposes, and Bob arranged the production of this, as well as putting stakes in the ground, later with the eight-figure grid references marked on them, where the 100-metre grid-lines intersected.

Securing of the boundaries was an urgent task, in some cases needing a survey to determine the exact line, and decisions on what form of fence or hedge was best suited to the site. There was no statutory right of way through the wood, but some riders and also some dog-walkers had liberal ideas concerning the width of the bridle-path along its edge. The hydraulic connections between the ponds needed investigation – there was clearly more than one generation of such works, and we had to find out what was the latest in time, and where and why it was leaking. Decisions were needed on the setting out of paths, bearing in mind future use as nature trails, and avoidance of dangerous features. A policy needed formulation regarding control of rhododendron, and the leaving of dead wood. Apart from these general requirements, the ornithologists wished to put up bird boxes, the entomologists to make glades, the herpetologists to create an open area of heather, the deer-watchers to make high seats, the pond-dippers (*Photo 28*) to make a platform, and so forth. It was surprising how all these things came to be done, sometimes by a numerous party, but often by only one or two enthusiasts working away at all hours. Possibly the heather area was the most ambitious, and when I first saw the straggly planting I thought success unlikely, but careful husbandry and spreading of seed ultimately produced a natural effect, complete with adders. Their introduction was unfortunately observed by a local dogwalker, which led to adverse comment, though there were later proved to be native adders in the wood. However this did help to keep villagers from encouraging their children to roam. The efforts to restore overgrown hazel to a coppice regime were at first thwarted by browsing deer, until a sufficiently sizeable area equated supply with demand. The deer also negated efforts to replace large sweet chestnut with young oak, until tree-tubes were invented, but meanwhile the supply of chestnut stakes and posts was always useful. Nigel, whose occupation as a farm supplies distributor allowed him considerable free time of his choosing, were made manager of the reserve, and his strength and resourcefulness were equal to all demands.

Fred took over control of the fishermen, who were mostly village boys whom he knew, and soon organized an effective licensing system. He also arranged for the adjustment of the stock of fish – at first there were far too many small perch. It was found that a pirate radio station had set up an aerial between two trees on the hilltop, which was the highest point for some miles around, and was broadcasting regularly. The pirates were not easy to trace, until we found that having set up their pre-recorded programme they then repaired to the local pub. Efforts to compromise with them were unavailing, since though these might have been successful on conservation matters, they could not be on the advocacy of drugs. Aerials were taken down, and replaced elsewhere, and the problem was not solved until Nigel, pitchfork in hand, happened to catch them up a tree, which resulted in a settlement whereby they went elsewhere.

By the end of 1975 a position had been reached where we wanted to wind up the purchase appeal, and move on to the next stage of providing permanent educational facilities. Little fresh money was now coming in, and we needed £2800 to complete the repayment of the interest-free loans. After discussion, and with Fred dissenting, we decided to accept the offer of one of the original co-purchasers to buy for £3000 two acres, including one of the lower ponds, subject to the Trust being able to use it for educational purposes. This was agreed by the Charity Commissioners, and went ahead. The part played by Brian, our Honorary Solicitor in this, and in all the legal matters concerning this and other reserves, as well as acting as Company Secretary, was enormous, and often unknown to the membership as a whole. Apart from the desire to move on to the next stage, the winding up of the appeal and the loans associated with it was becoming increasingly necessary with the deaths of some of the lenders and consequent repayment to their executors, while those who had kindly asked us not to pay their loan off until all others had been paid off, introduced a complicating factor. It seemed best to clear it all up when the 1976 repayment was due, particularly since in the absence of further funds coming to the appeal, the repayments would need to be made from the Trust's general funds, so this was done.

1976 therefore became a Janus year with the winding up of the purchase, writing of a guide leaflet and a management plan, and preparations for the next stage of setting up a permanent educational centre. We repelled an attempt to levy rates on the new car park, but we were thankful to be able to use it for the 200 members who came to the spring open day, and later for the visits of 14 school parties. We began to make enquiries about planning permission for a Centre building, and to look for possible candidates as a part-time teacher-warden, for whose housing my family were able to offer a small ex-agricultural cottage close to the wood. Also that year we found a new Treasurer, which allowed me to switch to being Chairman of our Educational Committee; a position that had become vacant the year before, which would allow me to continue involvement in the development of the wood.

Latterly I had found being Treasurer increasingly irksome, having successively had to master the complexities of Giro, PAYE, and VAT in addition to the routine book-keeping and keeping of checks on rents, wayleave payments, dividends, recovery of tax on covenants and so forth. A Treasurer, like a bishop in chess, is ineffective without the concurrence of more important figures, and needs to move obliquely, as the repository of dark secrets such as whose subscription is unpaid, and who is likely to leave a legacy. He has an excuse for enquiry into every sort of detail, on economy grounds if not otherwise, but interference can produce irritation, or curb initiative. I had already devolved membership subscriptions, covenants, ordering goods for sale, writing the newsletter, and various other ancillaries, but the basic chore had become increasingly time-consuming and more complex each year; the membership had grown tenfold, and the Trust's assets a hundredfold, though we did not let that show on the balance sheet. Eric was both younger and professional qualified; after nearly fifteen years I was glad to be able to hand things over to him, thinking it might well be another fifteen years before someone else appeared.

I should say something about the physical handicaps to setting up the Centre, apart from any financial or planning considerations. The ground rose from the level Chalk of the car park to form a cap of Tertiary sands, gravels and clays. The slope up was not very steep, but it was always wet, and if you dug into it, it got wetter, to form a spring. We had found that we could alleviate the problem a bit by digging drainage ditches, but it still remained. The only course was to build over it, which we did, making a series of squares of round timbers, and filling them in with hardcore topped with gravel. This made a tolerable flight of steps into the wood, and once we got past the really sticky bit, it wasn't so bad. But any form of excavation to make a level site for a building almost anywhere in the wood met the same problem, and it would be necessary to raise the building on piles of some kind to keep it dry. There was also difficulty in the absence of main services; there was no local sewage system; electricity would be very expensive to bring in; water might be possible if the site was not very far up into the wood, but above that there would not be sufficient head, and there was no telephone line near. Road access to the new car park was good, and mains services would be easier to provide there, but we were unlikely to obtain planning permission for any building within sight of the road. In any case we preferred to have it some way into the wood, so that children would get the feeling of being in rather different surroundings as they walked up to it.

At the first meeting under my chairmanship, the Education Committee decided to advertise for a part-time teacher-warden, preferably young and enthusiastic, rather than middle-aged, as the housing in the cottage was of low standard, and the infrastructure in the wood was non-existent. He or she would need to do a lot of the setting up of the latter, as well as writing the trail leaflets and other literature needed. We envisaged that initially it would be a part-time job, and include wardening of the wood and two other reserves nearby, as well as taking over the organization of the various school parties that had been booked for 1977. We had recently had a visit from the NCC's Regional Officer, and we now decided to invite one from the County's School Inspectors concerned with biological education. These too were very interested in the ways the wood might be used for school trails and study groups. Meanwhile John was taking soundings from the local planning department regarding a building.

Re-reading our advertisement for a teacher-warden, I am surprised that the £500 p.a. remuneration offered attracted any interest, but from the start we had decided that the warden's salary must be coverable by the admission fees paid by the schools who visited the wood, though it could be increased as these built up. About 15 applications were received; we interveiwed in March, when it was not an easy choice, and Doug and Beth moved into the cottage in July.

John had by now obtained planning permission to put up a 20 × 30 ft wooden classroom in the wood, for which he had received estimates of £3400 for the structure, and £650 for its base. We allowed £1000 for equipment, largely tables and chairs, though we hoped to cut down on these figures through gifts and working ourselves. We initiated an appeal for £5000, and could borrow £2000 from a recent legacy so that work could start as soon as we had raised a similar amount ourselves. To differentiate this new appeal, we had commissioned a fresh drawing of a woodcock, this time with a chick. The NCC provisionally agreed to provide £2500 if we could prove that the Centre would be used by schools, which was not very difficult to do, as we were soon able to show a letter from one source alone requesting 700 places during the next summer. The WWF would match £ for £ any moneys up to £1000 that the Local Education Authority gave, but the latter had no money to spare, though they could help with equipment and publicity. We received about £1500 from the other sources we had canvassed, so we looked like being £1000 short. Doug gave a talk in one near-by London Borough at which staff of schools with a total of some 10 000 pupils promised interest, and followed this by further talks and the mailing of 200 schools. The NCC accepted there was demand, and agreed to making the £2500 unconditional, subject to us providing education on conservation and not just on wildlife, and allowing their County Officer to come to our Committee meetings. The WWF reconsidered, and gave us £1000 outright. Further donations increased the total, but meanwhile the contractor's estimate had also increased. The building was erected in May 1978, but there was still a lot to do before we could use it. Delphine kindly offered to donate Sundeala ceiling panels, instead of using plasterboard, so that posters could be pinned to it, which also served to brighten things up a bit. A generator was obtained, and the wiring of the classroom was done by Trust members. Water supply had cost £150 to install, in the shape of a standpipe at the car park, with a connection from which we could run a polythene pipe up to the classroom, but this had to be dug in 2' 6" down, and inspected by the Water Co. I obtained the 150m of continuous 22mm piping needed, together with the fittings, easily enough for about £100, but it took a long time to dig the trench, and party after party took a hand until it was finally passed, and the pipe installed.

We decided to employ Doug full-time from September 1978 at £46 per week plus limited overtime. We had already got the 1979 booking application form in preparation; he had written one of the trail guides, and had plans for further ones. We expected to cater for both day visits from schools, and short courses. Later we were to find 'holiday workshops' a useful addition, as they filled up some of the potentially empty days between term times. Doug began to collect a number of volunteer teaching assistants, and our guesses at his interview that he would be the sort of inspiring person whom people would be willing to help and work with, turned out to be correct. His gift for drawing was also much employed. He had estimated £900 income from booked parties in the first year, which seemed encouraging, though we later insisted on raising admission fees when we saw the full extent of the demand. He prepared a lengthy list of equipment required, of about £1500 in essentials, and rather more in less essential items, which was somewhat reduced in discussion with teacher members, but we were encouraged by the high standard he obviously intended to set, and I think in the end he got nearly all the items by one means or another. Individually expensive ones, such as microscopes, or an environmental comparator, can easily be dismissed by a layman as inessential for school parties, but Barbara and others persuaded us not to be short-sighted about this, and they were proved right.

In our booking leaflet, costing £132 for the first 500, we emphasized the resources of the wood, with its ponds, the easy access, and the opportunities for practical as opposed to classroom study. We added paragaphs learnt from previous experience about requiring an advance deposit; availability of previous on-site discussion with teachers; discipline; non-collecting; quietness; recommended clothing; the sort of goods that could be purchased by visiting parties, and a summary of what the Trust was about. We warned them that sanitation was Elsan-based, for which I had procured a number of small individual wooden cabins at a sale, in which we installed the latrine equipment we already had from our earlier nature trails. We had also looked into the various requirements needed for fire insurance and escape routes, but there were many and expensive needs that would clearly have to remain unsatisfied for the time being.

Firstly vehicle access to the classroom was not easy. We had made a track to one side, between the trees, up which I could get my landrover at most times of the year, but not with a trailer except in very dry weather. A tractor could use it, but increased the ruts to an unwelcome extent. Heavy things, such as the broken paving slabs I had obtained from a County Highways depot for the hut foundations, could only be brought to site over a period, and any bulkier items were better man-handled up if possible. We tried to improve the access with Terram and gravel, but it didn't work, and the only permanent solution seemed to be a concrete track which we could not afford. The lack of all-weather access hampered us all the time, and meant that it was only on occasion that we could cater for physically-handicapped visitors, nor could we rely on getting any casualties out except by stretcher, or use any fire-fighting equipment beyond what hand extinguishers and our limited water could manage.

The primitive sanitation was sufficiently remote from what the school children were accustomed to see provided for them as to cause considerable comment and sometimes unruly behaviour, unless checked, but became accepted as part of the character of the place. It meant that someone had to empty the buckets into a form of cesspit, and clean things up each evening, which was a nuisance, but we had to put up with this.

The lack of a telephone was particularly difficult, and we ultimately had one installed. Using a generator for electricity supplies had its own difficulties in that the first model used needed swinging to start it off, and even when some years later we purchased a kind with a battery start, there was still the problem of carrying up daily supplies of diesel, with its liability to freeze in hard weather, and spread onto clothing at the best of times. We also had to trespass on the goodwill of a neighbouring farmer for a continual supply of small quantities, with accounting complications, until much later we managed to install a system of tanks, so that deliveries to one close to the car park could be pumped electrically, with the use of the generator, to another close to the classroom. The generator also required a separate shed, not too far from the classroom to give a good electricity supply, but far enough for its continual noisiness to be less intrusive. The heating of the classroom was also a difficulty in that calor-gas cylinders, when full, are not very easy to carry up a hill, and we also needed to use oil-stoves during chilly weather, so paraffin too had to be carried up.

The classroom (*Photos 29, 30*) had already been in use for some weeks when we held our formal opening ceremony on 12 May 1979, a date selected in the expectation that the bluebells would be in flower, but limited by Oleg's need to go to Sikkim on the 14th, and mine more prosaically to the Isle of Wight. It was a pleasant occasion with the first orange-tips flying, and I think everyone who meant to did get there, even those diverted because badgers had undermined one approach road. According to Arthur's careful listing, there were two mayors, whose chains of office did not seem out of place when combined with gumboots, the Regional Officer of the NCC, the Area Organizer and those of five local WWF groups, the County Education Officer, Chief Biology Inspector and County Youth Officer, the County Planning Officer, representatives of many of the firms and charitable trusts that had supported us, and a numerous contingent of representatives from the natural history societies in the County. In most cases those invited had brought their wives too, and a large number of Trust members and other friends had also come. Nearly all had contributed to the setting up of the classroom, which they now had their first chance of inspecting, though we had to limit numbers to thirty at a time. Others took the opportunity to join short guided walks in the wood, where at least some of the bluebells had come out. It was, as intended, more an occasion for thanking those responsible for the £6500 subscribed than to publicize the Trust, even though this Educational Centre, modest as it appeared, was the first that a County Naturalists' Trust had set up by themselves. Oleg appeared, photogenically as always, in the local Press, cutting the tape, while I figured less so, and getting rather bald, but at least having remembered to bring some scissors. We had many further contributions as a result of this opening ceremony, and in general I think that occasions of this sort are worth holding, apart from the chance they give to thank those who have contributed.

The classroom was very unlike that of another Centre in whose setting up I had been involved some five years earlier for another Trust. That had been a much more elaborate affair with expense unspared on the grounds that we could not afford to do it poorly. While the result had been successful in terms of impact, the main sufferer in the high-powered discussions had been the scientific content, and our efforts to introduce even a geological relief map had been vetoed, still more any diagrams of food chains, nitrogen cycles, or the like. I had been determined to do better this time, and with Doug as an ally, we were able to put over much more of the inter-relationships on which the life of the wood depended, and link it closely with the knowledge required by current school examinations. Some of the necessary jargon I found tiresome, such as the substitution for 'natural history' of 'biological appreciation in a countryside environment', but the effect of the change of approach was startling in that the bookings soon became full for a year ahead, and have continued so subsequently. While it had been made and maintained on a comparative shoestring, close attention to what the teachers needed, and the abilities of both Doug himself and the many he had attracted to help him (though there were never enough!) who were themselves practising teachers, combined to put it on a very high level.

There were numerous flies in the ointment. It is easy to estimate income in advance for budgeting purposes, taking a combination of day visits, field courses, and other offerings; to assume that they will be filled to capacity, and to base one's expenditure for the year ahead on that figure. It is much harder to live up to it, when days or half-days are not taken up, often for reasons completely outside the control of the schools or oneself; strikes, epidemics or weather difficulties being the most common. Even when matters seem to have gone as forecast, there is often a discrepancy between recorded figures, and those of the Treasurer, usually because of some altered interpretation of VAT liability. Expenditure is seldom subject to similar shortfalls, and one really should work to a 10 per cent margin.

We were unable to develop our sales of goods to anything like the extent of other Centres, for many of which this provides a major income source. This was due to this single outlet not being typical of the Trust's more usual sales pitches at shows and fetes, so that much of our normal range of goods was not suitable, yet there was unwillingness to make special purchases of more appropriate items, though some were tried. All the goods sold had to be carried up into the wood, there was little storage or sales space, and it was not possible for Trust members to pay a visit to the wood, as they might to other more accessible Centres, purely for shopping. Comparisons with other centres showed our figures to be only 10 per cent to 25 per cent of theirs, and later the competition in this respect was to increase much further as it became more generally realized that a leisured and wealthy public were glad of an opportunity to be able to do all, or almost all, their Christmas shopping in one place, away from the towns, close to their car, in pleasant surroundings, preferably with tea available, and the excuse of helping support a charity of which they approved. Unfortunately we were not in a position to set up such a countryside boutique.

There was always a latent source of difficulty, though it was overcome, between the responsibilities of the Teacher-Warden, who worked all weekdays (and most evenings too), and those of the Management Committee, who took over at weekends, either for working parties or to run monthly Open Days. Visitors at weekends expected to meet the Teacher-Warden, but he had to have some time with his family. He did in fact appear more often at weekends than was strictly due, but it was only because of the personalities involved being prepared to work together, that more trouble did not arise over the demarcations of whose duty it was to do what in the wood, either from the point of view of its use for teaching, or its maintenance as one of the Trust's larger reserves.

There were other more deep-seated difficulties. I have three times had experience of working with teacher-wardens, and in every case the wardening side has become very much secondary to the teaching. I now accept it as a fact that this will happen, and that such a post is not a practical combination of responsibilities.

There may be some, including myself, who would much prefer mending a stile to teaching children, but they are not likely to be found in such jobs. So I was not surprised when Doug wanted to give up the wardening in favour of spending more time on teaching, visiting schools, and planning the educational side, though it did raise a question-mark over his occupancy of an agricultural cottage. A warden is sufficiently akin to a gamekeeper to be accepted by a village, but a teacher is not. Fortunately such representations as I received on this were fairly easily suppressed, and Doug's successor wished to live elsewhere anyway.

However having been relieved of the wardening function, being simply the Centre's teacher soon led to an understandable wish to be the Trust's Education Officer; a post which had by then been instituted by other Trusts, though my personal grapevine led me to believe that such appointments, without an income-producing base, were likely to be a short-lived luxury. It is very useful for County authorities to be able to call on their Trust's Education officer for assistance at the many exhibitions, symposia, or other gatherings that they wish to stage, but few of them will grant-aid their Trusts to an extent that justifies this. It can be argued, as WWF had done, that education, including biological education, should be the provision of the LEA, and some Trust members also queried the extent of the Trust's financial involvement in educational matters beyond that directly required in the interpretation to the public of its work in maintaining its nature reserves. Others, however, thought that the Trust's pioneering work in this respect was well worth while, supporting their views by further donations, including one for the floor-covering of the classroom.

While these rather wider considerations were in many respects the result of healthy growth, this had also resulted in urgent needs closer at hand. To allow for the teaching of smaller classes simultaneously with the school day visits, a wooden contractors' site hut was obtained, and erected by BTCV (*Photo 29*). The cost of around £2500 was found from donations from charitable trusts. To help with the many routine tasks, a sandwich student from an agricultural training college was engaged yearly, partly grant-aided by the Countryside Commission. Doug's absence on visits to schools, or other matters, led to considerable strain falling on the volunteer teachers, and it was necessary to appoint Margaret as his official deputy, at a small remuneration. Frequent usage had led to some tracks becoming overworn, with increasing disturbance to the wood's wildlife in the areas near the Centre. There were still comparatively undisturbed parts further off, but the 25 acres to the east had now come on the market following the death of one of our co-purchasers. We could not justify spending the £25 000 asked, but we heard with relief that the National Trust was able to find this money. The fourfold increase in value over ten years was more than justified by that of the timber alone. The old generator suddenly gave out beyond hope of repair, but we were able to buy a replacement for £2000, following a further approach to our faithful charitable trusts. It was evident though that each year we were coming closer and closer to covering the Centre's running costs, including salaries, from admission and sales income, even by the Treasurer's stricter interpretation of the figures. We had originally estimated five years for this, but it was in the fourth that the Education Committee was able to report to the Trust's Council that a sustainable equilibrium had been achieved on income and expenditure, though there would always be risk of some disaster requiring a call on capital funds. We could also report that continued full forward bookings indicated a high standard, and a growing reputation.

The Education Committee had been somewhat depleted as members had retired or left the County, so it seemed opportune to replenish its numbers and in doing so, to add to its professional quality in the educational field. We decided to approach the County Inspectorate, and the three centres of learning in the County: the University, the Technical College, and the Agricultural College. All four willingly accepted representation, and the reconstituted Committee seemed more than adequately competent to deal with the various problems that might arise. As my commitments in other directions were increasing, and if this had been a business proposition it was clearly the right time to sell, I resigned the Committee's chairmanship at the end of 1981, almost exactly ten years from when we had purchased the wood as an educational reserve. I am glad to say the Centre's subsequent history has borne out my belief in its future.

THIRTEEN

Sheepdown and Hanger

I have a particular respect for Selborne Hill, not just because of its associations with Gilbert White, by reason of which it is one of the few places for which there are accurate records stretching back for 200 years, or because of its present natural history interests, and the way in which it is still capable of providing first records for Britain despite the two centuries in which it has been visited and researched by those "in pursuit of natural knowledge". My respect is based on the much more prosaic fact that not once but twice have I got myself completely lost there, and I mean lost to the extent that not only did I not know which way I should head, but I even doubted what my compass told me. This has happened to me occasionally in other woodlands, but for it to happen twice in a place that is under a hundred hectares in size is a lesson in humility. Later, under Judy's guidance, I got to know my way round it fairly well, though I am still cautious if on my own, because if you go down the wrong side of a hill, you have to walk a considerable circuit to get back to where you left your car, and at Selborne there are many tempting ways down. So be warned if you go there, because it lies diagonally to the compass lines, and there is no road or railway within audible distance to give one a bearing either.

In the old days it was much less overgrown, and like Gaul was divided into three parts. The 1842 Tithe map still showed the Hanger, running along the escarpment above Selborne village, and the open Sheepdown, stretching from there in a wide arc the whole distance to Newton Valence. By that time there was a fringe of trees shown along the southern edge of the hill, which have since spread northward, to join up with the third section, the High Wood, which covered the northern part of the hill, except for the Wadden and the other smaller enclosures which had been made in the wood. The earth banks of these enclosures, and that between the Sheepdown and the High Wood, can still be traced on the ground, but the trees have grown in so much that when I first saw it in the early 1970s, the common or Sheepdown was reduced to the appearance of a wide glade, largely covered with bracken, and interspersed with clumps of hawthorn. This first visit was a rather hurried one, because I was due to meet the management committee the next week, and I thought I could not then admit to never having seen such a hallowed place at first hand. Not wanting to meet anyone, until I did so officially, I left my car near Newton Valence church and walked carefully into the woodland for a couple of hours, seeing enough plants of indicator status, butchers broom, spurge-laurel, Tutsan and the like, to give me an idea of the values. Later I found I had parked by the house of one of the Committee.

The first work on which I was engaged there was the repair of the famous Zigzag, which with increasing use by visitors, needs to be put in order every few years (*Photo 33*). On that occasion we were trying to prevent the short-circuiting of its twenty-seven zigs or zags, which had been caused by the making of short cuts between the various legs of the track instead of following the easy gradient of this to its next turning point. These short cuts seemed to be started by dogs, and later adopted by children, on their bottoms or otherwise, which was no doubt good exercise, but on that steep slope was soon followed by rainwater channels and spreading erosion. Our first intention was to peg down chicken-wire over these, to allow the vegetation to recover, but we found this was frustrated by both parties. The children, with fingers and toes, found the wire to be a capital form of scaling ladder, while the dogs nosing under it from above, formed in the case of those of retriever size, a most efficient wedge shape on the very steep slope, well capable of tearing up any such impediment. So in the end we put in stretches of low chestnut paling, which the vegetation, largely of sycamore seedlings, soon hid, and we then cut this off at waist height. Meanwhile we renewed the logs that formed the kerbs of the path, and re-staked them in position. Actually I should not say 'we' because on this occasion the work, which was grant-aided by the Countryside Commission, was done by contractors, who were allowed access by means of the private drive to the group of houses at the top of the zig-zag. These houses to my mind completely spoil the view of Selborne Hill from the

23

PLATE 9 *The Orchid Bank*

23 A 1959 view from the lucerne looking over the road to baling hay in the strip field, with the bank beyond gradually becoming covered as shrubs and trees seed out from the wood behind.

24 Clearing the bank in the autumn of 1984. The strip field has been incorporated in the reserve.

25 △   26 ▽

PLATE 10 *Wind and Tide*

25 Operations starting on 1 October 1975 to protect the neck of the spit by driving in 'soldiers'. The position of their line was governed by the tractor having to work on firm sand.

26 The step in the shingle (centre right) had been moving inland in July 1975. It had not far to go before the neck of the spit would be cut through.

27 By February 1977 the beach had risen almost to the top of the 'soldiers', aided by a break in the sea-groynes that allowed shingle to come round the corner into the mouth of the harbour.

27 ▽

28 △   29 ▽

30 ▽

PLATE 11 *The Fate of a Wood*

28 Top pond, with the dipping platform, constructed by volunteers, and the donated observation hide beyond.

29 The extended Forestry hut, and the Centre beyond.

30 David, the Trust's President, at home in the wood.

31 △   32 ▽

PLATE 12 *Sheep-down and Hanger*

33 ▽

31 Selborne Common in 1979 with the
ingrowing scrub gradually being driven back.

32 In 1974 an Acorn Camp cleared the
woodland fringe that had engulfed Wood
Pond since it was described by Gilbert White
in 1776.

33 Repairs were made to the Zig Zag in 1974.
Judy, Eric, John and Ian inspecting progress.

south, and should never have been allowed to be built. However some very charming people have lived in them, and at that time the lawn of one of these houses was all the open chalk downland that remained on the Hill to show the variety of wild flowers that had once been widely spread.

The publicity notice issued by the management committee gave the impression that these were the first repairs to the Zig-Zag since its construction by Gilbert White and his brother in 1753, but it was clear that it had been refurbished from time to time before, as it has been since. It must have been a massive undertaking in its original form, with its almost sheer rainwater ditches each side of the zig-zagging path. I have no doubt that the actual work of construction was done by an employed team, with the White brothers setting out the lines to follow, as it is certainly too big for two people to have done on their own. I never found out where exactly the hermit's straw-clad cell was sited, though I imagine it was where the path crosses about two-thirds of the way up, and a seat now gives a convenient place to get back one's breath. Nor did I discover the origin of the Sarsen wishing-stone at the top, though no doubt it is recorded in the Selbornian literature. Some years later, when volunteer working parties became available, we altered the direction of the upper part of the track, again because of growing erosion, and I think we found we had to put in an extra zig, or zag, to reduce this. It was done by a party led by John, an East London joiner, who through Scout associations had formed a group of families of all ages who were prepared to come out for a weekend to do conservation work once or twice in the summer, and they did a lot of useful work, with a bias towards construction, in many places. Later John led some of the Acorn camps (*Photo 53*).

At that time the Management Committee did not employ a warden, but shared out between them such routine work as litter clearance and the cutting back of vegetation that tended to grow across the paths. For smaller constructional jobs such as putting up notices, Eric, officially their Treasurer, and an expert on old clocks, was always available, and for larger jobs they employed a contractor. A great deal however fell on the Commons Manager in general oversight and checking up, and it is not easy for such committees to find someone young, active and available on week-days, at least between school-journey times, to do such work.

Judy was good news in all respects, not least in her geologist background, and the decade in which, until her re-marriage, she held this voluntary office, saw the Committee through what might have been a very difficult period of transition. Her enthusiasm led us to look for other improvements to be made, particularly in restoring the previous open area of the common.

Wood pond was still marked on the map, but when I was shown its whereabouts we had to force our way through the woodland edge to reach it, and though recognizably once a pond, it was completely overshadowed, with no water or signs of life in its muddy remains. Biologically it was dead. This had been the only pond on the common, and Gilbert White in his letter XXIX of February 1776 to the Hon. Daines Barrington describes it thus: "Now we have many such little round ponds in this district; and one in particular on our sheep-down, three hundred feet above my house; which, though never above three feet deep in the middle, and not more than thirty feet in diameter, and containing perhaps not more than two or three hundred hogsheads of water, yet never is known to fail, though it affords drink for three hundred or four hundred sheep, and for at least twenty head of large cattle beside. This pond, it is true, is over-hung with two moderate beeches, that, doubtless, at times afford it much supply".

Most volunteer parties, particularly the girls, enjoy cleaning out ponds, and we thought it would be suitable to ask the National Trust's Junior Division, who ran the yearly volunteer Acorn Camps that have done so much work on Trust properties, whether they could restore this pond in time for the two hundredth anniversary of this letter. They responded that they would be willing, so Judy booked the Selborne Village Hall for their week's accommodation, and they duly came in the summer of 1974. We had been able to arrange for two Trust woodmen to help for a couple of days in felling some of the larger growth, being careful to leave a representative selection of oak, yew, and thorn to give some shade, as well as the only 'moderate beech' present to help recreate the scene. We were lucky in the leader of this camp, Ann, who brought her own chain-saw too. The fourteen young volunteers, equally divided as to sex, worked very hard under her leadership, in digging out and barrowing away large quantities of silt, while about seventy roots of sallows were extracted by ropes and levers (*Photo 32*). Two young police cadets spent several days working with chromes to dredge out the quantities of leaves that had fallen or blown into the pond, and as they worked the area of water increased visibly. This was a most successful operation, and even in the dry summers that followed, the pond continued to hold water over a much greater extent than would have been thought possible in its previous condition.

A few years later, when the pond had begun to be recolonize, we carried out some further dredging operations, dividing this between two summers to avoid exterminating any species. This went well and after it had been done, the life attracted to it increased greatly in variety, both of water and waterside plants, and in the dragonflies and other insects that came to live there. This further work was undertaken because in its original state we found that the height of the banks was uneven, being consider-ably higher to the west than to the east, so we wanted to bank up the latter to hold more water. This may have been deliberately intended for the access of cattle, but as the east-west dimensions were considerably greater than the thirty feet of diameter de-scribed by Gilbert White, no doubt with his usual accuracy, I suspect that it had been enlarged by subsequent generations to the detriment of its original capacity. Certainly his description makes one think the pond was round, whereas we found it to be oblong.

As the first Acorn Camp had been such a success, the Manage-ment Committee suggested holding another the following sum-mer, with the object of doing some work in the Lythes. The meadow below the Long Lythe had been planted up with poplars by previous owners, and a thick growth of saplings of ash and sycamore had sprung up between their lines blocking the view of the Selborne stream and valley meadows from the footpath that runs below the escarpment of the Lythes. This growth was felled over a large section to bring in light and air as well as to give glimpses over the attractive valley. The saplings being stout and straight, were usable as faggots, of which some fifty were made, and were carried to the roadside on the party's daily journeys. They were thence taken to a coastal property, to be incorporated in the beach defences and sand-traps that were being constructed there.

While this improved the view from the footpath, the path itself was in need of attention, as were so many on Selborne Hill itself.

Clay-with-flints over chalk is liable to give difficult going at the best of times, and though leaf-fall may give a temporary improvement, these sloping hill-paths soon get into a slippery if not dangerous state as winter progresses. We were fortunate in being able to obtain one of the early Manpower Services Commission schemes, and equally fortunate in our choice of supervisor. Robert was very good with the four young men who formed the team, whom we chose from the available unemployed of the district, being careful not to recruit an obviously already-formed street-corner gang, but picking them from here and there. All were eager to come, but the original promises of how they would be able to get a lift from a neighbour, or borrow Dad's bike, did not often materialize, and frequently Robert had to drive round and more or less haul them out of bed. So we had badly underestimated the petrol he would need, but were able to make this up in other ways. The team worked extremely well under his supervision, with only one replacement being needed, and their physique and self-assurance both improved greatly, with all getting jobs at the conclusion of the period. Meanwhile the various tracks and paths round Selborne were put in better condition than for many years.

They were also able to do some cutting back of the fringes of the Common (*Photo 31*), which were still tending to grow in and reduce the remaining open area. Grazing rights were still held, and now registered, but none was exercised. In practice their exercise would have been difficult without constant supervision, and while grazing would have been for the good of the common, it would not have been worth much to the animals, still less the commoners. It became possible at first to hire a contractor to swipe the bracken each summer, and later to use the services of a warden and equipment from another Trust property for this work. Gradually this was increased and some reclamation of the surrounding area resulted so what had been reduced to a glade became a bit more of an indication of its former size. Species began to re-appear, including the marbled white butterfly, which in the good summer of 1976 extended its range considerably in Southern England, and in many places was able to hold on to its gains of territory.

Selborne is not a particularly good place for butterflies, and personally I never found many more than twenty species there. I never saw a purple emperor there myself, though one or two were reported, and though white admirals were around, there were not many sunny bramble patches which they could visit. Holly blues were sometimes abundant, but I never saw any of the hairstreaks there, though I was always hoping to see evidence of the brown one in the frequent blackthorn thickets. The silver-washed fritillary was to be seen occasionally, and there were plenty of the grass-feeding satyrids, and skippers, with the various whites and vanessids. The hill is not sufficiently open on top to be good for butterflies, as is the nearby Noar Hill. I saw grass snake, adder, and slow-worm, but not many mammals, apart from the roe deer of which one saw small parties on almost any visit. The bird list was good, and several comparative rarities were reported, with a total of over sixty species. The countryside around has altered very much, particularly in increased tree cover, since Gilbert White's time, so that the birds now are much more of woodland species, with a loss of those of open country such as the stone-curlews that intrigued him so much.

Selborne Hill has become rather an island in an intensively farmed and fertilized area, and there are days when the smell of sprays reaches far into it, which may be a factor in reducing the butterflies. Its present qualifications for status as a Site of Special Scientific Interest are based partly on the associations with Gilbert White, partly on the representative range of beeches in all stages from present regeneration back to ancient pollards, and their associated community. This includes some rare fungi, and the occasional appearance of some of the rarer helleborines, as well as many groups of the stinking hellebore, and the Italian lords-and-ladies. It is unusually rich in molluscs too. But even the common woodland plants are a joy, and the sheets of woodruff in flower above Coneycroft are particularly striking. Nevertheless the woodland spread has reduced the variety, and to this had unfortunately been added until recently a policy of planting up available open areas, often with conifers unsuitable for a chalk situation, so that the original bee-orchids and other chalk-down flowers were suppressed or extinguished under them. When the National Trust was offered a small triangular field at the south-eastern end in 1979, it was a revelation on forcing our way through the woodland edge to find a central clearing thick with marjoram and other chalk-down plants which must once have extended along the Hanger, in any unshaded places where the chalk reached the surface, uncovered by the clay-with-flints of the plateau of the hill. It is much to be regretted that Western Red Cedar was introduced to such places, and great efforts made to re-establish it after initial failures, particularly as the competition of the native old-man's beard is likely to prevent good growth. The background of such unfortuante plantings as this, or of the poplars in the Lythe meadows, did not improve relations with the naturalists at one meeting I attended when, after considerable misgivings, the latter were persuaded to assent to a thinning of beech to allow the copious regeneration to grow unchecked, as was sylviculturally much overdue, and when effected was agreed by all parties to have been beneficial. In that case the forester had suggested what was needed, but so often he is asked to suggest what isn't needed. If he is asked what trees may make a profitable crop in a given situation, he can only say from his knowledge what might grow there – whether it might be better left without any trees has already been decided, usually by non-foresters, and often wrongly.

Some of the plants mentioned in Gilbert White's letter XLI to DB of 3 July 1778, such as the "autumnal gentian or fellwort" on the Zig-Zag and Hanger, show what used to be there, and his "ladies' traces" of the south corner of the common have only survived on the lawn of Kite's Hanger. This list is remarkable however, not least in the paucity of alterations that have subsequently occurred in the names he gives, both in Latin and English, of which one or both are still immediately intelligible, but in that so many of those plants that he considered noteworthy are still to be found at Selborne. When we did a comparison, I think there were few of his locations that we could not still find. Taking Katherine round once, when she was doing her biological survey, we went down from the Lythes to the edge of the stream, where among the waist-high growth there were two slightly prickly stalks of a plant not immediately familiar. When I mentioned Gilbert White had recorded the small teasel near there, she at once confirmed it as that.

FOURTEEN

The Lily Patch

July 15th 1935

Dear Sir,

I am a lover of all the beauties of the wild – a Naturalist. I on June 21st went to seek out the beautiful Martagon Lily. I searched the top end of the little copse and was pleased to at last come on these beautiful plants, in numbers about 20 or 30, not yet in flower.

I had read of their existence here in . . . (a flora) . . . of 1856. (The author) . . . there states "From its appearance I believe it must have existed there for centuries; it extends along the copse for the distance of nearly half a mile".

As I proceeded further down the hill I saw men erecting a new chestnut fence and I stopped to ask of them if they knew of . . . Wood, as I was a botanist and wanted to find a rare flower there. The men did not know this wood by name but added, to my great joy, that they were erecting this fence to preserve a rare flower here! That thrilled me! I felt I must throw all etiquette to the winds and write and thank you for your thoughtful and kind action . . .

On July 11th I cycled over again to see if possible this elegant plant in flower. I alighted where I had seen the big number and every one had been picked; then I rode to the new fenced off portion and there to my great joy were two magnificent specimens out in full flower, thanks to you fully preserved . . .

Will you kindly treat this letter just as "a voice from the wild" appreciative of a kind thought of yours which has given such intense pleasure.

Yours truly
A . . . B . . .

This letter doubtless caused my father some satisfaction because the previous year he had heard, at a dinner party, a local landowner boast that he knew where the lilies flowered and that each year he cut them down to prevent their removal by others. This landowner did not know my father, or that it was on his ground that they grew, nor did my father inform him, but he privately decided that some at least should be fenced off from this method of preservation, and a chestnut paling fence was accordingly put round a long, narrow and vulnerable strip that lay between the road and the common. Here they still survive, though there are now none to be seen in the rest of the half-mile of woodland.

Most botanical authors now class them as "probably introduced, possibly native". This particular station is the largest in the locality, with usually 300 to 500 plants in flower. I know of at least six other places where they grow within a few miles, with up to 30 plants, most of them, including those on the ground that then belonged to the landowner referred to, almost certainly deriving from this main site. Sadly many were removed to peoples' gardens 'for safety', where they were correctly positioned in partial shade, only to be later stifled as the shade developed unchecked. There are other parts of Britain where they exist; Frank used to cross-pollinate ours with some which he also considered wild, on land owned by his cousin in Berkshire. CTW says it is naturalized in many counties; possibly native in Surrey and Gloucester. Ted told me that he could trace our colony back for over 200 years but my opinions about native origins in general have rather altered since re-visiting a chance discovery of grape hyacinths in an apparently remote downland situation, to find they had been joined by both trumpet gentians and edelweiss.

The fence survived the war years, though I suspect it was patched up from time to time, as the Canadian Army that occupied this countryside were no respecters of fences, nor were the Italian prisoners-of-war who followed them. However while these between them cleaned out the pheasants and ground game from our valley, they were not after the flowers, so the colony survived into the 1950s when it passed to my ownership. I had the fence renewed, and the brambles cut back occasionally, but apart from keeping an eye open for intruders in the flowering time, I did not do very much then to help them along.

The threats were really of quite a different nature, as unknown to the writer of the 1935 letter there were then at least two proposals for new roads, either of which would have destroyed the colony. One, which was probably never a very practical proposition, was for the widening of the valley road itself to take the London to South Coast traffic. This worried my father much at the time however, as there was a strong lobby of local landowners against the adoption of the obvious route down the main valley, of which ours is a tributary, two miles to the west. This lobby was however defeated in the later 1930s, when the County Council bought up one estate entirely, so as to allow the road to be made. More lasting was the threat posed by the London South Orbital Road, which was planned to cut over the common and through the middle of the lily colony making use of a slight transverse spur of ground in the valley side at that point, which would have reduced the work involved in the engineering of a viaduct over the valley. Although the lilies would have been at the lower level, the construction of the viaduct piers would have largely obliterated them. This threat hung over us for some thirty years, even after the proposed road's upgrading to motorway status as the M25 made that exact route less likely, since many alternative suggestions for variation were put forward by interested parties, several of which would have affected the site in one way or another.

Fortunately by then conservation interests were beginning to receive recognition. The common itself had been acquired by the National Trust, and was rapidly developing into one of the most visited open spaces in the Home Counties. A great deal of lobbying went on behind the scenes. Gradually thinking altered, pushed no doubt by better appreciation of the engineering costs. I was to some extent kept in touch by Frank, who was a member of the Trunk Roads Advisory Committee, though he was careful not to reveal anything confidential. However while in March 1966 he was sounding me out on the likely reactions of the County Naturalists' Trust to moving the bulbs by some 200 yds, only a month later he sent me an encouraging message that there was a growing feeling amongst those concerned towards a line that would allow the lilies to sleep in peace. All the same he warned me that he thought the site had shrunk considerably, and that efforts should be made to spread the seed into other areas of the woodland. When the new line came to be revealed, I understood his discretion, since while avoiding the lilies by a quarter of a mile, the route ran through the middle of our village, within a hundred yards of my house, and would have obliterated our farm buildings!

Needless to say this aroused a great deal of local antagonism, in which I had to keep a low profile, since I was accused of being among those responsible for causing the alteration, although there were many other interests involved besides my concern for the lilies. Indeed at that time the presence of rare plants, doubtfully native at that, would not have been likely to receive the consideration that might have been the case ten years later. Lobbying and counter-lobbying continued on a massive scale, with a series of public inquiries, and it was not until 1973 that it seemed fairly certain that the route finally adopted would lie a mile to the north. Even so there remained some doubt whether this would not be reversed, and it was not until actual construction started in the 1980s that we felt secure.

Meanwhile the site of the lilies had been included, as an outlier, in a nature reserve agreement with the County Naturalists' Trust made in 1967, with John and me being made the managers. At that time there was great enthusiasm among County Trust members for practical work in the field, giving us considerable volunteer assistance. We made it a practice to programme a working party date for early each year, with the object of clearing the bramble and other overgrowth from the site; or reducing any excess of shading from nearby trees; and of replacing any sections of fencing that were in poor condition. This was usually a well-attended day, being close to the road, and with the element of obvious benefit to an uncommon and spectacular plant. Numbers at first allowed us to carry out all the tasks needed, but after about 1980 they began to fall off, so that sometimes we had to postpone some of the clearance until next month.

We did not consider it safe to work after February, as it might harm the plants even though the shoots might not have emerged. We normally asked any children present to collect into plastic bags all the dead heads remaining from the last season's flowering, which usually resulted in quite an amount of seed, and we broadcast this elsewhere in the reserve. This was surprisingly ineffective, and I only remember three plants resulting, though all reappeared for many subsequent years. The seed takes two years to germinate, but even so, it seems a poor result. The three plants that came up did so in situations where there was almost complete overhead shade about 15 ft up from old coppice, but no competition at ground level except from dog's mercury.

The enclosure is a long narrow rectangle running from North-East to South-West, 150 yards long but only 25 deep, with the south-west end being down-valley, and thus slightly lower. It is fenced with 4'6" chestnut paling, of the style that has a central wire as well as top and bottom ones. The individual pales are 3" apart since a wider spacing than this allows a foot to be put on the central wire. The front long fence runs along the side of the road, and there are bushes or trees at intervals: hazel, field maple and ash. We try to cut these off at about 8ft height to allow them to spread out and form a screen from the road, but not to get high enough to shade the lilies. This screen is by no means complete, and it is not difficult to see the lilies from the road, especially as the ground rises rather, forming a terrace along which the back fence runs. In the 1960s the lilies that flowered were mostly at the lower, south-west, end, usually some 20 to 50 plants, with only ten or twenty at the upper, north-east, end. There were never any in the middle section, which we therefore used as a convenient central site for our yearly bonfire. We thought the paucity at the north-east end might be due to overshading, combined with the presence of two large oaks that grew on the terrace just outside the enclosure on the common. We had cleared their lower boughs, but John thought that their root competition could be affecting the lilies. I approached the Chairman of the National Trust Committee with the problem, and was pleasantly surprised to receive almost immediate agreement to the oaks being felled. A contractor was found; who cut them down in the autumn of 1967, for the sake of the cordwood, which he took away. The trunks were left lying, and as they were in the way of renewing the back fence, which had been breached in the felling, we needed to move them. There was no question of being able to get in a matador or crane lorry, as the site was only approachable down the steep slope from the common, but we were able to clear a route along which I could get my landrover, which was fitted with a capstan worked from the power take-off. Recollections of hauliers in my youth parbuckling tree-trunks onto horse-drawn timber tugs came back to me, and we found that by taking a couple of twists with a 3" rope round the trunks, the capstan was just strong enough to roll them, even though it was slightly uphill

(*Photo 34*). The success of this operation raised morale considerably, and we soon got them clear of the fence-line, blocked them securely, and restored the fence. This was in February 1968, and in the following June, the martagons were flowering at that end of the strip in a profusion such as we had never seen before. In fact ever since, that end has been the one with most flowers by far.

Usually they come into flower in the last week of June and last well into July. Comparison of photographs of them with some I have taken in the Alps leads me to think that the Alpine plants are a slightly deeper colour, yet I have come across some wishy-washy ones there, and I doubt if there is really much difference. When they first come out, they are very bright, but the first rain tarnishes them duller, and there aren't many summers when this doesn't happen within a few days. One might think that they would be so conspicuous as to attract attention from passers by, but curiously they do not seem to be noticed except by those who actually recognize them. For most people a tall red flower in a woodland edge does not apparently seem so exceptional as to arouse comment – possibly this is due to people being used to seeing foxgloves, red campion, rose-bay willowherb, and the like. Picking is perhaps also deterred by the petals being so obviously prone to dropping – normally they have fallen off the lower flowers before the higher ones have begun to open. The dangerous time for human intruders is a month earlier, particularly the bank holidays that we nowadays have at each end of May. At that time the lily patch is a sheet of bluebells and wood anemones that could well attract pickers, while the lily plants are about a foot high, so that they could easily be trampled. In former times, when we used to have a Whit-Monday holiday, we had to be on the watch if it fell late in June in an early season, and there have been years when some special extra holiday in mid-summer has caused a similar problem. However increased traffic on the road deters stopping, and the growth of travellers' joy in the fence is fairly thick by then.

Of the natural hazards, badgers sometimes cause breaches in the fences wide enough to allow roe deer to penetrate. In 1985 we had ten plants sliced off by roe with their unmistakeable slantwise cuts, before we noticed this was happening and blocked up the gaps. This was under 3 per cent of the plants that flowered, so it wasn't serious, but we didn't want our local roe to get the habit. Of the occasional plants that come up outside the enclosure, I have sometimes seen some that have been bitten off by roe, but not really very many. I am inclined to think that despite their addiction to garden lilies and roses they may not like martagons enough to jump the 4'6" fence deliberately, though they could easily do so. But if it did start happening, we could always put in higher posts, and run wire mesh round it.

Competition from other vegetation is minimized by our yearly clearances (*Photo 36*), but if these were not carried out, the brambles could soon reach blanketing proportions. Bracken invades from the common from time to time, but I have found that spraying with asulox late in the year (September) has been effective, by which time the lily plants are less vigorous than earlier. I try to avoid them of course, but one cannot entirely do so, and it seems better to make sure of covering all the bracken than to worry about the odd lily – I have not in fact noticed any effects on them. In 1985 I became concerned about a strong build-up of ferns (*Dryopteris filix-mas*) at the north-east end, which seemed likely to be preventing the lilies from expanding into that corner. I sprayed them with asulox that September and as the next year showed them much reduced, but with some plants that I had missed still vigorous, I sprayed them again in 1986. Nettles have fortunately not been a problem there, but I am worried by the increase in rose-bay willowherb as although this has not yet been shown to be affecting the lilies, one suspects that anything with a close root system could be inimical to their seeding.

In June 1973 I was taking a well-known botanist and photographer round some of our local plants for the plates of Ted's new County Flora, and while he was setting up his apparatus I was intrigued to see a large skipper butterfly visiting the lilies. It moved from flower to flower in the sunshine, spending several minutes at each, and drinking deeply from one or more of the furrows. To do this it alighted in the upper side of the flower, and walked down a petal until it was upside down underneath the flower, from which position it extended its proboscis upwards into a furrow. It seemed quite accustomed to this manoeuvre, and I wondered how many other of our native lepidoptera visited the lilies, and took them in their stride. I had recently read a book in which it was suggested that it needed some rather special sort of moth, such as a humming-bird hawk moth, to penetrate the narrow tubes on the perianth segments, and had thought that this was unlikely to happen in the case of our lilies since such moths rarely reach us sufficiently early in the summer to have found the lilies in flower. It was a surprise to me that a common butterfly like the large skipper could apparently reach and enjoy the nectar (*Photo 37*).

A few days later, I had an afternoon spare, and spent a couple of hours in the lily patch. It was sunny for most of the time, but shade gradually moved over the flowers, so by 5.30 pm I gave up, having seen only one butterfly, a meadow brown, visit the flowers, and that only briefly. Several moths, geometrids and pyralids, were present, but none seemed to feed from the lilies.

Bees however were continuously active, though in small numbers. There were usually two or three bumble bees and one or two hive bees present, flying from flower head to flower head. These alighted on the underside of the flowers, normally with the head outwards, and spent only a few seconds on each flower head, moving about under it. The hive bees and the smaller bumble bees did this without disturbing the anthers, but a few larger bumble bees had their posteriors coated a rich chestnut from the pollen. The bees visited each flower of each spike in turn, usually going first to one of the lower ones, and proceeding upwards, with a slight bias towards a clockwise direction. Many of the spikes were however sufficiently close for their flowers to intermingle. Few flowers were left unvisited, and few were visited twice, in fact the bee seemed to know as soon as it got there and that it had been there before, and flew on to another.

Small numbers of Diptera were visiting the plants, but no particular species was preponderant. Although they spent a longer time on the flower heads than the bees, they seemed to do little other than sit or crawl about. In some flowers white crab-spiders were present. Two were on different flowers of one spike. They lurked in between the curve of the petals, keeping their bodies hidden and peering over the edge if the flower was touched. One was feeding on a small fly. Both were transferred to plants under easier observation. One did not have a visit from any possible prey while I was there. The other dropped in the process, and I saw possibly the same spider half an hour later in the same place crawling up a grass stem to reach the lily flowers, not up the stem of the lily itself, where the stout ruff formed by the leaves might have presented an impediment to its corpulent body.

That evening, 23rd June, I visited the plants again about 10.30 pm remaining there until 11.30. Air temperature was 14.5°C. It was apparent immediately on arrival that a number of moths were present, at least a dozen being visible in the first sweep of my torch. The moths were upside-down under the flowers into which they had inserted their probosces. In the case of the geometrids, their wings hung down below their bodies, and these were therefore conspicuous in torchlight. When disturbed, the moths were reluctant to leave the area of the flowers, usually flying to another plant. Two moths had been caught by crab-spiders.

Sixteen moths of ten species were collected from the flower heads and identified, all being common moths of the neighbourhood. There were three each of the Clouded-bordered Brindle (*Apamea crenata*) and of the Silver-ground Carpet (*Xanthorhoe montanata*), two each of the Burnished Brass (*Diachrysia chrysitis*) and the Mottled Beauty (*Alcis repandata*), and singletons of the Setaceous Hebrew Character (*Xestia c-nigrum*), the Ingrailed Clay (*Diarsia mendica*) the Bright-line Brown-eye (*Lacanobia oleracea*), the Common Marbled Carpet (*Chloroclysta truncata*), the Common White Wave (*Cabera pusaria*), and the Pale Oak Beauty (*Serraca punctinalis*). Species were thus equally divided between noctuids and geometrids. Some of the larger geometrids had pollen dusted on their wings, which hung down low enough to catch the anthers.

On a visit the next morning I noticed that of several particular plants closely observed the previous day, a further upper bud had opened, and a lower flower had lost its petals, indicating a total flowering period in days of the number of florets plus the length of time an individual floret remains on the plant. Thus a plant of 13 florets, the highest number present, would have a total flowering period of say 16 days. This seemed to tally with previous notes of a total flowering period for the colony of three to four weeks, with some plants that are in less sunnier positions coming out a week or more later than those in full sun.

I wrote this up for the County Naturalists' Trust magazine, and I intended to make further visits, but it was not until 1986 that I was able to spend any time there when the lilies were in flower.

In that year however on 30 June, I spent an hour there, counting 70 plants in flower at the lower end, and 400 at the upper. Butterflies were more numerous, with several large whites (*Pieris brassicae*), one or two male brimstones (*Gonepteryx rhamni*) and at least half a dozen large skippers (*Ochlodes venata*). the large whites and the brimstones had their wings heavily stained by the henna-coloured pollen, though this did not seem to incommode them in the least. One wondered how they got it off; or perhaps it made them more attractive to the other sex.

I felt satisfied that there were ample pollinators among our normal common insects not to have to introduce any special measures, though no doubt cross-fertilization with another colony would be useful, as Frank had suggested. But it certainly does not seem to be one of those plants that is near the edge of its range because it is outside the area of any possible pollinators (*Photo 35*).

The most serious threat to the lilies is undoubtedly the recent spread in Britain of the bright-red beetle, *Lilioceris lilii*. We had searched in 1986, when it had reached the neighbourhood, but the first we found were in 1989. I was taking the friend of a friend into the enclosure on 23 June to photograph them, about mid-morning, cutting a track along the back edge that wouldn't be noticed from the road, and we found two of these beetles mating on a lily leaf. We photographed them, and then I removed them in a pill-box to kill. They lost their bright colour when killed, and in a few days were only a tawny brown. We saw no others, though we looked, and John came that afternoon and sprayed the plants with malathion. We had counted about fifty plants in flower at the lower end, and over 200 at the upper, but with the hot weather they were past their best, and I had to search to find some bright ones for Caroline to photograph.

The only butterflies were meadow browns and large skippers, and there were few bees. The upper part of the enclosure was in shade from birches that had grown up on the common behind the fence, and there were no lilies in it, I thought probably because of this shading or the root spread, and made a note to cut and poison these birches next winter. We also found three groups of two or three stems with flowers on them, bent down and blackening, which looked due to mechanical damage, though we couldn't see any obvious agency, and I was sure in cutting out the track that no person or animal had been in the enclosure. In fact it was quite hard work to get through, and we were glad of a swim afterwards. I cut off some of these blackened stems and sealed them in a plastic bag, but nothing emerged from them, and the damage could possibly have been caused by a pheasant pitching into the enclosure – I couldn't think of anything else. We didn't think that it was connected with the beetles, though it happening on their first appearance seemed suspicious.

Next year, in 1990, the threat really materialized. On 29 May I went into the enclosure when the lilies were in bud in this early year, and removed sixty of the red beetles straight into a killing bottle. I knew some had dropped in the process, and I rang John who came up the same afternoon, when I was busy elsewhere, and dusted all the plants with malathion. He told me he saw as many beetles again. Two days later we went through them again, but the malathion powder was still present in the fine weather, and we only saw two beetles. The lilies flowered well, but we thought it advisable to give them another dusting, for which I had by then got NCC permission, in early August, when we found six beetles remaining. Several of the seed-heads had been eaten into by them, but the great majority seemed to be seeding satisfactorily. Clearly this dusting will have to be done annually, but it needs to be done when there aren't any bees coming to the flowers.

I should add that legal protection has now caught up with this colony – it was in 1975 included in a SSSI under the 1949 Act, and in 1986 was notified as such under the 1981 *Wildlife and Countryside Act*. The various threats from new roads and the like, which fifty years ago were very real, and against which at that time one had really no protection, apart from private lobbying of those who knew one sufficiently well not to think one was being crazy in suggesting such plants were worth preserving, would, if they should recur in present times, come up against considerably more powerful opposition. One is always at the mercy of political horse-trading, but nowadays it is not considered eccentric to put up a case on nature conservation grounds. However other things have altered too, and I don't think nowadays I would have got such ready agreement to felling those two oaks!

FIFTEEN

The Tunnel

It was a couple of years before I got involved myself, though I saw the records of the annual counts of the bats by the experts. However it became increasingly clear that something had to be done for their protection from vandals and collectors, and that I was in the best position to arrange this. So the following January I joined them. I didn't know much about bats, but I thought this would be a good opportunity to learn.

The first thing I learnt was that I had a recognition problem, but not only with the bats. In the dark of a half-mile tunnel, with eight or so people, all in balaclavas, mufflers, and the like, it isn't easy to tell one from another, until after a while (and we only met once a year) one got to know that so and so was a distinctive shape, or always wore a hat with a peak, or one of those helmets with a torch in it. The bats mostly looked alike too, what one could see of them, and half of them were in crevices in the brick-work. I didn't know how Bob could do it, when he could only see a bit of one limb, and whenever I thought one did look a bit different, more often than not it was due to moisture on its fur making it seemed an altered colour in the light of our torches. So I realized that bats must be one of those things that some people can do, and some can't, like micros or grasses, unless you really set yourself at it for a year or so, with daily practice. As I would never get the opportunity for this, I kept quiet, and listened to the experts.

It was fascinating to watch the way they could take bats down and unwrap their wings gently to measure the length of the bones or hang them on scales to measure their weight, and then fold them up and put them back up again on the tunnel brick-work without waking them more than to make the sort of slight protesting noise that a child makes when you turn it over in its sleep. It was also clear when you saw their bodies uncovered by their wings, that they were fellow-mammals, and one felt more kinship than, for instance, in ringing birds. Some of the bats were out of reach, but by bringing up a stick with a bent wire behind their legs, they could be made to transfer their grip to the wire, and then be lowered down. Sometimes the bats were in groups of two or three, not necessarily the same species, but far more often they were roosting singly. They didn't seem gregarious, or wanting to huddle together for warmth. There were smaller bats all along the tunnel, and the few larger ones were to the south of the middle, but again not close together. These larger ones were always higher up and hanging freely, heads down. It was mainly the larger ones that Bob ringed and recorded, measuring some of the bones, and looking at the condition; most of the others he just counted by species. Smoking was not allowed, but flash photography apparently didn't disturb the bats. The camera I had then wasn't equipped for this, and efforts to open the aperture to use someone else's flash didn't work as there were too many flashes. I was very kindly given some copies of his slides by someone better equipped, that I could use for lecturing, and later I got a better camera. But it wasn't easy to focus and so forth in the dark, and I never got more than a handful of good pictures (*Photo 39*).

From time to time a bat would be passed to Tony who squatted down to examine what fleas they were carrying. I knew bats had their own kinds of fleas, like birds, but I didn't expect to see much in the way of other insect life in a cold and rather damp tunnel, so I was surprised to find several Herald moths as we neared the south end. Later I was to read that this is a well-known habit of this species, and also of one of the Tissue moths. One Herald, which I kept, had chosen an unfortunate place under a drip, so had turned into a sort of stalagmite – a sad end to its hibernation. There was no other life visible in the tunnel apart from occasional plant roots in the roof, but there were signs of digging in the ballast of the floor near the ends, so it looked as if rabbits or foxes came in from time to time, getting under the metal doors at the ends.

These doors, which had been installed by the railway company when the line was decommissioned, were falling into a poor condition, and this was the problem (*Photo 38*). The line had been double-track, and when this work had been done, the top of each of the arches of the ends had been partly bricked up, so as to make a trapezoid which was filled with metal plates cut and welded, reinforced by angle irons, and with an angle-iron surround. This top section was still sound. Below this, brick piers on each side carried the pair of almost square doors, like garage doors, of similar construction, but not only were these rusting low down, but they had been holed in places. They could also be got under by digging out the ballast. The amount of graffiti both all over the outside of the doors, and on the tunnel walls inside, indicated that this was a local custom, particularly to Kevin and Andrew, whoever they might be, and the danger was that if they could get in, so could others, or they could be employed by others, with more nefarious motives. Bats were collectable, and there was a high price on their heads.

Bob explained to me what he thought should be done. The land at both ends was owned by the National Trust, as now was the tunnel itself, and the Trust was prepared, within reason, to help protect the wildlife of its property. The Nature Conservancy Council would grant-aid, and there were various funds available for bats, though these were limited. Briefly he wanted the lower three quarters of each end completely walled up, and a grille of thick metal rods or bars put above this at both ends, with a vandal-proof lockable entrance at one end. Preferably this should be the north end, which was easier to reach, since the approach cutting that end was shorter. He gave me the sizes of bars needed for the grilles, and the distances apart they must be. The bars had to be 1½" wide by ¾" thick, and the rectangular holes between where they crossed needed to be 9" wide and 7" deep. Actually the wing span of the larger bats could be as much as 15", but they would know they had to close them while flying through, and in any case they were at the time having to get through the holes in the doors, or under them. The grilles would give them much more room to get in and out, at either end, but any larger size of apertures might tempt small boys to do the same. Ian suggested some likely local contractors, and one of these was more than co-operative in suggesting how the work could best be done. It was to be undertaken in the following summer.

Bats turn things upside-down, not only themselves, and I can't think of anything else for which the conservation work needs to be done in mid-summer, but the bats are then elsewhere. It meant taking a JCB in, because the floors of the cuttings had to be cleared of the large chalk boulders that had rolled down from the sides over the years, and now were overgrown with mosses, so that they looked a bit like the shore at low tide. The JCB then brought in the building materials in its bucket, and could be used as a crane in getting down the remains of the heavy doors. Ian had been promoted by then, but I stayed with him that June, and told him all was going well. When I got back, I found that the foundations were completed, the metalwork and the additional brickwork removed, and it was now simply a matter of building up the wall course by course, with reinforcements through the holes in the blocks, and putting in the door and grilles, which had been pre-ordered. It was a fine summer, and the work went well. I visited from time to time, but there were no problems, and it was finished by August, when I checked it over (*Photos 40, 41*).

The concrete was still a bit raw, but the important thing was that it looked strong enough to deter any attempt at vandalism. The graffiti artist had been there already, and 'Beware of low flying vampires' decorated the new wall beside the entrance door. This however was both robust and narrow, and I had to contort myself agonisingly to open the second padlock, which one could not see, and had to find by touch. Walking through the half-mile of tunnel by myself, to check that the inside of the far end was sound, was rather an eerie experience, but one could now see the light from the grille at the southern end getting larger as one walked towards it, and vice versa on the return journey.

I had noticed a silver-washed fritillary in a patch of sunshine in the cutting at the north end, which was getting rather overshaded by ash and other growth on its sides. These trees, as they grew up, would also be likely to give trouble in ultimately falling across the entrance, as well as bringing more of the sides of the cutting down in the process. So that November I got a BTCV party to cut them off, which would open up the cutting more to the sunlight. I thought too it would give more flying area for the bats. I also put a max-min thermometer in the tunnel, which then registered 10°C. This was a bit north of the tunnel centre, and I had fixed it to a white board, with a loop to hang it on one of the series of hooks which ran along the side of the tunnel, about 7 feet up, that no doubt had carried telephone cables once, so that the thermometer itself would be at eye-level. I tied on a gem-marker so that one could write successive readings on to the board, but this never worked because of the condensation.

Next January when Bob came again, this thermometer showed 4°C and had been down to 2°C. We decided that the grilles were letting too much draught through, so next summer John and I fixed some planks over the bases of the grilles at each end. This seemed to help, but a year later there still seemed to be too much draught and I wondered whether we ought to put in some form of screen or baffle, though doing this would be difficult now the ends were closed. Bob wanted to instal a form of continuous thermometer throughout the tunnel, but my superiors decided that this was going too far – it was the Trust's responsibility to protect the bats, but not to seek to improve their lot. So instead I put in two more max-min thermometers at each end. I think it was at that time that as an experiment I put in some beer crates, hanging them on the sides of the tunnel, thinking that their partitions might appeal to the bats as roosting sites. In fact they didn't. It was also notable for the appearance of a new species – I must have been in front when I saw what even I could recognize as a horseshoe bat ahead of us, and said so, in what I hoped was a matter-of-fact voice, to be greeted by a chorus of 'First County record'. However there was only the one, a female, and though we saw it again in some succeeding years, no other came to join it.

The next summer John and I decided that before we embarked on baffles, we would first put boards at the top of the grilles too, sawing them to approximately the right curve outside, and then fixing them up inside. This needed a ladder, and a carrying party to do the same the far end, so some of my family were enlisted to help (*Photo 41*). The addition of this extra boarding meant that the top two as well as the bottom one of the six rows of openings in the grille over the north end were now covered by the boards, leaving the three middle rows clear. At the south end, where there were only four lines of openings, the top and bottom were now blocked, leaving the two middle ones clear. This turned out to be successful, because although in later winters the temperature at the middle went down to 1.5°C, the total number of bats of all kinds using the tunnel steadily increased from that year on, and had tripled by six years later.

The thermometer at the north end showed falls to below

freezing, but the one at the south end kept above 4°C. We thought later that these thermometers were not recording accurately – they were the ordinary kind one can buy at ironmongers for greenhouses, and after nearly ten years in the dark and damp of the tunnel, they may well have gone on the blink even if they had been accurate to start with. So though they gave a trend, and a contrast between the ends, we didn't accept their absolute figures, which Bob thought might be up to 3° too high. We reset them on each winter count and if John or I went in during the summer we took the readings and reset them then too. When we were in the tunnel, we always left the door open, and took the keys with us, but I also left a pick inside the far end, just in case someone got shut in. We counted people in and out of course, but sometimes people joined late or left early. Counting the bats could take two to three hours, as you had to search all the crevices.

When we did this blocking of the top sections of the grilles, we had taken more planks than we really needed, in case we made a mistake in cutting them to shape. So we had two or three lengths over, and by way of having them handy for spares if the ones we had put up got vandalized, we left them inside the tunnel. We found that bats liked these, although they hadn't liked the beer crates, possibly because the wood was too smooth, or perhaps they didn't like the partitions. These planks were as sawn, not planed. So John got together a load of timber offcuts, many still with the bark on one side, and put loops on them so that we could hang them from the hooks that had carried the telephone wire. Dave and Carol brought a YNT party that spring, as well as their own children, and everyone helped carry the offcuts in. We had enough to hang them up at intervals all through the tunnel. This was in April, rather a compromise in timing between summer work for the bats, though we only saw one in the tunnel then, and winter clearing of the cutting sides which I thought needed doing again after eight years. Bob had said clearing the sides wasn't necessary for the bats, who weren't worried by vegetation, but I thought it was needed for other reasons, and I wanted to leave it all in order as this was my last year. We had a bonfire in the cutting with the ash growth we had cleared, and it was rather a pleasant spring day, with the primroses out, as well as the violets and wood anemones. Looking round after our picnic lunch we found false oxlip as well, and some early orchids starting to put up spikes.

The bats liked the offcuts; there weren't many on them the next winter, perhaps because they were new, but after that I am told they have become increasingly used. I haven't been there again myself, since I retired, because the tunnel is a long drive from my home, and early morning starts in January have lost their appeal for me. The fortifications have lasted well, and I only remember one attempt at getting through them. It must have taken some hours of work with a hammer and cold chisel for whoever did it to make a hole through the south wall, and I was surprised he hadn't been heard bashing away. I could see the hole from half-way along the tunnel, as the light came through it, but it wasn't really so large, about wide enough to get a hand through. It couldn't have been widened much more without running into the reinforcing bars, and it didn't take long for the warden to concrete it up again. But it showed there was still a danger.

There is a sad side to this story. When we first walled up the ends, the tunnel had regularly contained in winter a strong colony of the large bats. Bill had found this colony by chance some years earlier, and it had been quite an exciting event as they are not often seen in Britain. They were using the tunnel for their winter quarters, and in spring they went off elsewhere for the summer, the males by themselves, and the females and young elsewhere. It was not known how far away the summer haunts of either the males or the breeding cluster were likely to be – it could have been several miles. However after we made the walls and grilles the number dropped, and it gradually became apparent that some tragedy must have wiped out the breeding cluster that same year since we only found a diminishing number of the previously ringed males in the tunnel each winter. Two years later two of these were found killed after the felling of a beech tree only three miles from the tunnel in August, so it seemed likely that the summer quarters of the breeding cluster may not have been so far away either. It is still not known what might have caused this disaster to the colony, but there was certainly one barn destroyed by fire in the neighbourhood about the time the tunnel was being strengthened, and there were no doubt other possible causes. In a countryside where farming was then prosperous and commuters were coming to live, there could have been any number of changes, such as concreting of farm yards, that might have covered over the entrance to hiding places; renovation of buildings; alteration of water-supply arrangements; as well as destruction of buildings by fire, which might have wiped them out. Looking through the files for the period covering the National Trust property alone, I could find at least five possible events, any of which might have been responsible. Over the possible area in which the summer quarters may have been, there could well have been twenty or thirty such events. Possibly, if some concealed hiding place had been concreted up, it may one day be discovered, but if fire was the cause, we shall never know. The surviving males continued to use the tunnel in winter, but their numbers dropped to two, then one, and the chances of them being joined by a fresh immigration are remote.

SIXTEEN

Advice to Countryside Managers

1) Your staff should work as a team, of which you are the responsible leader. All reports, leaflets, etc. should bear your name only, and contributions by them should not be separately identified.

2) A useful indication that you have taken up your appointment is to redesign your office notepaper. A striking logo or slogan, in a second colour, will impress your personality.

3) Your office wall map is an indication to callers of your wide range of responsibility. You should update it regularly. This can often be done without visiting the sites personally.

4) It is dangerous to admit to specialist knowledge, since this may identify you with particular interests which will detract from opinion of you as a competent all-rounder suitable for promotion.

5) Always encourage your staff to attend courses on their particular expertise. They will then know more and more about less and less, and become too boring to offer competition.

6) Impress on your colleagues how experienced you are in interface with the media, and encourage them to entrust to you all aspects of publicity.

7) Your hard-hat should accompany you at all times, since you do not know when you will need it for press photographs. If carrying it through the office daily does not give it a sufficiently worn look, try dropping it down the stairs.

8) Keep your vehicle mileage claims constant, as the computer may throw up variations. Deviations for liaison purposes in a frequently-made journey should therefore be included each time.

9) Make your name known to others in your field by contributing short articles to journals. Use your staff to do any necessary research, and include accounts of projects or trials initiated. Do not include those that were unsuccessful, since this would not benefit others.

10) Such articles should end with a list of references, preferably longer than the text. This list should include all previous articles published by you, and should also indicate the wide reading undertaken to keep abreast of developments in your field. If any well-known expert has recently passed the time of day with you, include his or her name with 'personal communication' in brackets.

11) Remember the important part played by your boss's secretary in the smooth running of the organization, and how difficult life must be for her. You can help lighten her burden with occasional kind words or small gifts, such as free passes.

12) Although word-processing your applications for jobs to further your career indicates your familiarity with management methods, intended employers might presume that you use official equipment for private purposes. Do not compound this by using the office franking machine when posting them.

13) Support in the form of sponsoring, or discounts, is often obtainable from the local business community. It is preferable to contact them in their off-duty moments, such as at golf courses.

SEVENTEEN

Midnight Sun

On the whole the sun seemed to shine more at night than during the day because the weather was more settled then. In daytime it changed so much, and I seemed frequently to be shedding clothes or putting them on again; sometimes in jerseys and anorak, sometimes in shirtsleeves, as it altered so quickly from rather cold to very hot. Rainbows were a big feature, and on occasions I could see two or three at once, according to the location of their preceding showers of rain or sleet. I soon learnt the need to apply insect repellant immediately after, if not before, taking off any clothes, but we had come prepared with stocks of this, both in tubes as supplied by chemists' shops, and in little bottles containing a syrupy liquid we called Worm Oil, made to the secret formula of a well-known entomologist and chemist.

I had come to the Arctic out of a sense of filial duty, because my father had arranged to go there with George, who had been there two years before, and wanted to go again at a slightly earlier time of year. George was rather younger than my father and I thought he might walk him off his feet. As I frequently stop to take photographs, or to light a pipe, or just to look around, I hoped I might adjust the balance. We had joined forces with George before in various parts of Europe, but then there had been our wives with us, as a restraining influence, and with two cars it was always possible for one section of the party to go on a long trip, or stay out longer, without involving the others. Going by air and rail, without wives, I thought there might be occasions when things could get overdone, as George's enthusiasm was unbounded, and the mention of a rare bird or butterfly in a distant valley was enough to make him set off straightaway. It is recorded that when he escaped from an Italian prisoner of war camp, he made his way south to the Allied lines wielding an improvised butterfly net.

We had flown to the northern airport, and spent a night in the city, with the next day for stocking up with any provisions, which included alcohol since our destination was teetotal. We also spent some time in the local bookshops looking for illustrated field guides to the plants, birds and insects. For reasons of weight, we had cut down those we had brought with us to the minimum, taking just a few of the smaller-sized general works, with photostats of the more likely pages from larger ones. I had also photostated such accounts as I had come across of previous visits by naturalists to the area. These we now supplemented with a number of excellent illustrated Scandinavian books, though in most cases we had to pencil the scientific names onto the illustrations, by cross reference to where they were given in the text. We filled in the afternoon before the train went at a sort of open-air museum, which had re-erected rural buildings of various types from different parts of the country, and a selection of native animals in large enclosures. The bears were particularly impressive as they ranged about, very unlike the pot-bellied creatures one sees in some zoos, and showing clearly who was head of the food chain in the country for which we were bound.

The train was the most comfortable I had ever been on, with the seats designed for reclining. It did not go fast, so there was plenty of time to look out of the windows. In fact it took nearly 24 hours to travel the 1000 miles to our destination, and there were not very many stops on the way, so it cannot have frequently exceeded 50 mph. The route was lined with conifers, mostly spruces, giving a somewhat monotonous outlook, perhaps accentuated by steady rain, though it was noticeable how they altered from a dense and broad-based form in the south to a sparser and thinner shape in the northern regions which had greater snow-fall in winter. The stops were enlivened by the usual sale of comestibles on the platforms, and particularly by the convolutions of the students who had achieved their ambition of acquiring a set of reindeer antlers. Nature has ordained that such antlers are conveniently carried attached to a back-pack either so that the horns hang on each side of the owner, or else project upwards to his rear, but it is another matter entirely to manoeuvre the assembly through the door of a railway carriage and put it on the luggage rack over one's head. It is possible but it takes practice, and a degree of contortion that not all were able to achieve unaided.

I suppose there are many countries in which it is possible to travel for 1000 miles thorugh a virtual monoculture, but I was at a loss to understand why at one period everyone appeared to be looking expectantly out of the windows, if not projecting themselves out of them. There seemed no alteration in the landscape, and the spruces appeared to be all set to continue for ever. However the reason for the excitement was explained when we passed some form of monument or gateway on each side of the track, which indicated that we were now within the Arctic circle, having passed 66° 33'N. There was then a period of anticlimax, as there seemed nothing different in sight, and we continued our slow but unrelenting journey through the spruces. Later the spruces did at last come to an end, and we left them behind, apart from occasional clumps, so that the scenery was of more open country, tundra, and drifts of birches. The rain too had stopped.

George's home was at the first camp on Hadrian's Wall east of Carlisle, so he referred to all upland moorlands as 'fells', just as, when we had been in Mediterranean lands with him, any dry valley was a 'wadi'. We naturally tended to adopt his nomenclature. 'Fell' sounded appropriate anyhow, where moorland would have induced conceptions of remembered heathlands quite unlike the wide russet expanses we were now traversing. For one thing, moorland to me would have indicated heather, which here was replaced by other, though still ericaceous, growth. We had previously seen what we took to be *Ledum* from the train, but here it seemed to be principally *Phyllodoce*, with the warm chestnut and brown tints deriving from a variety of mosses. We could only speculate on the identity of the various flowering plants until we reached our destination. Beyond these russet slopes the ground rose on our left to a series of low ridges of grey rock, on which snow lay in wreaths and bands lower down, and continuously along their summits. Further off, we could see higher snow-covered hills, though none very high, and all smoothed and planed by past ice-sheets. To the right, between the drifts of birches, we had glimpses of a long low lake, unfrozen, with its steely water reflecting the hills beyond. The direction of the railway had now altered, and we were travelling westwards, along a single track, with long sidings at the occasional stations for trains to pass each other.

We arrived at our destination in afternoon sunshine. It was not accessible by road, only railway, by which means all the material for the construction of the scattered village, and for its provision had come. There were, however, a number of small vehicles in evidence, though not many appeared to be in particularly serviceable condition, apart from a few light motor-cycles which could negotiate the rough tracks, at least for a while, and a rather larger number which were clearly designed for winter use, and at present were abandoned until the short summer was over and snow returned. Rather sturdier, and in more continuous use, were some ingenious mechanisms designed to fit the gauge of the railway, but capable of removal from it as a train approached. One type, four-square with a wheel at each corner, needed a crew to work the up and down crank which supplied the motive power, and presumably also to lift it out of the way of trains. Another, on the pedal cycle principle, allowed the rider to bicycle along one of the rails, while a wheel on an extended arm stabilized it by running along the other rail – this type could be quickly removed from the line by its rider dismounting, tipping the machine up and wheeling it off the track. We were however reassured to see that a horse and cart awaited to take our luggage to the visitor centre.

This was a three-storied building, the only one of such proportions; about a mile from the station. Having seen our luggage onto the cart, we walked to it unencumbered along a grey gravel path. We passed the Lapps who had spread their goods out on reindeer skins under the birches by the station. They were pear-shaped men, very broad in the hips, dressed in buff trimmed with scarlet, and with scarlet cockades in their hats. We did not venture to buy anything from them at the time, though we noted that their displayed goods were mostly derived from reindeer skin or horn, and that their trade with the students seemed to be less roaring than haggling. We passed a cabin with a pied flycatcher's nest, and some pines in which fieldfares were nesting. It was the third week in June, and spring had arrived.

Our rooms in the visitor centre were simple but adequate, with mosquito netting on the windows supplemented by black-out curtains to give a semblance of darkness. When we had set out our luggage, we went for an evening walk, since the sun was shining although clouds were thickening in the distance. We first explored our immediate surroundings, then, with the aid of a large-scale map we had bought at the hotel, we made our way towards the long lake that bounded the reserve to the north. At first we followed a track which marked the eastern boundary of the reserve, but we found this occupied at one point by the large tripod of a film crew, who were photographing a family of three-toed woodpeckers – charming small black and white streaked birds with yellow crests – which were nesting in a dead birch trunk. To avoid interfering with these activities, we struck through the woodland of birch, sallow and alder, in which George soon spotted a Tengmalm's Owl. This, rather larger than our Little Owl, twisted its head to follow our movements, as it sat dumpily on a low sallow branch, and allowed me to approach within a few feet before we decided that I had taken its picture enough for the time being, and left it in peace. We continued and soon came out into a clearing close to the lake, where we could see something of the flowers and insects of the area. Mosquitoes had already been more than noticeable, but their effect did not seem, at least at that time of year, to be much more discomforting than that of a Highland midge, and with frequent applications of deterrent and antidote, it was possible to co-exist, as long as one had something else to take one's mind off them. Here there was plenty such, and we soon identified three of the northern butterfly species that we were to find were fairly widespread, though far from abundant, in the district. The first we saw was the pale arctic clouded yellow, *nastes*, rather resembling the *phicomene* of the Alps, which was particularly attracted by the plants of alpine milk-vetch, blue, red or white. More camouflaged was a small fritillary, *freija*, not much smaller than our small pearl-bordered, and with a zig-zag pattern on the underwings. Less easy to see, but more frequent, was one of the grey skippers, *centaureae*. In an hour or so of relatively sunny weather we saw one or two each of the clouded yellows and fritillaries, and perhaps half a dozen of the skipper, which gave us an indication of their frequency. In between these appearances, and during the cloudy intervals, I photographed some of the flowers, butterwort, bog rosemary, moss campion, a dwarf rhododendron (*lapponicum*), a yellow lousewort (*lapponica*), mountain avens, and dwarf cornel – this last with its black-eyed cream cups grew in profusion in thick tufts of green foliage. I thought it an entrancing

△   35 ▽   36 ▽

37 ▽

PLATE 13 *The Lily Patch*

34 Parbuckling the oak trunks (1968).

35 Small Tortoiseshell feeding from the nectar.

36 Annual clearance (1986).

37 Large Skipper about to land on a floret.

38 △   39 ▽   40 ▽

41 ▽

PLATE 14 *The Tunnel*

38 South end, before alterations.

39 Long-eared bat, *Plecotus auritus*.

40 South end, walled and grilled 1975.

41 North end, with baffle boards
added, 1977.

42 △

PLATE 15 *Midnight Sun (1)*

42 My father following one of the tracks through the birch woods in the reserve, where planks had been laid over soft ground.

43 We were in sun on the mountain, but could see rainstorms below, where the lake and railway stretched eastwards. Note the reindeer on the lower slope.

43 ▽

44 ◁

45 ▷

PLATE 16 *Midnight Sun (2)*

44 One of the lochans near the nunatak.

45 Dwarf cornel, *Chamaepericlymenum suecicum.*

The Island (1)

46 The undercliff near St. Catherine's Point, with the Upper Greensand cliff above.

46 ▽

flower, and one that is consistently undervalued by botanical field guides which lump it, and many other gems no doubt, in the 'white' section at the end, for which the expense of coloured illustrations can be avoided. This and the red arctic bramble, (*Rubus arcticus*) were the two plants that really hit me on this visit (*Photo 45*).

I had not been expecting flowers; at least not flowers like that. My mental expectations had been based erroneously on a low grey windswept countryside, like some extension of Caithness, and though I had known there would be flowers of a sort, and had even undertaken to photograph some for a friend who was preparing a book on the European flora, I had expected them to be hiding disconsolately in crannies. It was a revelation to find such a profusion of colour, with a background of russets and reds rather than grey, and I experienced the same feeling as I had when, somewhere in France, I had strayed into a local museum to encounter a display of Lurçat tapestries.

We were now outside the boundary of the reserve, so we were not inhibited from taking a representative selection of cuttings to identify and press, and we walked back to the hotel for the evening meal. The restaurant was cleverly laid out, with all the provisions being placed on a central table from which one could help oneself, according to one's appetite, and inclination, vegetarian or otherwise. Plates and cutlery were similarly placed at a side table, again overcoming differences in usage and habit between the various nationalities – these being particularly noticeable at breakfast. Having made our choice of plates and cutlery, and then helped ourselves from the central spread, we took it to eat at one of the numerous smaller tables round the edge of the room. It was not a very large room, and the atmosphere was friendly. Scandinavians predominated, and though we were the only English people present, there were usually some Americans. I heard French occasionally, and it was clear that while almost everyone could understand German as well as English, they preferred not to speak German for choice. The variety of fish dishes was large, if one includes shell-fish, and very good, but meat was less varied, deriving almost entirely from tins. This hotel was not as teetotal as alleged, since a supply of red wine, but not spirits, was forthcoming though it had to be fetched from the cellar, so we soon made a standing order for three bottles each evening, to save trouble and delay. It was perhaps on the second or third such bottle that we were engaged one evening, when the addition to the menu for that day of some almost indigestible fresh reindeer meat, led my father and George into a discussion of the various kinds of meat they had eaten during their lives, and which was the most tasteful. This engaged them for some time, and various suggestions were made by one, to be dismissed by the other, ranging through all the normal domestic animals, cooked in various ways, and, since they had both travelled extensively, through many kinds of deer and antelopes, before agreeing decisively that the best meat of all was impala. It was at that moment that I became aware that everyone in the room was listening attentively, though I don't think either of them noticed it themselves. I had known the glamour that Africa has for the Germans, but I had not realized before that it extended to the Scandinavians.

Naturally that first evening we waited up to see the midnight sun, which obliged by sinking until it was just visible above the distant ridge to the north, and then slowly starting to rise again. The Americans present were particularly in evidence at this time, with a large array of photographic equipment, and it seemed to be the principal reason for their coming, since I seldom saw them elsewhere in the district. A composite photograph was on sale in the hotel, taken at hourly intervals, which as well as giving a panoramic view, showed how the sun moved down and up again in a low swoop-like motion, illustrating rather than explaining how it happened, but having verified once that it did happen like that, it did not seem necessary to us to make nightly observations. Though one felt rather sorry for those who happened to make their visit on occasions when the critical period was obscured by cloud. There was however a good deal of opportunity to compare different makes of camera, and this between kindred spirits may have made up for the disappointment.

For myself, I had recently acquired a 16mm cine-camera with an electric eye, and a telephoto lens, but I had not really practised with it enough to compensate for the many occasions on which I was looking at a bird on a branch, but the electric eye was looking at the sky behind. However some of the films came out, and after editing on my return, I had a passable 400 foot reel. I also took my 30-year old Zeiss Ikon, with its very good lens that had served me

well, and a supply of 127-size Ferrania colour films, each of which
allowed 16 slide exposures near enough the same size as 35mm to
fit into mounts for this, when I was unable to get the 'bantam'
size which really fitted them. This camera, with its bellows,
folded up easily to go in a pocket, and I also had a close-up lens
which allowed me to take photos at just over 9" range from the
subject. This gave good results with plants, though was not close
enough to give the detail that Oleg required, and I don't think he
used any of them in his book. I also had a 120-size camera for
colour prints, again of bellows vintage, but I did not use this
much except for views, or carry it all the time. The cine-camera
and film fitted, with my field glasses, inside a case with a sling
strap, which was solid enough to sit on on wet ground, or I could
lighten the load on my shoulder by putting the field glasses
round my neck, and carry the cine camera ready for action. One
was however inclined to be rather laden, with clothes, food, field
guides, map, and other equipment, so a haversack or rucksack
was also needed. Everyone else was in the same state though,
and one met people, whose total burden, if one included their
boots, appeared to weigh as much as they did themselves.

We had dull, cold and windy weather for the next few days, so
we confined ourselves to within a few miles of the hotel, chiefly
exploring the nature reserve area, and familiarizing ourselves
with the country. The reserve, a National Park, was rectangular
in shape, about 3 miles in width, and ran southwards from the
big lake up the river valley for some 9 miles, until it reached the
two matching mountains, about 5000 ft high, that formed the
impressive skyline. The head waters of the river lay beyond this
majestic gateway, in Lapp country. We did not ourselves go further up the valley than the lake which lay about half-way up it,
whose cold water and windswept sides appeared like many other
mountain lakes, to be attractive but rather lifeless. We found
more of interest in the lower valley, particularly in the moraines
that had formed where tributaries joined the river. Here great
sheets of boulders extended, that had been washed down by
these torrents, and in the interstices between them we found a
large variety of plants in flower. They were not in sheets or
clumps, but singly, between the boulders, and you had to clam-
ber over these to find them. It was rather like climbing over a
rocky shore looking for pools with sea-urchins or lobsters in

them, or as if they had been dotted about in a rock garden. It was surprising to me to see such colours there, bright reds, yellows, whites, and occasionally blues, and I spent some time in photographing individuals, with the reflection from the rocks giving good light even on a dull day. I soon realized that we were in a different world, and a globally extensive one, that goes all round outside the arctic ice in a wide band, from continent to continent, so that the flowers and insects we were seeing could equally be seen in the north of Asia, or of America, without very much difference, and that from this northern world the few survivors that we cherish as rarities in the mountains of Scotland or of Central Europe were merely waifs, left behind by the ice ages. This was their real home.

The National Park was well served by footpaths and tracks, and these were well maintained, though we never saw anyone at work on them. Where a track ran over a marsh, or a stretch of boulders, long planks had been laid as a footwalk (*Photo 42*). We seldom met others, though the tracks were well used. Sign posts at intersections were clearly marked, with the posts supported by boulders, and coloured markers were frequent along each route. These were not painted on rocks, as in the Alps, but were on tin lids nailed to branches of the trees so that they projected vertically, and could serve equally in winter, when snow could not lodge on them. There were even occasional wooden loos, again built on stilts, so as to be usable, though presumably uncomfortable, in snow-cover. There were bridges over the tributaries, mostly of the suspension kind, though these naturally lay on the chiefly-used tracks, and one often had to divert back to these if one tried to strike out on a line of one's own. It was however inviting to attempt this, since the trees, almost all birch or willow, did not form a complete screen, and tempting glades lay between them. Although the valley floor was composed of boulders, these were covered by mosses, so that one could if one was careful walk off the paths. Sudden noises, or glimpses of movement, in the mosses or between the rocks made one aware of a life that is the foundation of the Arctic ecology – the lemmings. I did not see very many, perhaps a dozen in all, and none clearly except for one very small one I found dead, and we skinned. But their tunnels through the mosses and between the boulders led everywhere, and snow cover could only give further protection to their lives in the deep moss.

Away from the noise of rivers or streams, it was very quiet. There was not much bird song, or any other sound. We walked along the tracks in virtual silence, and for long distances. Perhaps every half-hour there would be some incident – one met a small-bird foraging party, or one thought one had heard a larger animal, or one passed other walkers. It was all very spread-out, giving plenty of time, aided by the knowledge that there was plenty of it with twenty-four hours of daylight. We did not in fact see any larger animals, but we frequently came on their traces – usually in the form of a patch of droppings, possibly from an elk, or tufts of hair from reindeer. These were not infrequent, and we found that they were much used by birds, particularly blue-throats, for lining their nests. One began to appreciate the numerous links between the species, and the interdependence of them all.

After these first few days, the weather turned better, and we spent most of our time outside the reserve. Reserves are all very well, and I have spent much of my life establishing them, but there is no doubt that they do induce a feeling of being in a sort of zoo, and one feels freer outside them. The pale arctic clouded yellow, *nastes*, was the most evident butterfly, because one could see it at a distance, but we found that the small fritillary, *freija*, was fairly widespread. We also discovered two other small fritill-aries, *frigga*, rather similar but with a darker chocolate underside pattern, and *iduna*, the Lapland fritillary, which was not unlike our marsh fritillary but without the row of spots on the wing-band, and similarly preferred marshy surroundings. Most of these butterflies were named not by Linnaeus himself, but a generation or two after his death in 1778. When he made his epic tour of Lapland, in 1732 at the age of twenty-five, he seems to have just about reached the large east-west valley where we were, at 68° 25′ N coming through the Lapp country to its south, after visiting the west coast possibly by the route which is now an established long-distance footpath. Collecting must have been extremely difficult in those days, and his first interest was the plants, of which he named so many. He did not visit the Arctic again himself, and though he named an incredible number of insects from more southerly and accessible countries, many of the purely arctic species were not named until later.

We were anxious to get up onto the fells, so when a day came that looked fine, though it was to rain in the evening, my father and I started off towards an inviting nunatak to the south-east, with a choice of routes to the slopes beyond it. Unfortunately he ricked his hip on the way, and thought he had better return to the hotel, or at least stay near it. Rather against my will, he persuaded me to go on by myself, so as not to lose the good weather. Having seen him out of sight, and being convinced that he could get back alright, I did go on, and soon found I was above the treeline, and on the open moorland.

This extended gradually upwards before me to the rocky ridges in the distance, and was delightfully unlike British moorlands in that the absence of any heather, either Erica or Calluna, allowed the underlying rock to be covered with much lower growth, not uniform in colour, but in sweeps of various greens and warm browns. It was as if I was walking on a luxuriant carpet. I could not begin to tell what all the plants were, apart from the obvious patches of dwarf birch, and their generally ericaceous look. *Phyllodoce caerulea*, the blue mountain heath, was in flower, as was the Lapland rhododendron, *R. lapponicum*, but the rest seemed a variegated mixture of the whortleberry tribe. Between the drifts of plants, the pattern of colour was taken up by the mosses, from green to chestnut and russet, all glowing in the sun.

The slowly rising ground had various hollows and changes of level, ground out by the ice-sheets. With solid rock below, these held water, and so were filled by small lochs, fringed by marshy edges with rushes, and backed by low bushes and stunted trees. There were probably a dozen of these in the area, and my route passed close enough to deviate and explore three or four of them (*Photo 44*). Some of these lochans were several acres in size and had a wide surround of marshy ground, but with sufficient dryer humps to get to the waters edge; others had little open water. There were whimbrels at one and tufted duck at another, while others seemed only to have smaller birds nesting in the bushes around them. It was tempting to visit each of them, and see what they held, but I also wanted to go on while the weather was good, and I reached the nunatak about midday.

It was only a small hillock really, perhaps 150 feet above its surroundings, but its harder rocky core had allowed it to remain in the general planing of the slope, and the ice-sheet had flowed round it. Stunted birches grew in its shelter, forming a last refuge of trees. Looking back northwards towards the great lake, the main tree-line seemed to end as a solid wall, though having come up through it, I knew that it was not really so. Over it, I could see the grey lake stretching east and west until hidden behind the snow-wreathed hills, while beyond to the north stretched further hills, more snow covered, into the distance. The roofs of the few village houses shone along the edge of the lake, while on the further shore there were no buildings to be seen. Looking south the moorland continued to rise gradually until it flowed through the gap between the two sharply etched mountains that formed the gateway to the Lapp country. A cairn had been piled up on the rock of the top of the nunatak and I could see a file of people coming up from the trees towards it. Clearly it was a popular objective for a day's walk from the hotel.

I went on higher up the slope for a while, but I knew I had spent too long round the lochans to reach the pass, so I cut across westwards thinking I would reach one of the tributary valleys in a mile or two. I recognized a new butterfly, one of the mountain-ringlet family, the dewy ringlet, *Erebia pandrose*, which is a high-ground inhabitant of most of the European mountain chains. It is the highest flying of its tribe and one has normally passed through the zones of many others of the family before one sees it. But when one does, one knows that there will be nothing else higher up, so one might as well turn round. It is curious that this butterfly should remain as a relict on many of the European mountains, whereas its only close relative, which much resembles it in appearance and life-style, has only survived in one area of the Pyrenees. This was not the only new butterfly I was to find, because when I reached the valley of the tributary stream, I found this was confined as a raging torrent between steep cliffs, and one had to take a path that ran parallel to it through what had been birchwood. This had however been defoliated the previous year by caterpillars of a micro-moth, and most of the trees were dying in consequence, which allowed sunlight to reach the ground more than normally. As I passed along one small gulley, I disturbed a number of butterflies which were sheltering on its side, like graylings, and they were in fact one of the northern representatives of the primitive-looking *Oeneis* family, the Norse grayling, *O. norna*. There are only four European species of this genus, all rather resembling each other, and probably taking two years to complete their life as a caterpillar. One of them is a not unfamiliar sight in the higher Alps, while the other three are largely circum-polar. They are not well-studied, though their food-plants are believed to be grasses or sedges, and one of them, which frequents pinewoods, occurs as far south as the south of the Baltic. When I got back to the hotel, I found that my father had discovered a colony of the pearl-bordered fritillary, *euphrosyne*, near the hotel, so between us we had added considerably to our list of species.

The weather had closed down the next day, and my father wanted to rest his hip, so I took the opportunity to go by the train to the sea-port on the western coast to buy some more film, do some shopping, and see a town of which I had heard much during the war from some friends who had survived one of our brilliant though disastrous expeditions. Allowing for the two hours each way, and possible customs difficulty at the frontier, I would have about three hours there. I had a very pleasant journey, sharing a compartment with two Danish women, one of whom spoke good English, and the other French, while we could all fall back on some German if needed. I was very sorry not to be able to accept their invitation of hospitality when we reached the terminus after a long run along the steep side of the fjord, which showed me something of the difficulties my war-time friends had met. The town was very different to the hinterland, with the patches of waste ground between the houses deep in meadow flowers. The shops were well-equipped and modern, though I did not see any large stores, and as I worked along the main street from one end to the other, I had no difficulty in finding articles for sale, of a kind that one would not see elsewhere, as presents for my family, as well as the films I wanted, and further books on insects, flowers and birds. The currency was easily changed, and almost every shop had someone who not only could speak English, but seemed delighted to do so. There was continuous noise, both from building construction, and in export of quarried stone and metal, and the whole place was alive and bustling. It was very different from the soporific impression that is given by some Scottish sea-towns, and in the fish market I was surprised by the size of the sea-fish compared with those one would find at a Scottish market place. I had brought a hold-all but this was soon filled, and I returned to the station laden with carrier bags only just in time for my train back.

Being the last to enter the carriage, I had to take what seat was available, and found myself opposite a corpulent Lapp, whom everyone else had avoided. This was not so much because of his smell, which was significant, as that he was clearly much the worse for drink. He finished his last half bottle of brandy and tried to converse, but finding we had no common language, and I was not prepared to play cards since I was anxious to look through the books I had bought, we sat smoking our pipes while the rest of the carriage gradually abandoned their interest, until we reached our station, when he rejoined the traders outside it. I wondered whether the Lapps had some form of lay brotherhood, like the monks, authorized to make the necessary transactions with the outside world, and whether this was a privilege or a debasement, or whether the one always led to the other.

The next fine day, George went off to look for the place where I had seen the Oeneis butterflies, and my father wanted to climb the hill that lay to our west bordering the lake, and through which the railway ran in a tunnel. From the hotel it did not look too much of a walk, and through glasses we could see the reindeer on it, showing up grey, whereas red deer would have been difficult to spot with that background unless on the sky-line. We started out, at first along a track, but then through the lower woodland of the hillside. My father was then over 70, and though he was to live for another ten years, physical difficulties were becoming apparent, and he kept worrying to himself, and apologizing to me, how slow he was getting on the hill. I was very glad of the frequent stops, as it gave me a chance, now I had plenty of film, to photograph some of the commoner plants that I had neglected – the chickweed wintergreen, yellow wood violet, a white-fruited bilberry, roseroot, butterwort, junipers and others. But the ground was getting steeper, and we were making slow progress, particularly when we ran into patches of snow, and had to cross them at an angle to avoid slipping backwards. At length we struggled up to the top of the wood, to find our way blocked by a willow belt. Trying to get through this was very hard work – the dense hard stems rose to about shoulder high, and forcing a path between them was extremely difficult – I wished I had something more effective than a sheath-knife. It was not continuous, but in belts and thickets, with open spaces between in which we found plants such as frog orchid, *Cassiope tetragona*, and alpine rockcress, but one could not, looking upwards, see what was the best line to take. Morale was now getting low, and I feared that we would have to turn round, though I did not relish the prospect of trying to get back through this belt when I thought we must have come through at least half of it. We stopped again, and I think we would have turned round, but at that moment a grouse called, quite close to us. This was enough to revive spirits and make us go on. In a short while we were through onto the low turf and moss of the open hillside.

I don't think we ever saw that grouse, though we saw several others later on. The willow grouse is conspecific with our red grouse, though it looks different with much white on the body and wings. Certainly the call we heard was most familiar. It must find the belts of willow a considerable protection, though I believe it nests in the open, and later we found a deserted egg on the hillside. We should probably have expected to find a willow-belt, as it is a well known feature of the zonation of the vegetation, and stuck to the path, but by the time we got to it, we were a long way from the path, and did not realize the willow would be so fiendish to negotiate. I don't know how many species of willow it comprised – the woolly willow, *Salix lanata*, featured largely, but there were probably others too. No doubt it helps protect the woodlands by stabilizing the snow above them.

Above, the ground was easy and bracing walking, with wonderful views back over the lake. I photographed matted Cassiope (*Cassiope hypnoides*), Lapland rhododendron, cloudberry, mountain heath, mountain avens, creeping azalea, moss campion, diapensia, purple saxifrage, and *Ranunculus nivalis*, all in flower, fir clubmoss and lichens. The actual hilltop was flat, with small snow-sheets and patches of bare rock, or fragments of scalpings size, alternating with the drifts of flowers. The reindeer allowed us to approach them until they got our wind, which perhaps being unlike that of their Lapp master, caused them to stampede past us in good filming range, led by the bell-wether. We saw no other creature, except for a frog, and surprisingly, no birds. We were in sun throughout, but we could see a rainstorm over the hotel, and further off, a number of others (*Photo 43*). From our height of about 3500 ft we could see range after range of hills to the north, gradually seeming to diminish in height, and becoming increasingly covered with snow.

We had by now walked over to the north-east side of the hill, which fell steeply to the lake, and it seemed simpler to carry on down northwards, where there was a track, to the station beyond the tunnel, and take the train back. This we did without incident, except that as we came down through the woodland, I noticed something apparently glowing in a near-by clearing. It was a small bush of bird cherry, *Prunus padus*, in full flower in the middle of the clearing, which it seemed to light up like a candle in a darkened church.

We had intended, given a fine day, to go two stations eastward down the line to a place where there was extensive bogland, recommended by George. The complexities of the single-line train system meant an early start, but we achieved this, and alighted at a deserted platform in comparatively low-lying country. Following George's sketch map, we all walked some way back westwards along the line to avoid the swamp behind the station, and then struck due north for some six hundred yards across rather nondescript land, increasingly wetter, until we came to what George called a 'moss'. This was an extensive tract of highly treacherous country with peat-hags, and pools of water large and small, more or less interconnected, but with occasional rocky islands protruding on which birches and sallows were growing. It was possible to make one's way on firmer ground between the pools by following an indirect route, with a good deal of going back and forth, like a maze. A fringe of bog-rosemary in flower decorated the dryer land on the edge of each pool. Here we split up, each taking a section, with the purpose of watching out for one of the larger members of the mountain ringlet family, with the forbidding name of *Erebia disa*, the arctic ringlet. This, like its relatives, only flies in sunshine, and then singly and erratically, looping its way over the pools, where we could not follow it, and our only course was to stay in one place and hope it came in our direction. We saw about one of these butterflies in each hour, since a cold wind was limiting their activities, and it would have been a boring day had it not been for the birds. We could hear redshank calling and snipe drumming, and I was lucky to have a phalarope pitch in front of me, where it swam round and round in circles for an hour or so. It allowed me to approach close, so that it was spinning round practically at my feet, occasionally taking off for low skimming flights, and then returning. It would have been easy to hit it with a stone, and I wondered how such a confiding species had survived. So many of these arctic birds seemed far too tame for their own good. I was so engrossed in photographing it that I would have missed the appearance of one of the butterflies, had it not been for a warning shout that one was coming my way.

Apart from the Erebia, there were a few other species in the bogland, though not commonplace. We saw the fritillary *frigga* there too, and it seems to be met with more frequently in boggy areas. We also found the bog fritillary, *eunomia*, which we had last seen in Andorra, but here it assumed a smaller and brighter form. However around midday the weather clouded over, and it soon began to drizzle, so we went back to the station and sat in the shelter, though it would be over three hours before we could get a train back.

After making sure this was so, I left my cameras with my father and George, put on a mack, and had a look at the swampy woods round the station. Globe flowers and kingcups were out, as were dwarf cornel and chickweed wintergreen, but the chief attraction was the spread of the low-growing arctic bramble, *Rubus arcticus*, all over the station sidings. I dug up a few young plants to take home, where they grew for several years, though never flowered in the full red colour of their homeland. Apart from finding a portion of reindeer horn, there wasn't much of interest, and I went back to wait for the train. This returned us to a sunny evening, and I photographed the various shades of alpine milk-vetch and red campion round the hotel.

While we were walking about in the bogland, we had come across one individual each of two of the smaller tiger moths, *Orodemnias quenselii*, and *Hypharaia festiva*, both attractively patterned. We had seen the broad-bordered white underwing of the Scottish mountain tops the day before on the hill with the reindeer, and at other times we came across small day-flying noctuids of the *Sympistis* genus. In general however, the local moths, as might be expected, were chiefly geometers, particularly carpets and pugs, and pyrals and tortrices. As usual we kept a look out round any overnight lamps there were, though in the absence of darkness these were not many. One or two of the alpine members of the annulet family were seen, but probably we were too early in the season for many moths.

The next morning, 2 July, my father and I walked not far out of the reserve, keeping to the low ground, looking for flowers, though apart from two species of wintergreen and the one-flowered fleabane, we did not see any new ones. The first of the green-veined whites was flying, rather a dark form, and we found the Idas blue and the cranberry blue, *optilete*, asleep on grass stems. We were passing through a fairly sparsely wooded patch, where I had just photographed a dewy ringlet, when we noticed movement, and I was subjected to a furious attack from a willow grouse. Leaving her half-grown chicks in cover she hurtled at me, as fierce as any turkey, and pecked violently at my legs. As I was wearing half-length gum-boots, and waterproof overtrousers, as usual. I was well-protected, but since I was carrying a walking stick, butterfly net, and two cameras, none of which I dared put down to be further targets for her assault, it was very difficult to focus down or change lenses to point-blank range. Her method of attack was to slink round me in close circles, crouching down and trailing her wings so that their white edges hardly showed, and then suddenly fly at me, flailing, when she showed much more white. This went on for nearly twenty minutes, so I was able to get shots with both cameras, though it was difficult to avoid stepping or dropping something on her. My father, ten yards away, was laughing his head off, but we were worried about the chicks, until we saw that they, keeping to cover, had stolen round us, and were now awaiting their mother further on. I tried running away, but this only encouraged her to pursue, leaving the chicks further off. Finally by moving slowly to one side, I gradually managed to shake off her attentions, and with the chicks co-operating by cheeping loudly, she at last desisted, and joined them victoriously. Again I wondered how some species survive, as even without using my stick or butterfly net, I could have rung her neck in seconds.

We had intended to explore the gorges further that day, but the weather was turning bad again, so we returned to the hotel in mid afternoon to do our packing. This involved a good deal of redistribution of weight caused by my purchases, and the geological mementos that I tend to accumulate. However, after the long train journey south, when we reached the airport the staff were lenient over this, and with an hour to wait for the plane, I walked out into the surrounding pinewoods in which there were glades bright with meadow flowers, campanulas, yellow rattle and the like. It was alive with butterflies, and in a half hour I had seen sixteen species of which half occur in Britain, against the dozen we had seen in our ten days in the Arctic, few of which I had seen before, or will probably see again.

I meant to go back, of course, but this was over twenty-five years ago and family concerns and other preoccupations have always prevented it. The arctic summer is so short, and uncertain, that it is too much of a gamble to risk the expense and the pleasure of others, in what may well be a succession of drizzly days. We really had only two sunny days of our ten, though the frequent fine periods in the evenings or at night disguised this. George had not done much better on his previous visit, two years before, with four good days out of eleven, and on his visit then, though it started at the time we left, the first week of July, the season had been about two weeks earlier than on our trip, so that butterflies were then flying which we were too early to see, and the ones that we saw were over. It is very much taking a chance to go there, and then there are all the discomforts one forgets – the unrelenting mosquitos, the long distances, and the absence of interest if one is not a naturalist. There is a road there now, so it is probably more frequented, but the birds and plants and insects cannot have changed, and still give the opportunity of stepping out of Europe into an older world. I have always been glad to have had the experience, and I feel I can as a result understand so much easier how the European fauna and flora have moved and developed from the time, only 10 000 years ago, when the species we saw there would have been those of Britain.

EIGHTEEN

The Island

When my grandfather's head chauffeur saw a raincloud ahead, he would stop the Daimler, and take an apple out of the glove compartment. This he would cut in half vertically with his penknife, and one half he would use to smear the outside of the windscreen carefully in parallel lines from the top to the bottom. The other half he would give to me, who had meanwhile got out of the rear compartment, glad of an excuse to escape for a moment from its sick-making atmosphere. "'Ere you are, 'Umphrey," he would say, and "Thank-you, Mr. Wilson," I would reply. Thus fortified we would proceed slowly through the rainstorm. I feel sorry for small boys whom the invention of the windscreen-wiper later deprived of this chance of refreshment.

It was not often that my grandfather's visits to the Isle of Wight coincided with the times I was parked there, during summer holidays when my parents were abroad or otherwise occupied, and he was then chiefly engaged in visiting his properties where he attempted to grow trees that would not flourish on his Sussex land. But occasionally I would be summoned to accompany him on such a drive, if he intended going somewhere that was good for butterflies. On Brading Down for instance, I would be released to capture marbled whites and graylings with my butterfly net, and bring them for his inspection, while he continued to occupy the back seat of the car, on which he tended to spread laterally. Those I wished to keep as examples he would kill by squeezing their thorax between the nails of his finger and thumb, which I privately considered an inferior method to my cyanide killing bottle, especially as he was not manually dexterous. However there was no room for argument with such a formidable figure, and some years later I had the opportunity to replace the more mangled specimens.

More often I was left to roam the extensive garden, making a daily round of the flower beds on the upper terrace in the hope of seeing a humming-bird hawk-moth, and the less cultivated undercliff below the low escarpment of rock. This was rough grass, with a mown path giving a walk, with branches off to where various statues had been positioned. These white marble figures of draped or undraped nymphs stood life-size on pedestals, but apart from opportunities to add touches of colour by rubbing them with geranium petals, they did not hold interest compared to the strictly prohibited smugglers' caves leading back into the rocks on the one side, and the two or three hards that ran out on the other through the fringe of trees onto the foreshore. The beach was muddy and uninviting, but at very low tide there was the chance of finding a lobster as rock pools became exposed. From these hards one had a closer view of the liners coming up Spithead to Southampton, and on one occasion we had a grandstand view from them of the sea-planes competing in the Schneider Trophy.

Part of the escarpment had been made into a rock garden, and here if one sat still enough, which was not an easy matter at that age, one could see the big green lizards come out to bask. Or one could try, with a bent pin and breadcrumbs, to catch the large goldfish that sheltered under the leaves of the lily pond, and knew very well only to expose themselves tantalisingly when one had less nefarious intent. I can remember only long summer days then, but always with plenty of things of interest to fill them, while for nourishment an occasional peach would not be missed from the conservatory, if one was careful to shut the door again.

At that time we went to the Island by a boat which brought us to the end of Ryde pier just in time to see the train puffing out of the station at its other end. For us, with only a short taxi ride to go, this did not matter, but for others the vagaries of the four different railway companies that divided up the Island between them, must have been infuriating in their absence of any attempt at co-ordination. Bus services, each of a different colour, also abounded, and I remember one particular small purple kind which made a practice of nipping in ahead of the more ponderous yellow or chocolate double-deckers, to cream off the queue before the latter arrived.

War-time brought intense activity to the Island, but this was localized to areas of military importance, while the rest enjoyed the advantage of quotas based on a non-existent holiday population. On occasional trips when home on leave, it was a good place to stock up with tobacco. After the war, as family demand for seaside holidays increased, we made a succession of visits, but these were largely to the eastern coast or staying with relations. It was not until my conservation work was extended to include the National Trust's properties on the Island, that I got to know and appreciate its sharp end.

Visits then were difficult to plan to give sufficient time for covering, or uncovering, the many conservation problems, and usually involved looking at something in Hampshire on the way, so in contrast to the eastern ferries, which for me had become associated with a holiday approach, it was more convenient to slip across from Lymington. The Trust owns comparatively more of West Wight than of East, and much of it is visible as different ridges of high ground from the ferry, so one got tuned in as one came across. Even then I sometimes felt I had to stop the car and get out for a few minutes once on the Island, to adjust to the slower rhythm and unaccustomed quiet.

There is always interest along a coastline, even a familiar one, and particularly so where the geological formations are up-ended, as they are in so much of the Island, so that a short walk can take one from chalk to clay or greensand with the plants and animals varying to correspond. One is inclined to think that cliffs, of the kind that have ledges inaccessible except to the experienced climber, may harbour surviving examples of all sorts of rarities that no longer can be seen elsewhere, as in fact they sometimes do, but more often do not. Undercliffs are more accessible and fascinating in that they are perhaps the nearest approximation that we have to wilderness of a sort (*Photo 46*). Looking down over one once, in mid October, I noticed a chocolate brown animal apparently the size of a cat, stalking something in a jumble of rocks. It sat up on its haunches on seeing us, and we could see it had a sharply-outlined white patch on its chest. As it turned we saw its tail was black. It disappeared from our sight, but a few minutes later a rabbit jumped into view, hurtling through the air in the way they do after they have been bitten in the back of the neck by a ferret. There were four of us there, but we could not agree on what the animal had been. It had seemed larger than the rabbit, but looking through binoculars there had been nothing to give us a scale – there were no plants, and the rocks could have been any size. We could not even estimate how far away it had been. The black tail indicated a stoat, but the size and the dark body colour confused us. I later described it to a former gamekeeper who said it undoubtedly was a stoat of which the local males have such white chest patches at that season, and possibly it had been through a pool in the rocks so that it appeared so dark. But at that angle, we must have completely misjudged its size.

One gets this fore-shortened view as one looks down over an undercliff. The fallen debris lies in what seem to be a succession of terraces reaching to the beach below. One can pick out a possible route down, only to find halfway that the terraces are higher than estimated, and direct descent is ruled out. One has to traverse, and in the end one reaches the beach by a series of zigzags. Coming back is even harder, as one cannot see to plan a route to the top. Often one ends by walking a mile or so along the beach until one can find a trodden path. Some of the terraces are soft clay, with pools of water, or marsh, that one has to edge round, others have a thick growth of scrub that one cannot climb upwards through. Occasionally a layer of limestone is interspersed, carrying a colony of orchids, or other plants, and some of these may well be worth investigation, since not many people go that way, and there is always the chance of finding something unfamiliar. Each winter brings new landslips, and although some of the terraces have clearly been there several years for young trees to be growing on them, others are still raw after a recent fall, or have only two or three years growth on them. What you can see may have gone by next year, as some new slip may have removed it, or overwhelmed it.

Such a changing habitat favours the short-lived; plants that can colonize quickly and seed before the next landslip, or insects that can complete their cycle within a year. But they have to be equipped to survive the winter storms, the salt spray, and the sea mists, so it is a precarious existence. One such insect is the Glanville fritillary, now only found in Britain on the Isle of Wight, though it is widely, but locally, distributed through much of Europe and Asia. There was some confusion about whether it was declining or not. Jeremy and others were doing research on its current distribution and status, and whether conservation measures could be devised to make it more secure. The position was complicated by the known habit of various people to collect caterpillars, and breed them, releasing the surplus of the adult butterflies more or less where the caterpillars had been found, or possibly not. This does not always help matters, because it can overpopulate the area beyond what the foodplant can support. There was also some doubt about which species of plantain was the foodplant, and overall there was more general opinion than ascertained fact. Papers began to proliferate and in April 1982 most of those interested came to a 'cinxia conversazione' which Frank and Maretta hosted at the Noah's Ark (*Photo 47*).

Jeremy explained the result of the studies by ITE, and local naturalists, who had possibly felt that they had not previously been kept in the picture, added from their own observations. It was prickly at first, but general harmony was achieved in the interests of a common objective. One eminent local entomologist explained how some twenty years before he had painstakingly and systematically eradicated one of the main natural parasites of the species, by collecting up the caterpillars, then not nearly so numerous, breeding them up, and destroying the parasites, which at first were a high proportion. Others spoke from their own local knowledge of the insect's proclivities. The consensus was that the current population of the butterfly centred more to the south-west coast of the Island than had been the case before, largely because this coastline was still subject to landslips, whereas some former areas had now been stabilized artificially. The foodplant was the ribwort plantain, but only in the early stages of its growth. This plant quickly establishes itself on fresh landslips, and was ready for colonizing by the insect within a year or two. If the ground did not alter, and the plaintains grew larger, they became unsuitable for the caterpillars to eat. Of the total number of plantain plants on the Island, only a small proportion were of the right size. Successive landslips every few years were thus a requirement in perpetuating the insect's occupation of the undercliff. This also explained why it had not spread inland.

As to conservation measures, a certain amount could be done by re-locating caterpillars from overpopulated areas, and there were suggestions for the land-scaping of suitable ground, to give patches of bare earth for colonization by the plant, and thus by the insect. In practice these were difficult to arrange. Some of the land that might be used was hardly accessible to machinery, and if made accessible would also be opened up to the holiday crowds. Other suggested areas would conflict with long-established and legally inviolate farm tenancies. Meanwhile a sufficiency of landslips seemed likely to continue to provide new ground on a larger scale than could be contemplated by land-scaping. However there was clearly a future time when the land-slips might cut so far into the coastal lowlands as to lead to pressure for stabilization of the remaining coast, and when that happened the future of the butterfly would be in jeopardy.

While attention had rather focused on the Glanville fritillary as a particularly spectacular inhabitant of the undercliff, it is by no means the only one. In fact after the discussion when we went to look at one of its main locations, where we needed to pick our way between the concentrations of the furry black caterpillars with their russet heads that were taking the opportunity of the fine April weather to spread out from their conspicuous larval webs and nibble the plantains, we also saw caterpillars of two species of moths crawling about, and no doubt there were many others. The first flowers of the many species that make the under-cliffs so attractive, were coming into bloom and on the level sands of the beach below us, the first of the holidaymakers were also beginning to emerge.

It is surprising how high the spray reaches. The edge of the Downs where there is a sheer fall to the sea, both at the western and eastern ends of the Island, is so much richer in species than even a few yards inland, though there are rarities there too, unfortunately often exposed to trampling by horses as well as holiday-makers. When the Needles fortress was being adapted to become a visitor attraction, and one could still get out from what is now the observation platform at the end of the tunnel, there were maritime plants like sea heath on the narrow strip, nearly 300 ft above the sea level. The coastal influence also extends to where there is a further cliff inland, such as is formed by the cutting that carries the military road on Afton Down, above which the turf is particularly rich. But it is on the main chalk cliffs themselves, wherever there are ledges or footholds for plants, that the most colourful flowers can be seen, with the help of binoculars from the beach below, or less safely craning over the edges of the cliff-top. The purple of the hoary stock and the orange of the wall-flowers survive only on inaccessible parts, but there are clumps of thrift everywhere, and horse-shoe vetch and bird's-foot trefoil form sheets where the turf is sufficiently stabilized, such as round the former rocket platform behind the Needles headland.

Some of the horse-shoe vetch has a slightly different colour form, more lemon than golden, which I have also seen elsewhere, on the North Downs for instance, though it is more prevalent on the Island. Like some other examples where a species has two colour forms, these clash, and form an exception to the usual harmonious medley that wild flowers afford. I have seen the same clashing effect with red and pink valerians, or the occasional pale blue viper's-bugloss in a patch of the normal deeper colour, and no doubt it occurs with other plants. The normal colour seems usually the more effective in such cases, and the 'sport' – if it is that – a mistake, unless it is a completely different colour altogether. Then it can seem as fitting as the original and if all primroses or scarlet pimpernels were blue, no doubt we wouldn't wish for anything else. Occasional white bluebells, or thistles, or clumps of heather give a contrast, and one accepts them as they are, or rogues them out if they displease in one's garden, but to find two close colours together in the same wild plant strikes a discord. One wants to know what causes it and how deep it goes – do they have the same chemistry, or chromosome number, or taste alike to caterpillars?

Protection from the wind is at a premium on any coast, and the clumps of hawthorn and gorse, themselves sculptured lopsidedly by the onshore winds, assume great importance for insects. So too do the dells of old chalkpits, or the hollows of ancient track-ways or encampments, or, particularly for the moths, the patches of longer grass. Even so, there are more insects by far over the crest, on the landward side of the chalk ridges, but here the scrub grows thickly too. There are not many places where the turf sward is both sufficiently open and wind-protected to support colonies of the blue butterflies, but where it is, chalkhill, Adonis, and small blues are still about in summer. They are localized by the wind more than by their food plants, which are spread widely over the downland slopes and cliff-faces.

We tried to increase their possible habitat by making bays in the scrub, working from the tracks that follow the edge of the downs on the north side. The slopes soon become too steep for machine clearance, and hand-cutting is necessary. It is not easy to clear enough at a time by manual work alone to give a sufficiently large area for animal grazing to follow and consolidate the ground recovered before the scrub regrows. It requires a succession of working parties year after year to reverse the trend, but where it can be done, the result is to give a much greater opportunity for the butterflies and other insects of downland to survive. Sufficient sun reaches them, but they are protected by the down from the sea wind, and on less windy days they can use that too.

The scrub itself harbours other insects; mammals and birds too, though it is itself a passing stage as ash and other trees seed in and reduce it to the same form of mainly ash woodland, of lesser wildlife value, that fringes the South Downs beech woods. It is difficult to persuade people that to perpetuate the scrub stage, such tree seedlings must be weeded out. A good mixed scrub is of great value for wildlife, provided it is broken up enough to allow gaps and give edge effect. Coming over the top of the down, I once surprised a family of fox cubs as they played in a clear patch between the drifts of gorse. The hardy chats of the downs are here replaced by warblers. It is sheltered enough for the weaker insect fliers – the blue damselflies and the great green grasshopper. Craneflies abound and there is ivy for the holly blues. It is a very different community from that of the seaward side, so short a distance away. If you follow the ridge track, as most people do, you see little of either, though you have the benefit of a bracing walk, and the best of the views. An alternative is to go along the slope of one side, and come back on the other. A fine day's walk is that from Freshwater along the slopes of Afton, Compton and Brook Downs, and then back in the lee of the hills. In the spring on the seaward side the green-winged orchids cluster below the gorse drifts; above this and on the landward slope the early purples take over, forming patches of red in the sheets of cowslips. In summer these are replaced by the purple of saw-wort. There are botanical rarities too on this, almost the most southerly chalk ridge of Britain, so well exposed to both the influence of the sun and the sea. Often sea-mist or wind make it far from pleasurable, so one has to choose one's day, but if you get it right it can hardly be equalled. Coming back one day, having seen some plants and insects I had expected to see, and some I did not, I came across two or three palish blue flowers of a bell shape that puzzled me, which I looked at and photographed with care at first. However going through the possibilities I decided that they were simply Spanish bluebells that had been brought up with a load of earth intended to bank up the side of a recently extended reservoir, and which were trying their best to flower in such inappropriate surroundings, rather than some more fabulous kind of squill – in fact what the ornithologists call a hoodwink. However it was quite a good effort on their part, and made me look closely.

The ridge track is part of the Tennyson Trail, which continues along ridges to Newport. Some poets have been given to walking, others seem to have been more of an ambling or pub-crawling disposition. Tennyson clearly preferred bestriding the heights, and his footsteps have been followed by the National Trust, which owns so much of this chalk backbone of the Island. There are some gaps in its ownership, but not many. Rod and I had a plot to abolish one once, involving the sacrifice of an unfortunate plantation of Corsican pines, which should never have been planted in such a situation, and had suffered greatly from chlorosis. Though we have both left that paticular scene, it may still come about, linking the Trust's ownership up with the next section, and removing an unnecessary barrier to the free spread of species along the line of downs.

To the south is greensand country, of somewhat similar formations to those of the Weald, though called by different names. There are differences however to the geologist, and even to the layman it is a surprise to find the normally rather subdued Upper Greensand making such commanding cliffs as it does near St. Catherine's Point, high above the undercliff of clays and sandstones. However an even harder rock occurs to the north of the spine, in the shape of the Bembridge Limestone, of Oligocene age, which gives the lie to one's usual impression that hard rocks ended with the Jurassic. It is not thick, but one can see it at several places along the north coast and where it is falling into the undercliff, as at Headon Warren (*Photo 48*). There it is responsible for some of the terraces carrying a limestone flora, in contrast to those of their neighbours, and even more with the bell heather of the hill above. From this now rather eroded ridge one has a fine view towards the Needles, over the cliff from Alum Bay, where a chairlift can be seen taking a continual procession, like the souls of the damned, to nether regions out of sight, where they can fill little jars with coloured sands from the fourteen or more varieties available. The chair-lift also brings them up again, though descent is more evident than redemption, to where the stallkeepers in the crowded coachpark exert themselves to sell a corresponding number of shades of candy floss.

Beyond the bay, a buoy marks the edge of the deep-water channel, which runs surprisingly close to the cliff of Needles Headland. Most of the width of the Solent to the promontory of Hurst Castle is shallow. To command this channel more effectively than could be done by the guns of the Needles fortress, a shaft was sunk to a gallery almost at beach level where Oerlikons were mounted. The armaments have long been removed but the gallery remains and forms an interesting area of dispute between those who wish to conserve a part of our maritime history for public viewing and those who wish to make it a safer refuge for the bats that now occupy it in winter. Frank showed me photographs of the entrances taken from close inshore, since an altered date due to weather conditions had meant I had not been able to accompany the party. They clearly could be grilled up given a suitably amphibious expedition over a succession of calm days at the right tide. Scheduling both as an ancient monument and a SSSI had however led to an impasse, in which it was not clear which would ultimately prevail.

The Isle of Wight is so small, and contains so much, that such clashes are inevitable. Even more threatening to the life that its coastline supports is the ever-increasing risk of major pollution, from a tanker or off-shore drilling, both in the effects of such a spill itself and in the measures that would follow to restore the profitableness of its beaches for the tourist industry. Oil is far from being the only possible pollutant in such a scenario. The ecology of the Glanville fritillary, dependent on timely landslips, is an illustration in miniature of the hazard to which so much of coastal wildlife is exposed.

NINETEEN

The Dark Sentinel

I felt rather complimented when, although a non-local, I was asked to write much of the text for a fresh edition of the map and guide to Black Down, but of the Wealden hills it appeals to me the most in having kept its individual character despite its present coverage by pine and rhododendron. I wish I had known it before this happened, and the other hills too, of the great arc of the Lower Greensand that encircles the basin of the Weald. Black Down was among the last to fall victim to the evergreen spread, and several people still alive have told me how in their childhood they enjoyed the open heathland it then possessed. Eric Parker in his *Surrey Naturalist* published in 1952, recalls how Hallam Tennyson had written, in 1892, a description of the hill as it had been known to his father on his regular walks from Aldworth "a mile out and a mile in, over Black-down", and the two summer houses facing east and west that he used increasingly in his later years. The western one looked out on Blackdown's "bleak ridges fledged with pine", but the pine did not get a real hold until much later, and Eric Parker would undoubtedly have remarked on it if it had been so altering the character of the hill in his time. E.C. Matthews in 1911 (*The Highlands of South-West Surrey*), describes thick hanging forests on pine on the south sides, but the summit plateau was open, and clothed, like Hindhead, with the three heathers, two gorses, bracken, and whortleberry, with clumps of harebells by the roadsides. Solitary pines, stunted by the winds, stood here and there in the heather. When King's College, University of London, started mapping it in 1948–49 most of the hill-top plateau was still heathland, but by its 1956–57 survey pine had reduced this by some 50 per cent. By 1969–70 only small and widely separated areas of heath still survived. These interesting maps were shown by Professor Yates at the Southern Heathland

Symposium arranged by the Surrey Naturalists' Trust in 1974, and are published in their report, which is still obtainable.

So the explosion of Scots pine (*Photo 50*) did not happen until the early 1950s, after half a century of build-up, and was not directly related to immediate events such as the myxomatosis of 1954. I think this compares with the time-lag in other places between the cessation of grazing, and the explosion of pine; there is a long period when the danger is not perceived. It is only after consolidating its hold on the lower slopes and valleys that the pine makes a mass assault on the higher ground. It brings its own fauna with it: the wood-ants, and the pine-eating insects, including the pine beauty moth which has wrought such havoc on the monocultures of lodgepole pine in the north of Scotland. The kestrels still hang at eye-level as one looks over the Weald, but the fauna is now more of woodland than heathland.

The rhododendron has similarly spread outwards, but rather later. It is not mentioned at all in Hallam Tennyson's description, and it does not seem to have been noticeable when Black Down was given to the National Trust in 1944. By 1974 however, I was to estimate that it covered some 30 acres densely. There was considerable local opposition to the many working parties we enlisted to endeavour to control its further spread, and satisfaction over the difficulties we experienced. It was not an easy site to work on, as camping was severely restricted by the topography, as well as by the objections of the local residents. It was not possible for a machine to work on such uneven terrain even to extract the roots, without undue damage to the surface or the trees. To pull out whole bushes would have needed a machine so large as to be well beyond our financial reach, quite apart from the local uproar that would have ensued. So we cut the branches off low down, and burnt them when and where we could, but that too was severely limited by the danger of sparks being blown afar and igniting the bracken of the hillside slopes. We tried to poison the stumps, but Hythe Beds soil is a very good growing medium, and we had to treat them repeatedly, using whatever formulation of 245T our latest advisors recommended. The only way of ensuring a kill seemed to be to pull up all the roots that could be pulled up, and hang them on the birches clear of the ground until they died of exposure. The growth from the large roots of the main clumps, which from their rings were, as expected, about 30 years old, could only be cut off repeatedly, which at least controlled its spread, until some more effective herbicide was obtainable. The amount that we could clear with available working parties was only a fraction of what was really needed, and the need for a site where they could be based closer to this work was one of the main reasons for establishing a base-camp in the Haslemere area. Even with such a near-by base, it will take many years to reverse the spread of the rhododendron by volunteer effort alone. Enthusiasm wanes after three or four days of such work and some alternation with other tasks is usually needed in the week that the parties are at the base camp.

There is no lack of other jobs, even on Black Down itself, where the remaining patches of heather need frequent weeding out of the invading pine seedlings. There are also many wet patches where the underlying chert has interrupted drainage so that small ponds can be made. Most of these irregularities, which give the hill so much of its character, derive from the extraction of the more accessible pockets of chert for roadstone, though some are formed by the ancient trackways which cut over the hill, and are now sunken lanes. These bear witness to their use over the centuries for a variety of purposes, probably often illicit, and one that still bears the name of Pen-y-bos, suggests a pre-Saxon origin. Though when I asked Ian to obtain a translation, his Welsh Clerk of Works, although a bard, could not reconcile it with my suggestion of the track of the ox, and it seems that either I was trying the wrong language, or that the Pen referred to a headland, as in so many Welsh place names, while the bos was unexplained. Another mystery is how the German word for a spring, Quell, came to its appropriate site on Black Down's southern face.

The maintenance of the views too needs frequent work, and the views from Black Down are really superb. It is these, perhaps above all else, that have allowed its character to be kept, and they themselves are due to the geology. The water drains freely through the sandstone, except where impeded by a patch of chert, so that the tracks dry out quickly after rain. Lower down however it is stopped by the layer of Atherfield Clay, with the Weald Clay below that, so a spring-line is formed all round the foot of the hill. This makes the clay slippery, and thus a land-slip zone develops. It is most extensive at the southern end of the hill, resulting in the sharp angle of pitch of the slope there, which is so prominent a landmark from as far off as the Kent border, and with other geological influences has caused the east and west sides to fall steeply. From the west side these springs form the headwaters of one of the main branches of the Wey, thus flowing to the Thames, while from the east and south sides they drain to the Rother, and thus, via the Arun, to the Channel. Black Down is therefore a watershed, and the views are commensurate. From the east side, only a few minutes walk from the upper car park, one can see, over the Hambledon Hills, which also have this steeply-angled character, along the whole Greensand ridge as it stretches into Kent. From the west side of the hill one has a perhaps even finer view over the jumble of hills at the western edge of the Weald and far beyond. These are more intriguing because they are less easily identifiable. One can pick out Selborne, Noar, and perhaps the Wealden hangers down which Cobbett and his horse descended so precipitously, but beyond that one loses direction, and even some familiarity with the Hampshire hills has never enabled me to sort them out. At the southern point of Black Down, where there is what we seldom remember to refer to as a toposcope, and the French more sensibly call a *table d'orientation*, one can see an even more extensive horizon, almost a complete circle, including the range of the South Downs, with Chanctonbury easily identifiable by its clump of beeches, Bignor and Butser more regrettably by their superimposed radiomasts and other artefacts of modern technology, and can argue whether or not one is seeing a glimpse or glimpses of the Channel between them. Having seen all these, one can then consider which of these views one likes best, and from the location of the various seats that have been put up to departed friends and relations (including in one rather charming case, the lady's dog too) it is clear that there has been no unanimity on the subject. My own preference for the western view is based more on associations than aesthetics.

Although we may regret the various pylons and similar objects that crown our hills, particularly our southern hills, and for a real horror of a wirescape the view from St. Catherine's Down in the Isle of Wight is not easily surpassed, they do help in recognition, and they have a long history, even though the individual objects may fortunately not last as much as a century. The naval telegraph system and its later shutter version, which must have been even more unsightly than most of them (always excepting the horrible lop-sided excrescence on Butser) went by Black Down, and thence to Telegraph Hill north of Woolbeding, on its long and expensively maintained route from the Admiralty to Portsmouth. Before that there were chains of beacons, as well as gibbets and other such decorations of our heights, and no doubt the custom goes back to when man first came to our shores.

Black Down, at 919 ft, is second only to the 967 feet of Leith Hill, in the heights of south-east England, though the tower on the top of the latter extends the possible human elevation to 1029 feet. So there is only some 50 ft of difference between them, and it is intriguing to speculate what might have been the consequences if, when there was a need for a place to put the considerable excavation from enlarging the reservoir above the end of Chase Lane in 1977, and the Chase Lane residents objected to it being lorried out past them, it had been put on the highest point of Black Down, so stealing the crown from Leith Hill. Such an opportunity to upset accepted doctrine in the geographical textbooks does not often occur. One can think of many people who would have relished in quietly doing just that, and waiting to see what would happen next time the Ordnance Survey paid a visit. The Black Down Committee soberly set aside the temptation, and found a declivity that could harmlessly be filled in, specifying only that it should afterwards be seeded with heather.

Black Down is the National Trust's spelling, and also the Ordnance Survey's, but Blackdown is also commonly used. There are several other Black Downs and Blackdowns in England alone. But one wonders why it was black, before the pines, "the dark sentinel of the Western Weald". Possibly the way the shadows fall, or could it be a corruption of 'bleak'? Certainly it shows as a dark outline particularly from the east, and has been likened to the jutting prow of a ship. From the south, from Duncton Hill for instance, it looks much less stern and forbidding, and it was from the south that the smugglers would have seen it. All the Greensand hills look different from the south, and their outlines are distinct and recognizable even in moonlight. Yet although it is by some way the highest peak in Sussex, many Sussex people do not seem to acknowledge it as part of their county, despite the poets, and one wonders why. Perhaps it is so different to the general run of Sussex countryside, that it appears foreign to them. Tennyson's "demon-haunted hill" is not easily reconciled with the cosier image of the downland villages, or the shopping arcades of the seaboard towns.

It is still little visited. I have seen coaches there, but usually they have turned out to be from some college, more intent on scientific pursuit than tourism. It does not attract the crowds as Hindhead does, though it has far more character, and more to offer in walks and views. Some would not agree to this, but at Hindhead one can only walk down, and then climb out again; at Black Down one can walk up, and see out, with marvellous views all the way. The road access is mercifully not good. It is quite a pull up Haste Hill from Haslemere, though less by Scotland Lane, and this no doubt keeps people away. So it is left to the few, and all the better for so being.

One doesn't see many butterflies on Black Down – I have never seen either the grayling or the silver-studded blue there of the heathland species, and I don't know if they were there before the pines came. It must have been rather windy for butterflies then, and it is only in sheltered valleys or down on the roadsides or in the Quell that one sees many, even now. So I was rather surprised to be rung up one day in April 1975 by a lady who said she had seen two Camberwell Beauties there. She described them closely; they couldn't have been anything else, and she told me exactly where she had seen them. The next weekend I had arranged to meet Ceres and Bill to look for large tortoiseshells that had been reported several times at a place on the North Downs. It was a very hot day and after we had walked fruitlessly up to the ridge and back, we had lunch in a pub below. I told them of this call, and we decided to go and have a look ourselves. We left the car by Chase Lane, and walked up Boarden-door Bottom, where the chestnut had been coppiced a year or two before, so it was quite open. I couldn't see anything much for Camberwell Beauties to eat, except the old sallow bushes round the edge of the coppice, so we walked towards those. There were a number of brimstones, small tortoiseshells and peacocks about in the spring sunshine, and we looked twice at all the latter as they flew over us showing their black undersides, just in case. However when we saw the Camberwell Beauty (we only saw one) it was so much larger than our usual British butterflies that there was no mistaking it. Ceres saw it first, as usual, and called to me – we were rather spread out. It came past me fast and low down, and I could see the white border of its wings. We went on a bit, and thought we saw it, or another, once again.

Ceres wrote it up in her column, and got a letter which made her furious, from someone who said he had bred some and let them out the previous autumn. It was from a Fernhurst address, but when I found his house, it was actually north of Kingsley Green, so only a mile or so from where we had seen it, and there was no doubt it was one from his release, though it was interesting that it had survived the winter, which had been fairly mild.

I didn't do anything further, except to ask Johnny, the Warden, to keep an eye out and discourage collectors. Later he did tell me he thought he had seen one or two others about on the southern side of Black Down, which would be more suitable country for them. Next year there really was an invasion of Camberwell Beauties with a weather pattern indicating that they had come over from the Baltic countries. I heard that an entomologist I knew was writing this up, so I felt I had to come clean and let him know of this introduction, some of whose progeny, if they existed, might confuse his records. That spring I had not been able to get to Black Down on a suitable day, but Johnny told me he thought there were still some about, and in the autumn both Ceres and I had reports of some at various places in the Surrey/Sussex borders, though we didn't know whether these were derived from the Black Down release, or the new invasion. A report duly appeared in the *Entomologists' Record* for April 1977, which was later amplified by further records, listing in total some 300 sightings all over the British Isles, but most thickly in the eastern counties – this being the largest invasion of this species since 1872. Some of these survived the winter, and were seen in the spring of 1977, when John saw one near where we had walked on the North Downs. However no permanent colony resulted at Black Down or anywhere else, since these butterflies do not pair until spring, and although some come over almost every year, even when a larger number do, the few that survive the comparative warmth and damp of our winters are so widely scattered that they have little chance of finding a mate.

With so many encroaching evergreens it might be supposed that the flowers of Black Down are merely the relics of the former heathland. This is far from the case, as the tracks and roadsides of the lower slopes all round the hill, and particularly in the Quell, bear a rich flora, especially striking in spring. The clumps of the white greater stitchwort seem to stand out the more in contrast to the darker background, while the primroses, blue-bells, woodsorrel and others of the many common woodland plants that flower before the trees are in full leaf, can be seen here in as attractive a setting as anywhere. I don't think there are any great rarities – the ivy-leafed bellflower and the beech fern are no longer to be found on the property, while I have some doubt whether the cotton-grass and sundew are still present round the much-photographed and much-trampled tarns above the car park (*Photo 49*). But it is a most attractive spring drive to make the circuit of the hill, as one can by metalled roads, even though it has had to be forbidden to take cars up onto the hill itself; and if one stops to listen, there are many warblers, and perhaps a night-ingale still.

Black Down excels in the smaller trees and shrubs too: black-thorn and crabapple at the lower levels, hazel and alder for catkins, and alder-buckthorn for its berries, pink at first, then turning black as the leaves turn yellow. Rowan is everywhere, with great masses of scarlet berries, and there is a famous example of its hybrid with whitebeam beside the eastern track from the upper car park to the Temple of the Winds, with leaves more like rowan in one part and more like whitebeam in another. This hybrid also bears berries; at least until, like the others, they are devoured by the flocks of winter thrushes. But it is not so much the individual features that make Black Down such an attractive hill to visit, at almost any time of the year when it is not shrouded in mist or rain, as the sense of well-being given by the upland atmosphere, the changing colours, and the tremendous views. Looking down one sees a landscape, almost toy-like from this height, entirely patterned by man, and looking up, the sky and the wind in the pines. The easy walking along this plateau between earth and heaven may be the nearest to Nirvana that some of us will reach.

PLATE 17 *The Island (2)*

47 The "cinxia conversazione" at the Noah's Ark in April 1982.

48 Katherine recording at Headon Warren for the National Trust's Biological Survey, August 1982.

48 ▽

PLATE 18 *The Dark Sentinel*

49 Cotton-grass, bog asphodel and sundew survived by the small tarn at the northern end of Black Down until the dry summer of 1976 (Photo taken in 1974).

50 The pines that now cover the crest of Black Down give shady walks, but are fairly recent arrivals, since 1950, and all are first generation trees (photo taken in 1976).

50 ▽

51 △ 52 ▽

PLATE 19 *The Ring (1)*

51 The East Gate in 1975, before erosion repairs, looking towards the Ring from outside.

52 Erosion above the Nepcote Lane car-park in 1977, after the first barrier had been installed.

PLATE 20 *The Ring (2)*

53 Lunch-break for an Acorn Camp, led by John in 1982, to clear scrub from the sheltered southern coomb.

54 The gabions used to repair the eroded sides of the West Gate soon turfed over, and are hardly visible in this 1988 photograph.

54

55 △

PLATE 21 *The Water Soldiers (1)*

55, 56 13 June 1983. Operations were going to plan, with the thick covering of water soldier (*Stratiotes aloides*) being systematically removed from the pond and wheel-barrowed well out into the field.

56 ▽

PLATE 22 *The Water Soldiers (2)*

57 I had got the planks too short, so it was easier to bring the emptied wheelbarrows back over the field to one side of them.

58 On the last day David strung a net across below the remaining weed, and we concentrated on clearing up all the loose bits downstream of this.

57 △

58 ▽

PLATE 23 *Canary Blues (1)* 59 △

59 View south-westwards along the spine of Tenerife at about 2000m towards Mt. Teide, 3715m. Subalpine zone with brooms, etc. on tufa soil. Cloud drifting in from both sides. May. See also the cover photo, taken looking northwards nearer the volcano.

60 Forestry track about 1700m in the remains of the evergreen forest zone of Tenerife just below the pinewoods. Rather Mediterranean type flora. Looking east, in July.

60 ▽

61 △   62 ▽   63 ▽

64 ▽

PLATE 24 *Canary Blues (2)*.

61 Milkweed butterfly, *Danaus plexippus*.

62 Canary Blue, *Cyclyrius webbianus*.

63 A blue-cheeked lizard.

64 Indian red admiral, *Vanessa indica calliroe* on wallflower.

TWENTY

The Ring

The lady was indignant as she returned to the Storrington Rise car park and decided to unburden to us as we sat finishing our sandwiches before our tour assembled. In efficient English she complained how she and her husband had walked up the hill in the direction the signpost said, and they had not seen any trace of old walls or anything of the sort one would expect. I was trying to make out what nationality she was, but it was not until they drove off and I saw the HH numberplate that it occurred to me that her guide book may have referred to a Schloss, so she would have been looking for a Norman keep, or perhaps something in the style of Ludwig II. Going up that way from Findon, one comes on the earthworks piecemeal, and it would not necessarily be easy to appreciate that they run all round the hilltop to enclose over 65 acres – a castle of a kind, though rather different to those one associates with the German landscape. Even if the sign had read Cissbury Ring, as several do, there would still be room for misinterpretation, as a ring might be formed of many different things, from standing stones to toadstools. Maiden Castle, so similar to Cissbury, might be even more misleading, and no doubt there will soon be an EEC directive that visitors must not be misled into expecting a castle when there is only chalk turf and sky.

Some would say there is nothing wrong with the latter, and many have wished for no more. But I had a feeling that there had been a failure in a matter of public interpretation, and that it would be retailed to their friends in Hamburg as a further example of the perfidy of Albion. Many years before I had been given some natural history notes on Cissbury, mainly ornithological, compiled by a friend, and asked to combine them with such archaeological and other information as I could glean, into the shape of a small booklet that could be made available to visitors. I wished that this had been published, and I could have given the lady a copy, but unfortunately after I had completed the text and obtained many of the illustrations, the project was abandoned since there did not seem to be sufficient places at which it could be sold to cover the costs of printing it. Perhaps one day Cissbury will have the interpretation centre it deserves, and a booklet produced, though over the last twenty years there have been so many changes that my original text would need considerable revision.

Again if the lady approached from the north side, from Nepcote Lane, as many do, she could hardly have failed to appreciate that what she was climbing was a segment of a gigantic earthwork. However the small car park there was established without the authorization of the owner of the land, who objected to its presence, so that the later official car parks indicated by the road-signs were sited to the west, where the outskirts of Findon run up to the base of the hill. At these there is ample parking space, but the approach to the Ring is gradual and much less spectacular from them, so that one reaches the earthworks without immediate appreciation of their immensity. Now that the Trust has acquired more land on the north side, a better arrangement may emerge in time, though there are considerable difficulties in the narrowness of the approach lanes; the botanical richness of the land on which any car park could in practice be sited; and the difficulties of screening it to avoid it being an eyesore.

When I first visited Cissbury the only place where one could park was off Nepcote Lane, where a number (I once counted fourteen) of roughly painted notices warned motorists of the likely fate of any car that obstructed the passage of the farmer's tractors. A choice of tracks led upwards; one steeply by an eroded and treacherously slippery trail, flanked by straggling juniper, to the rim of the counterscarp; the other less steep but apparently leading too far eastwards between high thickets of calcicole shrubs until it emerged in front of the east gate of the Ring. The steep ascent was naturally the one most used, especially by those who had not been there before, and was badly in need of erosion control. The other was more suitable for those who preferred a stroll to a scramble and appreciated the wealth of chalk flowers and insects in the numerous gaps betwen the bushes of wayfaring tree and privet, all overlaid by a tangle of travellers' joy. At that time this north-east side of the slopes did not belong to the National Trust, whose boundary, like that of the Parish and the District, followed the edge of the earthworks, as was indicated on the skyline above the steeper ascent by twin posts. One of these posts carried the Omega sign and by-laws of the National Trust; the other proclaimed management by Worthing District, and prohibited horse riding on National Trust land. That these posts, though contiguous and of similar height, were neither of them vertical, but inclined towards each other, gave an unfortunate impression of lack of co-ordination.

This was not however the case, since both parties worked together harmoniously in such management as the insufficient resources of each could provide, and relations were always on a friendly and co-operative basis. Both at that time had difficulty in coping with pressures on the periphery of their areas, even though, as a survey showed, visiting numbers to Cissbury were relatively static since they were controlled by the small holding capacity of the unofficial car park. Both Worthing and the Trust, and the County Council too, contributed what they could in the shape of volounteer or MSC labour, in the urgent work of clearing the scrub and sizeable trees, that then flourished in the vallum between the ramparts, and whose roots were causing an unknown extent of damage to such archaeological remains as lay below. Many years of work were needed in this task, and although the result was a considerable diminution of the birdlife that had used this refuge, as well as the loss of many of the more vigorous herbs such as hemp agrimony that had been a nectar source for a multitude of small tortoiseshell and peacock butterflies, there were less regrettable extirpations such as the clumps of deadly nightshade and in particular the growth of young ash and sycamore whose roots were the chief offenders. The clearance was essential for archaeological preservation, and also allowed people to see the double ramparts, with the intervening ditch, much more clearly, so that they were able to get a better impression of what the site comprised.

One really needs a diagram to visualize how these ramparts are thought to have looked in their original condition. The assumption is that they were vertical and faced with timber, so that they stood some 15 feet high, above a berm about 10 feet wide between the rampart and the ditch. These timbers would have projected a few feet above the rampart top, so as to give cover to the defending slingers. No doubt such other weapons as were available were also to be used but the finding of stores of beach pebbles show that slingers featured largely. The lower rampart, the counterscarp, would also have been vertical with the intervening ditch flat at its bottom, about 25 feet wide. Attackers would therefore have had to climb up the hill, exposed to fire from the slingers, and then be faced with crossing the ditch, no doubt furnished with obstacles such as pointed stakes, and climbing up the far side to the berm, before they were in a position to scale the main ramparts. One wonders whether pole-vaulting had been discovered! What we see today, though impressive enough, are only the fallen remains of the chalk rubble that was piled behind the palisades that have long ago perished. It has been estimated that some 60 000 tons of chalk had to be moved to form these ramparts, and that their revetment would have needed about 10 000 timbers, at least 15 feet (4.6m) long and 9 inches (0.25m) thick. The work was done in the Iron Age, about 250 BC, presumably by recent invaders under the compulsion to set up a strong base.

It seems to have been intended not so much as a permanently manned redoubt, but as a stronghold to which all the inhabitants of the area could retreat, with their cattle and belongings, in times of trouble. Whether this ever happened is open to doubt, since the Roman occupation in the first century AD appears to have been with the acquiescence of the local Belgic inhabitants. In Roman times the interior of the Ring was farmed, with the down-creep of soil from this cultivation piling up against the inner face of the banks or forming the lynchets one can see in the south-east part. At the very end of the Roman period, Cissbury was again fortified, perhaps against Saxon pirate raids, by the addition of a defensive wall of turves on top of the combined bank and lynchet.

Experience of military engineering leads me to doubt the detail of some of this, despite the teaching of the archaeologists. Clearly something of the sort happened originally, the chalk was dug out, the timbers were installed, and the backfill of rubble was pounded in. But timbers, even whole tree-trunks, do not last for ever, and the situation there is exposed. The selection of available material was not wider than the native hardwoods of today, and must have been largely of beech, oak or ash. Beech does not have a long life when cut, nor does ash; oak is considerably longer lasting (some three to four times) but unless grown in plantations is inclined to branch fairly low. I cannot think what else could have been used. Sweet chestnut, though as durable as oak, was not then introduced, and the even more durable yew could not have been found in the quantities and sizes needed. So it must have been oak, and to find, cut, extract and transport 10 000 of suitable size must have taken a good many years. The weather was warmer then, but if one assumes that four such trunks were installed on each day of say 250 suitable days in each year, which would involve a team of over 50 people, as well as their oxen, one is still faced with a time-span of 20 years, by when the first trunks installed would be beginning to warp and rot.

Consider too the mechanics. The prepared trunks would be towed on sledges or rollers, up the gentler slopes at the east or west ends and dragged to the required place where a hole in the chalk had already been prepared for their butts. They would be tilted into this, and pushed forward until they were vertical. They would then have to be secured by some tie to an anchorage behind so that when the chalk was filled and pounded in behind them, they did not topple into the vallum. Of what material could such ties have been made? Cord, or hide would have rotted. They could only have been of wood also, so that the whole construction must have been erected 'dry' and the chalk filled in behind afterwards.

Yet it was done, as one can see. But I do not believe that it could have been kept in repair, once the initial timbers had rotted. To have done so effectively would have been even more difficult than the original construction. It is far easier to ram chalk behind a new revetment, than it is to dismantle a decayed one down to its foundations, taking out the slumped chalk, putting in new timbers and ties, carrying the chalk up again, and backfilling as before. I believe that people then were in no more hurry to repair their defences than we are today, and were inclined only to do so in face of an obvious threat, when they would only have had time to do a patching job. So I suspect that if the ramparts were made in 250 BC, they were in disrepair within fifty years, and were much as we see them today by the time the Romans came. The quick raising of what was left of the defences at the end of the

Roman period suggests the sort of sand-bag effort that we would resort to, and I rather suspect that something of that nature is more likely than laying turves.

When the Saxons did come, in AD 477, Cissbury was probably in the wrong place for a defensive position; a situation not unknown in later military history. Aella sailed into Chichester Harbour and landed at Ellanore, in the Manhood, which then extended much further into what is now the sea. From there he conquered Sussex with his South Saxons, and on his death about 515 AD, he was succeeded by his son Cissa, whose name is perpetuated in both Chichester and Cissbury, though he does not seem to have been so strong a personality as his father. The Wealden forest still protected Sussex from the north, and no doubt formed a refuge for some of the defeated, though the South Saxon kingdom was only to last two centuries before becoming a puppet of its more powerful neighbours, Mercia to the north and Wessex to the west. From then on Cissbury's history has been that of much of the higher hinterland of the Channel coastline – wartime usage for lookouts and rallying points, signal beacons, and more recently anti-aircraft defences, and peacetime usage for sheep, recreation and neglect.

Although the ramparts of the Ring may seldom, if ever, have been manned in anger, they have defended, and still defend, Cissbury against the more insidious threats of peacetime. As well as preserving a large proportion of the relics of the very much earlier flint-mines, they have prevented the ready inclusion of Cissbury in the cereal cultivation to which the South Downs was subjected in the 1939–45 war, and which still holds sway over most of its former sheepwalks. The centre of the Ring has been cultivated from time to time, as have the flatter parts of the southern slope, but hay or grazing has been more frequent. On the ramparts, and the small areas between the flint mines in the western part of the Ring, no cultivation has been practicable. The chalk turf here has had two thousand years to develop undisturbed and establish a characteristic flora with its accompanying insect life. Its low-growing plants include field fleawort, frog orchid and dumpy centaury. There are large patches of horseshoe vetch, which have allowed the chalkhill blue butterfly to survive in quantity, and also the Adonis blue, though this species is now confined to the sheltered southern coombe. Cissbury has

remained an oasis of green turf and wildlife in a desert of cultivation, but it has been touch and go. When I first saw it in 1972 it
was deteriorating, both in its natural history and archaeological
values, and it went on deteriorating, mainly because of lack of
management resources, for another five years, before it was possible to turn the tide.

Concurrently with the removal of the trees and scrub from the
ramparts, there was need to control the erosion. There are always
people who say that erosion is incurable, and has to be accepted,
but this is not true – it can nearly always be localized to follow a
harder surface on a less exposed route. There are also people who
say that it has gone on for so long that it forms part of the
character of the place – this also is usually untrue. I was able to
assemble a series of airphotographs stretching back over some
fifty years which disproved this belief, and showed clearly that
the erosion was of fairly recent origin, but was increasing yearly.
They also showed the former presence, even up to the 1950s, of
considerably more large trees within the Ring than were there
twenty years later and the existence of a square 'gorse' in its
eastern part of the shape and size commonly planted in previous
centuries for fox coverts. Its former presence explained why there
were two tracks connecting the East Gate with the West, rather
than a single direct line; one had gone north and one south of this
gorse. The trigonometric point, at 183 metres, had been
established just off the northern one, at the highest point, since
the gorse had been put in, as usual, on a slightly south-facing
slope, and appeared to have been of the normal four-square pattern so that the central north-south ride would be open to the sun.
No doubt it had been one of the more exhilarating draws of the
local fox-hounds.

This feature was not, in the 1970s, apparent on the ground, and
was not even recognizable in airphotographs later than 1960. Nor
was there evidence of much erosion of the face of the ramparts
then, except at the two gateways into the camp. These, although
referred to as the East and West Gates are actually positioned
further south – the East Gate being ESE, and the West Gate SSW,
so that the track from the latter runs alongside the old woodland
of Cissbury Plantation. This wood is not National Trust property,
though the Trust owns a triangle of land to its immediate west
including part of this track, and this triangle when I first saw it

still had a small area of chalk heath, both ling and bell, which has since disappeared. It was also remarkable for its wealth of horse-shoe vetch, which survives, though in rather too windy a position on the south-west slope of the hill-top to be greatly used by Adonis blues as well as the hardier Chalkhills. There have been a good many adjustments in this area over the last twenty years, including boundary alterations, but it remains an interesting slope, with occasional orchids, early purple, fragrant and autumn lady's-tresses, usually only a few scattered plants, but well-grown, as well as a good mixture of other chalk flowers.

It does not perhaps have the potential of the southern coombe, which lies to the south of the East Gate, and runs down towards Deep Bottom, with its long narrow field, sheltered on both sides, that has not surprisingly been used as a rifle range, and possibly in earlier times for archery, since it seems almost designed by nature for marksmanship. The slope down from the East Gate to the field is fairly steep, though the winding farm track which crosses it gives a gentler descent. The sides of this track, which must have been made before the 1939–45 war, or early in it, since a friend told me that it had been her war-time pram walk, have now healed and developed short vegetation to the benefit of the Adonis blues. By the early 1970s, this slope was getting covered with scrub, though small patches of short turf remained here and there, and I thought, on what evidence I now forget, that it was used chiefly for snaring rabbits. On a visit in June 1976, I saw that much of the scrub on the slope above the track had been fired earlier that year, and while looking for the cause of the fire, though it was not hard to formulate a suspicion, I suddenly noticed a brood of grey partridges sitting closely, tails together, and facing outwards in a circle ready to burst out from the inade-quate protection of the low regrowth. They allowed me to take a couple of indifferent photographs, for which I wished I had a better camera, and I retreated leaving them as they were. Next year this area had a thick growth of thistles, with a surprising number of white-flowered plants, both spear and musk, and after that the farmer's sheep had begun to use the ground and pre-vented its return to scrub. It was on this slope in the next sum-mer, 1978, when a small party came to look into my recommendation that Cissbury warranted SSSI status, that we put up a cream-spot tiger moth, which caused some excitement.

Adders also liked this sunny slope, with its many scattered bushes giving cover into which they could retreat quickly if anyone intruded on their basking, and one I surprised there was of such an exceptional size that I looked for it again on subsequent visits, but without success. It was also browner than usual for Cissbury, where most of the adders are strongly patterned in black and white. Much of the scrub on this slope has now been cleared, by fire, grazing, or working parties (*Photo 53*), but there remains a hard core of it in the the middle of the coombe that has not yet been cleared.

Attempts to use Cissbury for modern trends in recreation have been spasmodic – there are other hills better shaped, more legally usable, and with easier access for the hang-gliders. Pop festivals were tried in several years, causing so much noise and annoyance to the people of Findon that the police took such strong action that they have not recurred. I am not sure that they were really a success either – when we cleared up after the first one, though it seemed to me that the participants had tried not to leave a mess, and we only filled half a dozen sacks, the small collection of fires they had made from dead wood and fenceposts only occupied an acre or so of the large expanse inside the ramparts. I could not think that it had been much of a party, shivering on an Easter Monday in the inadequate shelter of the ramparts, and though some people later told me they had enjoyed it, I felt this was more in retrospect. Cissbury does not have the numinous quality of sites associated with former religious ceremonies such as Stonehenge.

There were no statutory bridlepaths within the Ring, and though one not infrequently saw riders there, I do not think they were responsible for much of the erosion. Most of it undoubtedly was caused by foot traffic, and it was most severe in the neighbourhood of the statutory footpath that ran up from the Nepcote Lane car park. Various short cuts had been made from this, each developing into a line of white where the turf was worn down to the chalk, and one of these had been widened into a scree area attractive to children for sliding down by whatever means were available (*Photo 52*). This was barricaded off in 1977 by Tony before it had worn too deeply, but the main agent in controlling the erosion was the institution by the farmer in 1976 of a perimeter sheep fence, running along the centre of the ditch between the ramparts. This meant that access to the Ring was confined to the kissing gates or stiles placed in the lines of the main paths, and the various short cuts that had been made, none of which had been in existence long enough to become really gullied, were thereby rendered useless, and gradually healed. It did however mean that pressure was concentrated on the line of the main footpath and this clearly had to be improved.

Work on this started in the late 1970s with the benefit of current experience of dealing with the much more severe erosion at Box Hill. The same method was used of introducing steps of square-cut tanalised softwood. It was possible to bend the track above the sheepfence so that it followed a gully hidden from below, and conceal the obtrusive effect. There is always a problem that steps are easier for people to walk up than down, and if the slope allows them to do so, people descending prefer to walk on the turf alongside, rather than on the steps. However here the slopes were such as to induce people to use the steps for going down, as well as up, and this resulted in greater compaction and hollowing out of the chalk fill of the treads. They were topped up with more chalk, but the same problem arose again. Finally, several years later, and Glynn told me, after much agonizing, the decision was taken to fill the treads with concrete, and this was done in the mid-1980s. The result has been satisfactory, and its appearance is not so very different to the previous chalk filling as to provoke cries of desecration, given that no better method has been suggested for providing access up a steep and narrow path for increasing numbers.

There were two other main places where erosion was becoming a problem; along the ridge of the ramparts and at the two original gates of the camp. It was natural that people, having climbed up to the Ring, should prefer to follow the higher ridge of the rampart to east or west, with its short turf, rather than fan out into the longer grass of the centre of the Ring. For one thing, they could see the views better, and for another there is a human inclination to want to walk all round the edge of such a feature. Cissbury is so large that most visitors tire of doing this before long, and move instead on to the tracks inside the Ring, but there were parts of the ridge of the rampart, chiefly on the north-east side, where something was needed. Various forms of wire or plastic netting mesh were tried, some less satisfactory than others in that they caught high heels, or tore out at the ends unless these were somehow bent down and bedded into the turf. I don't think that an ideal material for this problem has yet been found, since it needs to become so integrated that one does not even realize it is there, and most of the materials come in rolls or sheets which are inclined to crinkle up or work loose along at least one edge, however carefully you try to bed them in.

The two 'gates' were really just gaps in the ramparts, and though they must originally have been fitted with posts and barricades, these had long since perished. The passage of tractors and farm implements was eroding the sides of these gaps, and this erosion was compounded by people walking or running up and down them (*Photo 51*). It was necessary to restore them to more vertical breaks in the ramparts, in order to protect any archaeological evidence before it was further eroded. Two different methods were used. At the East Gate timber barricades on posts were installed, and the gap behind these was filled in, using wire mesh as a retainer. At the West Gate, gabions were tried – boxes of wire filled with chalk rubble. The latter have been the better and when I saw them in 1988 they had turfed over so that the only erosion visible was of the track itself (*Photo 54*). The method tried at the East Gate had not been as successful, partly because some of the timber revetment had warped and could be caught and pulled out further by passing farm machinery, and partly because the side that was in sun shadow had not been able to turf over as much as had the other. It had fulfilled its object of preventing further archaeological damage all the same.

So these varying methods have all contributed to the lessons that can be learnt about how to avoid a daily stream of visitors destroying the object of their visit, and variants of them have been introduced at other places at Cissbury where frequent use was causing problems of erosion. By and large, it would seem that it has been a fairly successful exercise in the technique of control of visitor pressure. What is still lacking at Cissbury is a method of interpreting to the public the most interesting period of its long history, which was at a greater distance back in time before the making of the Ring, than the Ring is to us.

The particular accessibility and quality of the flint seams in the Upper Chalk gave Cissbury its first historical importance, as far back as 5000 years ago. It was in those Neolithic times a centre of the flint-mining industry, and the mines here are, in England, second in importance only to those at Grimes Graves in Norfolk. About 250 filled-up mine shafts have been counted, of which 200 are in the area enclosed by the hill-fort, forty outside it to the South-West, and others under the ramparts which were thrown up so much later. Freshly mined flint was more easily worked into tools and weapons than exposed nodules picked up from the surface. The axe-heads were roughed-out at the mines and then distributed far and wide, the eventual user presumably doing the final chipping to his requirements before grinding and polishing to make a smooth and highly efficient tool. The mine shafts were about forty feet (12m) deep and had radiating galleries to follow the flint seams; the chalk was dug by using red deer antler picks which were hammered in and then worked to break up the chalk, and the flint nodules were won from their bedding in the same day way. Antler was also employed as rakes and the shoulder-blades of oxen as shovels, for the collection and removal of waste chalk in baskets; this waste was disposed of into the shafts of previously worked-out mines. The antler and bone tools have been found in excavations, and also a rim sherd of brown pottery identified as coming from a Neolithic round-bottomed bowl with a distinct shoulder ridge. Also found was a miner's lamp, a shallow chalk cup with blackened edges. Two graffiti were found in the galleries, representing an ox and a red deer.

This archaeological account leaves out much of the socio-economic interest, and one can only speculate on such matters as why the Cissbury flints were among the market leaders of the time. Apart from Grimes Graves in Norfolk, there were flint mines in the Seine area of France, as well as in Holland, Belgium and elsewhere, and no doubt there were lesser centres of exploitation. What was so special about Cissbury, when Upper Chalk, with its flints, occurs in so many other places? It was near to the coast, but some sites are much nearer: the Seven Sisters for example. On the dates given, it would seem that the heyday of the Cissbury industry was after the opening, or rather re-opening of the Straits of Dover about 7500 BC, but the coastline would have been very different to the present and may still have included the Isle of Wight, with the ancient River Solent giving an access route. But it does not seem that Cissbury was in a particularly advantageous situation for its products to be marketed widely. Nor was there water for grinding. One would like to know the scale of the operation, how many finished products were produced per day and what and where the demand was. One wonders too how it all originated, whether it began as a sudden find, leading to a Klondike rush, with competing individual mines, or whether it was a collective effort fron the start. Man had been using flints for half a million years by then, so there must have been a considerable degree of sophistication in the appreciation of the quality of the finished products of the various sources. Clearly Cissbury had some advantage, or there would not have been such a concentration of industry there, but it is not easy to see just what it was.

Still it is a fascinating chapter of history, and one that could be demonstrated to the interest of the general public as it has been at Grimes Graves. Cissbury thus has two strings to its bow in this respect, in addition to the obvious attractions of the modern scene with its views, chalk flora and other attractions. Some connecting theme is however needed that serves to link together the highlights of its history, and this could be found in the sheep whose grazing has done so much over the millenia to produce the turf that is such an exhilarating feature of the South Downs, where it remains still unploughed. Cissbury is much transformed from when I first saw it, and there have been some regrettable losses, but it now gives the impression of being set fair to increase in biological value and be a prime example of the way that downland can be managed for the conservation of its natural wildlife.

TWENTY-ONE

The Ferrets

The wife of a colleague rang me one afternoon to say that she had just come back from a walk with her sons on a common I knew fairly well, where they had seen a small mammal in apparent distress. She described which car park they had used, and which way they had gone, and added that one of the sons had looked up a book and thought the animal was a polecat. I set off as soon as I could, putting cardboard box in the car, also a gun since I thought a mink was more likely. I doubted whether I would find the creature on a 600-acre common, even though she had asked someone to look out for me and take me to where she had seen it. In the event we had only gone a couple of hundred yards when we saw the creature coming towards us, unsteadily following two visitors with a small dog on a lead. They were glad to see us, as they were wondering what to do about their follower when they reached their car.

It was quite a large polecat-ferret, and in a bad way, with one eye covered in mucus, and a large matted tangle on top of its head. I picked it up with gloves, and put it in the cardboard box in the back of the car, but it soon upset that, and by the time I got home it had explored as much of the car as it could reach, not being too ill to be as inquisitive as ferrets always are. We put it in a chicken coop on the lawn, which had a wire netting run attached, and gave it some hay for bedding, and a meal. It drank a lot of milk, being clearly famished, and ate raw meat and egg. Then it made a nest in the hay, and went to sleep.

Next day I took it to a vet. The eye was not badly damaged, and soon healed, but with ether the scab on its head came away completely, leaving a raw gash the size of a crown piece. The vet gave me a puffer bottle of some green powder to spray on this, and over three or four months the wound gradually healed. It was an adult male; we could only guess it was at least two years old, and we came to the conclusion that it must have laid up when being used for ferreting, and that its previous owner had scalped it with a spade or mattock in attempting to dig it out, and left it for dead. It had most polite manners, though at first inclined to bite, but would always climb the side of the run to say thank-you before eating its meal. The dressing of the wound must have hurt it, since hard pieces of scab had sometimes to be removed, but it never seemed to protest even when I mishandled the puffer as it wriggled, and blew powder into its eyes or nose. I could soon leave off the gloves, which made handling easier.

We had not kept a ferret before, though we both remembered smelly hutches on stilts behind keepers' houses, but we soon discovered that such off-putting recollections were not borne out. In the absence of a fresh rabbit its preferred food was pigs liver, which had to be fresh, or if we had run out, a raw egg would do at a pinch. The routine was milk, which it preferred to bread and milk, in the morning before I went to work, and liver when I returned. It divided its hutch between bedding and larder, making a cosy nest on one side, and storing any surplus food on the other. This led to trouble with bluebottles and maggots, requiring fortnightly cleaning out with fresh sawdust and hay, also a good deal of the lice powder which we used for the chickens, as well as cleaning the run, which it always fouled in the same corner, before moving it to a fresh part of the lawn. This needed varying according to the season and weather to give more sun or shade.

When its wound had healed, we could let it out for short runs on the lawn where it would play about, chasing its tail, or playing hide and seek with us round the hutch. The dogs kept well away, and if it came up to one of them, it would bite the dog. Ferrets have no fear, though they are tremendously playful and inquisitive. Just putting a drainpipe on the lawn would tempt it to run through it, and any near object was immediately investigated. The lawn became rather cluttered with the ferret's toys.

Sometimes we took the ferret rabbiting, transferring it to an orange-box in the landrover, and setting it down by a warren. It would give a sort of bellicose snort before plunging underground, and we usually soon had shot two or three rabbits. We also learnt a lot about how the various warrens were connected underground; far more than we had ever realized before. But I wasn't able to take it out often, as one really needs to do this in the morning, when one has plenty of time if the ferret lays up;

also there are times in the spring to avoid when the chance of the ferret finding a brood of young rabbits is greater. There weren't many suitable days when I had the time available then, but we managed quite a few expeditions over the year and a half we kept this one. It died one November; we thought probably of pneumonia, and we reproached ourselves that though we had given it more hay and shelter, we had not thought to put corrugated asbestos under the hutch to insulate it from the damp ground, as we always did after that.

We had by then acquired a female, of the more usual small white kind, which my daughter and I saw late one night jumping about in our headlights in the middle of the main road across our local common. Fortunately there was no other traffic just at that moment, and we were able to scoop it into the car, though driving was hazardous as it explored under our legs until it got into the glove compartment. This one was also installed in a hutch on the lawn, and soon became tame and playful. We did put them together, but being taken aback by the Apache approach shown by the much larger male, we thought we must intervene, and separated them. This was probably a mistake, as this ferret also died after eighteen months with us, during which we frequently used it for rabbiting. There is a belief that a jill ferret will not live after its second yearly season (which is in spring) unless it has mated, and our further experience seemed to confirm this.

Once one gets known to be keeping ferrets, one soon finds oneself on a grapevine, and all sorts of people start offering you others, or exchanging information about them. Probably this is true of most kinds of pets – which is what our ferrets became really, and very good pets they are too. We got very fond of them all, though I forget now how many we had in total. We never had more than two at once, and we preferred the polecat kind with their appealing pansy-marked faces, but even with these the fur quality varied greatly, and some we had were almost like velvet in texture. They were all great fun to play with, and did not take a lot of time to look after, apart from the occasions when on their evening run one would make a beeline for the shrubbery, and take some time to find again. When they did get lost, they seemed to end up in sensible places, such as the fodder store, and we never lost one either through straying, or in rabbiting. But they are very short-lived creatures, so that the ten or twelve years during which they became part of our way of life, was punctuated by recurrent sadnesses when one of them fell ill and died. I don't think we had any that lasted for more than three years, and when we once had sisters, and kept them together, the second never was herself after the first one died and only lasted a further month. They were very tough in many ways, but seemed prone to virus diseases, and if they got scratched by a piece of wire, which one might not always notice, it seemed easily to go septic. After these last two, which were particularly attractive, we decided that we wouldn't start again. I was sorely tempted a few years later, when I met one coming towards me on the nature reserve, where it must have been left behind by some boys who had been ferreting. I stopped the car, at which it had a good look, climbing about in the undercarriage, and I had some difficulty in getting it to go far enough away for me to restart without running over it. It seemed a bit heartless to leave it, but there were plenty of rabbits about then, and it was probably better for it.

Ours are all buried, in biscuit tins for coffins, under a tree in the corner of the downland which was their hunting ground when we had the opportunity to take them rabbiting. Only a hundred yards into the big downland field from there is the warren where I had a memorable day with one of them. I had been ferreting with one of my sons, but there had been no action for some time, and we thought the ferret must have laid up. My other son joined us then, so I gave him my gun, and suggested they walked round while I waited for the ferret to reappear. Meanwhile I busied myself cutting with a slasher the growth of houndstongue and dogwood round the rabbit holes, so that I would see the ferret easier when it came out. After about a quarter of an hour, I heard a shot in the distance and then suddenly underneath me a terrific rumbling. A rabbit leaped into the air from one hole, and started to dance about. Realizing it must have been bitten by the ferret, I rushed after it, and killed it with the back of the slasher. This rumbling had been very deep down, and I thought the ferret must somehow have broken through to a lower level. Soon afterwards a further rumbling produced another rabbit from the same hole, in the same state, so I killed that too. A third followed, and then the ferret, which saw the last corpse, and made for it. Soon the boys returned, having shot another rabbit, so we ended up with four rabbits for one cartridge, and the ferret safely back. I don't suppose we will ever do that again!

TWENTY-TWO

Water Soldiers

A first camp at a new site is always a bit tricky, and this one had a good many things about it that could go wrong. The task was to clear water soldier that was choking a long narrow pond, and it had to be done in the first half of June. Earlier was no good, because the plant wouldn't have surfaced, and the water would be unpleasantly cold for the participants, who were bound to get very wet, even if they didn't fall in. Later was out because of the beginning of the fishing season, when the anglers would start pulling out the weed themselves in the haphazard manner they had done the years before, which had made it spread the more. The only hope was to start at one end, and work methodically along, taking out every bit. There were arguments against a later date too for conservation reasons. It was a particularly important botanical pond, and most of the rarities in it flowered in late summer. These were being stifled by the water-soldier, and it was desirable therefore to get it out in time to let them recoup with a good flowering season after its removal.

June however is not a good time for arranging camps that are to last a week. There aren't so many volunteers likely to be available then as during the holiday months, and conversely accommodation is difficult because school and college buildings are still in use during term time. The Thames Valley proved very inhospitable in this respect, and Eric had to try a great many places before he found anywhere for the camp to stay within reasonable distance of the site. In the end he had to compromise, in terms that were distinctly more expensive than usual, though he could justify the extra cost to his budget by the conservation importance of the work; and at a distance from the site that more or less necessitated some form of transport, since it was further than volunteers could be expected to walk, especially if they were wet and tired as was likely to be the case. However he had to settle for what he could get, though he was still uncertain whether he could provide the transport, or the numbers of volunteers at that time of year. In the event he managed to arranged things, despite many anxious moments, and having to divert people from other camps, finally supplementing the numbers through a radio appeal.

I too was having anxious moments. David had only recently come to warden this site. His previous experience had been as a gamekeeper, and though he was very keen to learn about conservation, he had never handled anything like a camp before, and I had not had the opportunity of working with him long enough to know how he would react to volunteers. I needn't have worried about this, as he and Sue, his wife, both rose to the occasion, but anything to do with boats always makes me anxious, because I have seen how quickly people can drown when something goes wrong. So I tend to be ultra-cautious with having life-jackets and ropes around, though it is difficult to guard against all possibilities, especially if high spirits lead to showing off or fooling about, which is less easy to handle in a civilian than a military situation, without provoking a reaction when one isn't there. The best way seems to be to start people off methodically, with the emphasis on the boat being used as a tool for doing a job, not as a means of self-expression, until they learn to handle it and appreciate that there are risks.

Bruce had let me have a dinghy some time before, because there are often conservation jobs for which it is handy to have one available. It wasn't a metal work-boat, but a normal dinghy, and a visit to a ship's chandler on the coast had sorted out the rowlocks and oars. Unfortunately, although two people could carry it, it was just too wide to go in the Sherpa van, so it meant taking it on a roofrack or a trailer. But though this would be useful, I needed something larger and more stable, that could carry the weed as it was hauled out. Bruce came up with a raft he had used for cleaning out locks on the canal he managed for the Trust, and moreover undertook to get it to the site. It was a curious wedge shape, but had big flotation tanks, and was ideal for the job, as it could carry several people and lots of weed as well. It duly arrived on site, though it got shifted by persons unknown in the interval before the camp started, but it wasn't damaged, and the incident at least impressed David with the need to lock things up. Bob and Jenny helped me take the dinghy over together with the wheel-barrows and the planks for them to run on, which gave them a chance of a talk with David about the habits of volunteer camps. The weather seemed reasonable and the weed had surfaced, so all was set fair for the camp to start on the Sunday. I met John, the camp leader, on site on the day before, and we all went over the requirements and procedure in detail.

Water soldier is a clever plant. It sinks down in the autumn and remains safely below ice level during the winter, coming up to the surface again in the late spring. I had known this pond for a long time, as it was the top botanical pond in the county, but there had never been any reports of water soldier there until about fifteen years before, when a few plants had appeared in a smaller pond a bit upstream, probably introduced by someone tipping in the contents of an aquarium. Nothing much happened at first, but ten years later it had got into the main pond, and had had a population explosion. In the last three or four years it had spread so that it blanketed about two thirds of the 400 yd length of the pond. Joyce had warned me three years earlier that this was likely to happen, and that the botanists were very worried, so at first we had tried to reduce it by parties from a local college using chromes and nets from the bank. However this had not been sufficient, and it was now not only covering the surface, but with another layer below that. We couldn't use herbicides, and the only course seemed to be manual removal from boats.

It looks a bit like a large artichoke, but the leaves are toothed, and one wants to wear gloves when handling it. It is quite easy to fish it out and one can do it with the handle of a walking stick. It doesn't seem to be attached to the bottom at all, in fact there is some resemblance to fishing out jellyfish, though it is not quite as slimy. If you put it on the bank, as the anglers did when they tried to clear enough space to fish, the cattle will eat it, or some of it, but they also tend to kick it back in again. It lives for a long time out of the water if it is kept moist and will recover if put in water again even though it looks dead. It bulks large, but if you pile it in windrows well back from the water, as we planned to do, it will melt away in time, and though we had thought we might have to level the windrows later, this wasn't necessary. It has a white flower, not very attractive, but is thought not to seed in our climate, and its spread seems entirely by vegetative means. Apart from upsetting the botanists and the anglers, the water soldier was also severely limiting the birds of the pond – mallard, coot and moorhens chiefly, that were still trying to raise their broods without enough open water for them to feed or learn to swim. The swans were restricted to the tail of the pond, that was still weed-free, but liable to dry out in summer. In fact this was no doubt the reason why the plant hadn't yet invaded that section.

The pond lies well back from the river, whose banks are crowded with people and cars most of the time. Not many people visit it, although it is so close to a historic site, as the monuments and the coach parks are some way off. The stream that flows through the pond has a high pH, since it derives from a chalk outlier, and here, where it flows over the gravel of the river terraces, produces the sort of growing medium that is the envy of all water gardeners. The important plants of the pond I am not able to describe, since they are the sort of things that you have to be a botanist to recognize, but even I could appreciate the wealth of flowering rush, arrowhead, and so forth, even if I couldn't tell which were the real rarities among the grasses and sedges. Joyce and Sheila had tried to teach me, but it was no use, though they had at least instilled in me how important the pond was, which was just as well as when it was transferred to us from another Region, it came together with a half-accepted proposal for the angling club to dredge it out with the aid of a large grant from the Sports Council. Luckily Ivor remembered I had told him about this pond, and we were able to alter the arrangements. It had soon been scheduled a SSSI, and though a compromise was made, as a result of several meetings between the botanists and the anglers, with the NCC and myself there to hold the ring, no dredging had so far taken place. This was probably as well, because later entomological investigation has shown that it is equally important for insects, quite apart from the ones that have been introduced perhaps in the same manner as the water soldier, including the water stick insect. I expect the molluscs are good too, and one often sees the big ramshorn there. The largest fish I have seen taken out was a pike of about 10lbs, and I rather doubt if they would get much larger there, as though it is so long, the pond is very narrow, more like a section of a canal really; I suspect that it was man-made originally.

However although visitors are not frequent, there are footpaths past it, and quite a number of locals go that way, as well as occasional explorers from the riverside crowds. So we put up notices explaining what we were doing, and that it had been agreed with the Nature Conservancy and the Trust. We had also warned the farmer, and he had agreed to keep the cattle off the north bank, which was where we intended to barrow out the weed. There were bullocks on the south bank though, which we had to drive back at intervals when they became too inquisitive.

When I got there on the Sunday, operations had already started, and were going well (*Photo 55*). There were twelve in the team, of whom ten looked more or less like other Acorn volunteers, in their mixture of sexes, shapes and origins, which included Hong Kong on this occasion. The two exceptions were girls who had responded to the radio appeal, both unusual at that time in having carefully groomed punk hairstyles, not then so often met. They were both hard workers, and enjoying it thoroughly, in fact they were rapidly becoming the life and soul of the party. The water level had dropped enough to allow one to walk round the end of the pond, which I did, to join them all on the further bank. The raft had begun as planned at the tail end of the weed, and was moving slowly upstream, manned by a crew of lads with chromes, who raked up onto it all the weed they could manage. The dinghy followed behind mopping up any detached bits that floated downstream. From time to time one or other pulled in to shore, and the weed collected was offloaded (*Photo 56*). It was then wheel-barrowed along the board walks to be tipped into windrows far enough away for it not to get back into the pond. I had made a bad miscalculation here, because in obtaining the hundred or so tanalised boards, I had specified they should be cut 5 ft long so that they could be carried inside an estate car, rather than on a roof-rack, where they would be too heavy. This short length was a mistake, as the field was uneven enough for them to tip up when the wheel-barrow came onto them. It was alright if one overlapped them endwise, but only for one direction, so that for coming back after unloading, it was easier to go over the field (*Photo 57*). Otherwise the equipment seemed adequate; the two wheelbarrows could clear each load before the next arrived, there were just enough pairs of waders for those who needed to stand half in the pond, and their wellingtons were adequate for the rest. There was enough for everyone to do; it was warm enough for shirt-sleeves, and the rest of their clothes were piled round a willow on the bank opposite, where they had embarked.

An agonized cry from one girl interrupted us, and we saw that the bullocks were not only investigating the pile of clothes but one of them was trying to eat the plastic carrier-bag in which she had left her purse. It took me some time to get back round the head of the pool, and by the time I had reached the bullocks, the dinghy had ferried some of the volunteers across too. The bullocks retreated, still munching plastic, but fortunately we found that the purse, which contained Valerie's return ticket, had fallen out in the process. After that we were careful not all to be on the other bank at the same time.

The next day I was working in Sussex in the morning, but was there able to borrow two more pairs of waders, which I took over in the afternoon, when Eric was also visiting. Valerie's boy-friend had slipped on the deck of the raft and hurt his ribs; after a medical check, Eric had decided it was best if he went home, and Valerie had accompanied him to look after him. This was the only casualty we had, but it reduced the team to ten.

I had to spend the next day in the office, and then a medical problem meant my visiting a doctor, so I didn't get back to the pond until the last day of the camp. Even if they had stayed at full strength, I don't think they would have cleared the immense amount of the weed that there really was. As they moved upstream, it got denser and denser, so David strung a boom of fishing net across about fifty yards below the head of the pond (*Photo 58*), and concentrated on clearing up all the loose bits downstream of this. We agreed to have another party later on to finish it off, and Dawn and Barbara had big plans to come again. Morale was very high and after mopping up all the remaining plants we could see either from the bank or the boats, we loaded all the equipment onto the tractor and trailer, with the girls driving it back to base.

TWENTY-THREE

Canary Blues

We didn't see milkweeds until our last day in Tenerife, and then it was by chance. We were using the hour we could spare between leaving the hotel in our hire-car, and reaching the airport, to go up a busy side road as far as the village in the nasturtium (*Tropaeolum*) zone, where we had seen a large white two days before. We had been up and down this road many times on this and a previous visit, going to and from the pine forest and the delightful sub-alpine country above it, but it is not the sort of road from which one can take one's eye for long. So we hadn't been certain whether there were large whites flying among the thousands of small whites, or whether the occasional one that looked larger was just an unusually large small white. Both species feed on the nasturtium that lines the verges, where it climbs over the stone walls, and spreads into the terraces of the small fields and vineyards, for some five miles length of the road as it ascends the ridge in a series of relatively gentle climbs between hairpins. The small white is like the form one sees in Europe, or other countries, and must be practically world-wide now, but the large white in the Canaries has developed a quite astonishing local form, very much bigger and better than anything in Europe proper, with enormous black blotches on its forewings. It used to be seen elsewhere in Tenerife, but it now seems only to occur in this one area. Certainly we had not seen it, although we had kept an eye open for it everywhere we had been, until two days before I had got out to look for caterpillars, or chrysales of it, for the few minutes before some lorry wanted to use the forecourt of a small firm in front of which we had stopped. I had only gone ten yards, when an adult female floated past me. By the time I had got my camera it had disappeared, but at least we knew it was flying. We couldn't stop longer then, but we did notice a place a bit lower down where we thought we could park if we stayed by the car, though it also seemed to serve as a villa entrance and a bus stop.

So, on our last morning, after settling with the hotel we drove up to this small terrace of tarmac, to wait hopefully. Penelope spotted a milkweed almost at once, sitting on the leaves of a rather ordinary-looking acacia-type bush just below us, where it seemed rather incongruous, and was too far for close photography. There it sat while we wondered how to get closer, but it then moved further down the hill. Meanwhile I had seen the first of the large whites fly over us and over the road, to whatever lay beyond a high fence on the other side. Some small whites were with it, and appeared to be mobbing it. We went on waiting, and found that there was some sort of pattern, with the large whites appearing from the same direction at about ten-minute intervals, and as each did, a cloud of small whites rose from the nasturtium to dance attendance. The road was as busy as ever, with cars and trucks going up or down, and we noticed larger lorries turning into the premises behind the fence. I went to its entrance which was a bit below us, to investigate, and found that this entrance had been planted up with lantana bushes, now in flower, on which a further milkweed was sitting, this time on much more appropriate coloration. It was undisturbed by another lorry coming in, and I was able to get some close shots (*Photo 61*), before returning to watch out for the large whites. We then divided our time between the two areas. We saw two milkweeds flying together at one moment, and there may well have been others. Finally a female large white came close enough to net, and examine, revealing that the black spots on the forewing were enlarged and fused together in an irregular blotch that ran into the streak of the inner margin, all on a greyish white background. The lower wings were tinged yellow centrally, changing to lime green towards the margins. The underside had the blotches of the forewings on the same background, but the apices and hind-wings were a pure yellow, unlike the greyish yellow of the European form. Our hour was up, and we turned to leave for the airport.

This form of the large white, which some consider a separate species, was first recorded early in the last century – a less extreme form occurs in Madeira, and it is also present in the Azores. The milkweed first reached the Canaries in 1880 from America, and is still extending its range eastwards, having recently established a colony in the south of Spain. Westwards it reached New Zealand in 1840 and Australia in 1870. Like other migratory species and, subject to winter temperatures, it can only hold the ground it gains if suitable food-plants are present, whether as introduced crops or garden plants. It is unfortunate that the best-known area for it on Tenerife was largely destroyed in making a motorway access some ten years ago, so now one has to take a chance on finding it. There are occasional milkweed bushes planted in the gardens, otherwise lantana seems to be a favourite nectar-source. The gliding flight is as different from that of most butterflies, as is that of a hawk amongst birds.

There are twenty-seven kinds of butterflies reported from the Canaries, all but one from Tenerife. Two at least have not been seen for some time, and about half are of migratory habit, so may well come and go. Many of the rest occur in North Africa, and the origin of the others is uncertain. Some have been there long enough for specific differences to have developed – the Speckled Wood for example, with its white streak on the underside. In most cases the forms present are rather brighter than those of Europe proper – the Mediterranean Brimstone striking enough with its splash of orange-red, here has the whole forewing col-oured an attractive apricot. The only species really unlike any-thing else is the Canary blue, *Cyclyrius webbianus* (*Photo 62*), the sole member of its genus, which abounds from the lower ground up into the lunar landscape of the National Park round Mount Teide, even penetrating the French windows of the Parador to drink the spillings of orangeade in the bar-room. But there are a good many puzzles in how some of them reached Tenerife, and how long they may have been there. While there are representat-ives of all the main families of European butterflies, they are by no means the sort of collection one would put forward as typical examples for preservation on such an ark as the Canaries repres-ent; where the oceanic climate has afforded survival to many plants of the ancient Tethyan flora, elsewhere squeezed out be-tween the ice-ages to the north, and the drying Sahara to the south.

For instance, there are two red admirals; the one familiar to us, *Vanessa atalanta*, and a subspecies of the Indian red admiral, *Vanessa indica*, with a much wider red band (*Photo 64*). *Indica* inhabits Asia, from India to Japan. The subspecies *calliroe* is in the

Canaries, and Madeira, but not in the Azores, and there is a slight difference between the form it takes in both Madeira and the Canaries, and that of the Asiatic species, in the arrangement of the white spots at the apex of the forewing, and in the colour of its chief feature, the doubled width of the red band on the forewings. This is a brilliant red, as it is in *atalanta*, but in Asia is distinctly duller, almost brown. This double red band is striking, and is apparent from a distance of many yards, if it is sitting, or even if it is flying past one. So there are these two species of red admiral, much the same size, as far as we could see in about equal numbers, (though *indica* was seen more often, but not that much, about 3 to 2) both using nettles as a food plant; flying together and often visiting the same group of flowers; co-existing as they have done for 200 years without interbreeding or one replacing the other. We saw one or other, or both together, in roughly the same frequency as one sees *atalanta* in Britain, given a good immigration year.

There are no peacocks, tortoiseshells, or other members of the group, except for two painted ladies, the cosmopolitan *Cynthia cardui*, familiar to us in Britain, and the American painted lady *Cynthia virginiensis*. Unlike the red admirals, these are far from being in equal numbers, with *cardui* commonplace, but *virginiensis* so seldom seen as for doubts to have arisen over its continued presence. It is a partial migrant, and is known to have reached Britain on nearly 20 occasions, but the Canaries records show that the species was formerly resident there, though it was becoming scarce and local in the 1960s. So we have parallel pairs of butterflies, red admirals and painted ladies, of which in one pair both are thriving, and in the other, one is not.

There remains the mystery of how the Asian red admiral, *indica*, ever reached the North Atlantic islands, since it does not occur anywhere in the intervening countries of Africa or Europe. While it is attractive to picture some early Spanish or Portuguese navigator releasing specimens on his way home, this could hardly have happened early enough for the differences in wing-markings to have developed. There is furthermore a species of red admiral in Hawaii, the Kamehameha (*Vanessa tameana*), which also seems to derive from the Asian *indica*, but now has the bright red extended all over the basal area of its forewings.

So one can only suggest that, in the remote past, *indica* had sufficient migratory tendencies, as are still present in some of its relations, to have colonized so widely, and that its intervening points of settlement have subsequently been lost. There seems no reason why some species, like some nations, should not have had periods of migratory urge, and then have settled down, having found somewhere that suited them. There aren't many threats to their continued existence in the equable climate of the Canaries.

Lizard predation is one threat however, particularly noticeable earlier in the year, where many of the butterflies one sees have chips in their hindwings. Speckled woods, we noticed, were particularly affected, so were meadow browns, and even one of the Indian red admirals I photographed. We stopped for lunch on a hillside once in May where there was a flattened area between some rocks and a small bridge. I threw a bit of bread into the rocks, whereupon a lizard immediately came out of hiding to seize it. We noticed other movement nearby, and by throwing other small pieces, we counted over twenty lizards within a few yards of the car park. I thought their density was about one per four square yards, which doesn't give much chance to a butterfly struggling up a stem to dry its wings after emergence.

There were two kinds of lizards, one very like the common wall lizard of Southern Europe, perhaps nine inches or so when fully grown. The other kind, about a third of those present, were blue-cheeked, longer and sleeker than the wall lizards, but growing corpulent and heavy when older (*Photo 63*). The older blue-cheeked lizards were dominant, taking food away from the younger ones or from all sizes of wall lizard, if these did not scuttle away before they reached them, but they were reluctant at first to show themselves, and seemed more attracted by the noise of movement of the smaller ones than by the bread. We saw these two kinds at many other places too, all over the lower part of the island, and we once saw, low down, an equally heavy kind of a dark reddish brown colour.

One would like to know more about the distribution of the various lizards, and whether they are endemic, or give a clue to how species reached these islands. The toll they take of insects is possibly a significant factor in controlling the spread of these. Bird predation, however, must be small, with the paucity of insect-eating birds in the pine forest, though we did meet one pair of blue chaffinches that seemed to have adopted a car park as a foraging area, like our chaffinches do. The original laurel forest zone, below the natural and supplemented pines, seems a better place for birds, but is now only a narrow belt (*Photo 60*). The plants along the tracks through it remind one of the Mediterranean maquis and include tree heath, broom heath and various cistuses. This level had the most varied butterfly fauna too, though there were frequent days on which it was shrouded in cloud, as the North-East Trade winds deposited the moisture which has given rise to the forest zones.

On such days, one could usually go up higher to the sub-alpine zone to find clear skies above the clouds. The ridge of the island at about 2000 metres was nearly always (*Photo 59*) in bright sunshine. Its tufa soil carries an attractive vegetation of brooms and other shrubs; yellow crucifers and white mayweeds in spring, a bushy pink scabious in summer. All are food plants or nectar sources for the local butterflies. Snow can lie here in winter which with the winds and the arid summer conditions limits growth, so that there are wide gaps between the clumps of bushes, though the tufa is not easy walking. Apart from the Observatory, the buildings at this height are all tourist-related, and confined to the main roads. There is a lot of country in between these to explore (*Cover photo*).

Glossary

Acorn Over 150 Acorn Camps are organized yearly by the National Trust's Volunteer Unit for work on NT properties. Each is ideally 16 strong, of both sexes, with a leader, deputy leader, tools and transport. Members have to be over 17, and pay about £20 towards the cost of board and lodging, for the week the camp lasts.

ADAS Agricultural Development Advisory Service.

Ancient woodland Land that has been woodland continuously since an arbitrarily chosen date. If the information is available, this may be Domesday (1086). Often AD1600 is adopted as a base-date as presumed to precede any deliberate forestry plantings such as followed the publication of *Sylva* by John Evelyn (1620–1706), or it may be the date of the earliest reliable map (usually Rocque *c*. 1760). Earlier map-makers did not always show woods that were not visible from the roads.

Angles Angle-iron fencing stakes.

AONB Area of outstanding natural beauty.

aposematic Warningly coloured, usually indicating distastefulness or danger to an attacker, and often mimicked by other species.

Autobahn, autoroute, autostrada, etc. None of the European variants seem as simple as our 'motorway' or the American 'freeway', so these may in time prevail, as already have so many English roadsigns, e.g. the ubiquitous STOP.

base-camp National Trust term for a hostel where volunteer parties can be accommodated, usually with its own warden, transport, and tools, for periods of a week or more.

BBCS British Butterfly Conservation Society.

billhook A short, heavy, edged (or two-edged) hand-tool for cutting woody growth as in coppicing, or laying hedges. An intriguing range of former individual county patterns are now collectables; modern catalogues give only three or four types, if that.

biomass The total weight of the living components in an ecosystem.

Brachypodium Tor-grass or Heath False-brome (*B. pinnatum*) and (more in shade usually) False Brome or Slender False-brome (*B. sylvaticum*).

BTCV British Trust for Conservation Volunteers. Formerly the Conservation Corps of the Council for Nature.

chespale Chestnut paling fencing. Sizes vary according to height, distance apart of individual pales, and whether there is a central wire connecting them as well as at top and bottom. All are factors in effectiveness for the intended purpose, and in weight and cost.

chrome A long-handled tool with tines bent at right angles in their middle, for use as a draghook. Unpleasant to travel with; best on a roofrack.

clearing saw A mechanical, hand-held, and optionally shoulder-slung, scrub-cutter, with the engine at the rear of a long shaft which projects in front of the operator, so that he or she can make side to side sweeps with the cutting end. This carries a rotating head, of interchangeable patterns from nylon cord up to various forms of circular saw-blades, so that it can be used for cutting vegetation from grass up to small trees. Also unpleasant in the car.

climax A self-sustaining state in which a community is at maximum development in equilibrium with its environment, and will not alter further unless some outside and usually disastrous agency (such as man) intervenes.

conifers A term normally used for pine, larch and the various introduced species, but the definition of gymnosperms includes the yews, junipers, and even the gingko. Currently conifers have a bad press, but they are useful in moderation in giving contrast, and winter shelter to wildlife.

County Trust There are 47 autonomous County Trusts within RSNC. Most started as the '. . . shire Naturalists' Trust' or the '. . . shire Trust for Nature Conservation', and the current fashion is the '. . . shire Wildlife Trust'. Most have a small permanent staff and a subscribing membership of around 5000.

CTW Clapham, Tutin and Warburg, *Flora of the British Isles*. Standard since 1951.

CUBG Cambridge University Botanic Garden.

edaphic Of the soil, or influenced by the soil

endemic Restricted in the wild to a district or region.

escarpment Steep slope or cliff at the margin of a flat or gently sloping area, such as produced by erosion or faulting, e.g. the south face of the North Downs or the north face of the South Downs.

FC Forestry Commission.

flail mower A power-driven machine for cutting vegetation, with the cutters operating in a vertical plane.

gabion A cage made of (nowadays) thick wire mesh containing boulders, flints, etc. Can be made up on site and filled with local materials as available, which it then holds in position. The word derives, through Old French, from an Italian word for a cage, of Latin origin, showing the antiquity of this

useful method of inducing stability in otherwise shifting materials. Presumably the earlier versions used wickerwork, or rope nets.

gallery woodland Woodland extending along the banks of a stream.

herbi A hand-held ULV sprayer for herbicide application.

herbicide Chemical formulation which suppresses or eliminates plant growth, either of 'blanket' type affecting all vegetation, or selective in affecting some categories and not others.

Hymac A tracked earthmover with a swivelling jib-arm able to rotate 360°, with a 30ft reach. Now many similar machines (Poclain, Leibherr, etc. and several Japanese makes).

ILEA Inner London Education Authority (now defunct).

inches, feet, etc. For the benefit of those brought up with metric weights and measurements, inches (1 inch = 25.4cm) appear as -in or " in the text; feet (1 foot = 30.5cm) as ft or '; yards (1 yard = 0.914m) as yds. For areas 1 acre = 0.405 ha; 1 hectare = 2.47 acres.

indigenous Originating in a district or country; native.

ITE Institute of Terrestrial Ecology (formerly, with the NCC, part of the old Nature Conservancy). The intention was to separate scientific and managerial functions, but the result has rather shown how the one needs the other.

JCB The familiar enlargement of a wheeled tractor with a bucket-blade in front and a digger arm behind. Now many makes and types, since the original by J.C. Bamford Ltd. Has advantages in road usability, avoiding the cost of a transporter, but also has limitations in application compared with a tracked machine.

jungle-buster A type of swipe, with horizontally revolving chains.

matador A heavy crane-lorry used in forestry.

MBGBI *The Moths and Butterflies of Great Britain and Ireland*, currently being published (since 1976) in ten (or more) volumes of which about half have appeared so far, forming the definitive work on the British lepidoptera for the foreseeable future.

micromoths Moths usually ignored, until too late an age, by entomologists because of their small size, lack of vernacular names, difficulty of identification and other excuses. Modern works, such as MBGBI, start with micros and end with the historically accepted (macro) moths, but the latter also include many genera taken from earlier families because of size, attractiveness etc. Butterflies come at about two thirds of the way through the total list.

Molinia Purple moor-grass (*M. caerulea*).

mycorrhiza Close physical association between a fungus and the roots of a plant, apparently to the benefit of both.

NCC Nature Conservancy Council, see ITE. Now subject to further dismemberment.

NNR National Nature Reserve. These are set up and managed by NCC, though privatization is sometimes threatened. Local Nature Reserves can be established and managed by local authorities.

NT The National Trust for Place of Historic Interest or Natural Beauty. Covers England, Wales and Northern Ireland – Scotland has its own National Trust.

Phragmites *Phragmites australis* (or *communis*) Common Reed. The giant reed (*Arundo donax*), of biblical mention, does not occur in Britain.

plagioclimax A stable state arising from a succession deflected or arrested by an outside agency, usually human, which would otherwise (if deflected) not have arisen or (if arrested) would continue to develop further by natural means. Examples range from lowland heath to mown lawns.

PTO Power take-off (of a tractor, etc.).

rendzina Earth soil that has developed over calcareous parent material, such as chalk.

RSNC Royal Society for Nature Conservation, formerly the Society for the Promotion of Nature Reserves (SPNR).

SBK Synthetic Brushwood Killer (now obsolete, or should be).

scalpings Crushed fragments of rock as used in different sizes for making up tracks. Often of limestone origin.

scrub Shrubby growth of which the user of the term disapproves – the equivalent of the gardener's 'weeds' – because he considers the biological value of the site (chalk downland, lowland heath, or whatever) would be higher without the scrub. This is often, but not always, true.

seral succession Stages in the development of plant succession from colonization to climax.

SSSI Site of Special Scientific Interest

swipe An attachment to a tractor with a horizontally revolving bar or chains for cutting vegetation in a rough and ready manner.

tanalise A method of impregnating timber to make it last longer, usually by treating it cold in a vacuum.

Terram An artificial material rather similar in appearance to Army blankets, supplied in rolls or rectangles for placing under gravel etc. in making up tracks, serving both as an insulating layer and distributing pressure.

Typha Reedmace or Bulrush (*T. latifolia*) and Lesser Bulrush (*T. angustifolia*).

ULV Ultra Low Volume. In herbicide spraying the droplets produced are too small to see, much smaller than those produced by the obsolescent knapsack sprayers, giving better coverage and reducing dramatically the amount of water that needs to be carried to the site.

WWF World Wildlife Fund, now the World-Wide Fund for Nature.

YNT Young National Trust groups normally start as an offshoot of one of the many National Trust Centres (supporters' clubs) based on large towns and later become semi-independent. They carry out practical work on Trust properties, within the radius of an hour's drive or so, mainly at weekends. Most have their own stock of tools. No age limits but usually under 40.